Fourth Edition

Business and Legal Forms

for Graphic Designers

WITHDRAWN

Business and Legal Forms
for
Graphic Designers

Tad Crawford and Eva Doman Bruck

Fourth Edition

ALLWORTH PRESS
NEW YORK

GRAPHIC ARTISTS GUILD

Allworth Press books may be purchased in bulk at special discounts for sales promotion, corporate gifts, fund-raising, or educational purposes. Special editions can also be created to specifications. For details, contact the Special Sales Department, Allworth Press, 307 West 36th Street, 11th Floor, New York, NY 10018 or info@skyhorsepublishing.com.

17 16 15 14 13   5 4 3 2 1

Published by Allworth Press, an imprint of Skyhorse Publishing, Inc.307 West 36th Street, 11th Floor, New York, NY 10018.Allworth Press® is a registered trademark of Skyhorse Publishing, Inc.®, a Delaware corporation. www.allworth.com

Cover design by Derek Bacchus
Interior page design by Douglas Design Associates, New York
Page composition/typography by Susan Ramundo

Library of Congress Cataloging-in-Publication Data is available on file.

ISBN: 978-1-62153-249-1

Printed in China

Table of Contents

A System for Success

The knowledge and use of good business practices are essential for the success of any professional or company, including the graphic designer and the design firm. The forms contained in this book deal with the most important business transactions that a designer or design firm is likely to undertake. At the back of the book is a CD-ROM that will allow the designer to customize and easily revise the forms. The fact that they are designed for use, and favor the designer if negotiations are necessary, give them a unique value.

The purpose of *Business and Legal Forms for Graphic Designers* is, in part, to provide information, systems, and forms that are useful to the organization and smooth functioning of the business side of the graphic design studio. It is possible to adopt (or adapt) the entire system or alter its parts to fit the particular needs of the individual studio. Each of these organizational forms can stand on its own or be used as a component of an integrated system. While an orderly system is essential to accurate record-keeping, flexibility is important to make the system responsive to changing circumstances.

Doing Business

The organization of the forms is based upon the typical chronology of events which occur in the course of doing business in the graphic design profession (with forms for the more sophisticated contracts coming last). As a starting point, the book begins with a very detailed estimate form for clients, which is used to assess the time and costs that a proposed job may require. This form can serve as an internal estimating form. It may also be a document that is shared with the client or it may be used internally or externally as a means of tracking the budget and time spent for ongoing projects in summary format.

Throughout the forms, by the way, there is a selective use of the words "job" and "project" because, while both words refer to the same activity, forms which the clients will never see use the word "job" and communications that the client will receive use the word "project." The slightly more formal tone that is used to communicate with clients need not appear on everyday internal forms.

Once the project has been estimated internally and fees determined, the designer is then able to draft a proposal, which the client may sign to make a binding contract. Or the project confirmation form, which is more formal, may be used once the client has approved the contract.

The credit reference form is used to ensure that an unknown client has a satisfactory history of bill paying. After this is confirmed and the client signs to commit to the project, the assignment may be considered a "job." Several steps are taken to open the system for tracking a job on its course through the studio. The job is first assigned a number via the jobs index, then a job sheet is opened to begin the process of recording time and costs expended on the assignment. Time sheets will show staff time expended. The studio production schedule is used to deliver the job on time.

During the course of the assignment, the project status report is used to keep the client informed of the ongoing work, and the work change order form confirms changes ordered by the client. In order to gather competitive bids for components of the job that are produced outside of the studio, the estimate request form is distributed to prospective vendors. The purchase order form serves as the designer's confirmation to a vendor to supply materials or services. It may be used to contract for illustration and photographic services, but needs to be modified for such uses. Large studios use internal requisition forms as a way of efficiently managing the purchase and allocation of needed supplies.

The payables index provides a way of tracking all incoming bills as well as a system for having these bills reviewed and identified as billable or not billable. The multi-use transmittal form has been designed for maximum flexibility and ease of use. The artwork log keeps track of all materials leaving the studio and their location within the studio once they have been returned.

Billing is an extremely important task, whether done during the course of the assignment or at its completion. The billing index provides the studio with invoice numbers as well as a handy guide for reviewing the status of payments due. Two invoice forms are provided, one in a generalized outline form and the other with a more detailed and comprehensive format. Monthly billing statements and collection letters are provided in a form that can be used directly.

Contracts

The forms then shift to focus more on the contractual relationships of the firm with clients and others in the outside world. Contracts with illustrators or photographers, printers, agents, lecture sponsors, and manufacturers of licensed designs are provided along with checklists for negotiating deals. Release forms are given for the use of images of models and property. A permission form to use copyrighted materials, a copyright transfer form, a copyright registration form (Form VA), a trademark application, employment forms, and lease forms are also included.

A contract is an agreement which creates legally enforceable obligations between two or more parties. In making a contract, each party gives something of value to the other party. This is called the exchange of consideration. Consideration can take many forms, including the giving of money or an artwork or the promise to create an artwork or pay for an artwork in the future.

All contracts, whether the designer's or someone else's, can be changed. Before using the contracts in this book, the designer should consider reviewing them with his or her attorney. This gives the opportunity to learn whether local or state laws may make it worthwhile to modify any of the provisions. For example, would it be wise to include a provision for arbitration of disputes or are the local courts speedy and inexpensive to use so no arbitration provision is necessary?

The contracts must be filled out, which means that the blanks must be completed. Beyond this, however, the designer can always delete or add provisions on any contract. Deletions or additions to a contract are usually initialed in the margin by both parties. It is also a good practice to have each party initial each page of the contract except the page on which the parties sign.

The designer must ascertain that the person signing the contract has authority to do so. If the designer is dealing with a company, the company's name should be included as well as the name of the individual authorized to sign the contract and the title of that individual (or, if it isn't clear who will sign or that person has no title, the words "Authorized Signatory" can be used instead of a title).

If the designer won't meet with the other party to sign the contract, it would be wise to have that party sign the forms first. After the designer gets back the two copies of the form, they can be signed and one copy returned to the other party. As discussed in more detail under letter contracts, this has the advantage of not leaving it up to the other party to decide whether to sign and thus make a binding contract.

If additional provisions that won't fit on the contract forms should be added, simply include a provision stating, "This contract is subject to the provisions of the rider attached hereto and made a part hereof." The rider is simply another piece of paper which would be headed "Rider to the contract between _____ and _____ dated the ___ day of _____, 20___." The additional provisions are put on this sheet and both parties sign it.

Negotiation

Understanding the business concepts behind the forms is as important as using them. By knowing why a certain provision has been included and what it accomplishes, the designer is able to negotiate when faced with someone else's contract. The designer knows what is and is not desirable.

Contracts require negotiation. The forms in this book are favorable to the designer. When they are presented to a client, printer, or supplier of creative services, changes may very well be requested. The explanation in this book of how to use each form should help the designer evaluate changes which either party may want to make. The explanation should also help the designer understand what changes would be desirable in forms presented to the designer.

Keep in mind that negotiation need not be adversarial. Certainly the designer and the other party may disagree on some points, but the basic transaction is something that both want. This larger framework of agreement must be kept in mind at all times when negotiating. Of course, the designer must also know which points are non-negotiable and be prepared to walk away from a deal if satisfaction cannot be had on these points.

When both parties have something valuable to offer each other, it should be possible for each side to come away from the negotiation feeling they have won. This win-win negotiation requires each side to make certain that the basic needs of both parties are met so that the result is fair. The designer can't negotiate for the other side, but a wise negotiation strategy must allow the other side to meet their vital needs within the larger context which also allows the designer to obtain what he or she must have.

It is a necessity to evaluate negotiating goals and strategy before conducting any negotiations. The designer should write down what he or she must have and what can be conceded or modified. The designer should try to imagine how the shape of the contract will affect the future business relationship with the other party. Will it probably lead to success for both sides and more business or will it fail to achieve what one side or the other desires?

When negotiating, the designer should keep written notes close at hand as to goals and strategy. Notes should be kept on the negotiations too, since many conversations may be necessary before final agreement is reached. At certain points the designer should compare where the negotiations have gone with the original goals. This will help evaluate whether the designer is conducting the negotiations according to plan.

Many negotiations are done over the telephone. This makes the telephone a tool to be used wisely in negotiations. The designer should decide when he or she wants to speak with the other party. Before calling, the designer should review the notes and be familiar with the points to be negotiated. If the designer wants the other party to call, the file should be kept close at hand so there is no question as to where the negotiations stand when the call comes. If the designer is unprepared to negotiate when the other side calls, the only wise course is to call back. Negotiation demands the fullest attention and complete readiness on the part of the designer.

Oral Contracts

Despite all the forms in this book being written, it is worth addressing the question of oral contracts. There are certain contracts which must be written, such as a contract for services which will take more than one year to perform, a contract to transfer an exclusive right of copyright (an exclusive right means that no one else can do what the person receiving that right of copyright can do), or in many cases a contract for the sale of goods worth more than $500. So, without delving into the full complexity of this subject, certain contracts can be oral. If the designer is faced with a party who has breached an oral contract, an attorney should certainly be consulted for advice. The designer should not give up simply because the contract was oral.

However, while some oral contracts are valid, a written contract is always best. Even people with the most scrupulous intentions do not always remember exactly what was said or whether a particular point was covered. Disputes, and litigation, are far more likely when a contract is oral rather than written. Do keep in mind that in many cases email and fax exchanges, even if unsigned, can serve as binding contracts. Stating the designer's intention either to create or not create a formal contract can be an important safeguard here.

Letter Contracts

If the designer feels sending a well-drafted form will be daunting to the other party, it is always possible to adopt the more informal approach of a letter which is signed by both parties. In this case, the contracts in this book will serve as valuable checklists for the content and negotiation of the letter contract. The last paragraph of the letter would say, "If the foregoing meets with your approval, please sign both copies of this letter beneath the words AGREED TO to make this a binding contract between us." At the bottom of the letter would be the words AGREED TO with the name of the other party so he or she can sign. Again, if the other party is a company, the company name would be placed beneath the words AGREED TO as well as the name of the individual who will sign and that individual's title. This would appear as follows:

AGREED TO:
XYZ Corporation
By: _____
Alice Hall, Vice President

Two copies of this letter are sent to the other party who is instructed to sign both copies and return one copy to the designer for his or her files. To be cautious, the designer can send the letters unsigned and ask the other party to sign and return both copies at which time the designer will sign and return one copy to the other party. This gives the other party an opportunity to review the final draft, but avoids a situation in which the other party might choose to delay signing and the designer would not be able to offer a similar contract to another party because the first contract might still be signed.

If the designer should ever sign a contract which the other party does not sign and return, it should be remembered that any offer to enter into a contract can always be revoked up until the time that the contract is actually entered into. The designer can protect his or her position by being the one who is last to sign, by insisting that both parties meet to sign, or by stating in the letter a deadline by which the other party must sign.

Standard Provisions

The contracts in this book contain a number of standard provisions, called "boilerplate" by lawyers. These provisions are important, although they will not seem as exciting as the provisions which relate more directly to the designer and the design process. Since these provisions can be used in almost every contract and appear in a number of the contracts in this book, an explanation of each of the provisions is given here.

Amendment. Any amendment of this Agreement must be in writing and signed by both parties.

This guarantees that any changes the parties want will be made in writing. It avoids the possibility of one party relying on oral changes to the agreement. Courts, by the way, will rarely change a written contract based on testimony that there was an oral amendment of the contract.

Arbitration. All disputes arising under this Agreement shall be submitted to binding arbitration before _____ in the following location _____ and shall be settled in accordance with the rules of the American Arbitration Association. Judgment upon the arbitration award may be entered in any court having jurisdiction thereof. Notwithstanding the foregoing, either party may refuse to arbitrate when the dispute is for a sum of less than $_____.

Arbitration can offer a quicker and less expensive way to settle disputes than litigation. However, the designer would be wise to consult a local attorney and make sure this is wise in the jurisdiction where the lawsuit would be likely to take place. The arbitrator could be the American Arbitration Association or some other person or group that both parties trust. The designer would also want the arbitration to take place where he or she is located. If small claims court is easy to use in the jurisdiction where the designer would have to sue, it might be best to have the right not to arbitrate if the disputed amount is small enough to be brought into the small claims court. In this case, the designer would put the maximum amount that can be sued for in small claims court in the space at the end of the paragraph.

Assignment. This Agreement shall not be assigned by either party hereto, provided that the Designer shall have the right to assign monies due to the Designer hereunder.

By not allowing the assignment of a contract, both parties remain more certain with whom they are dealing. Of course, a company may be purchased by new owners. If the designer only wanted to do business with the people who owned the company when the contract was entered into, change of ownership might be stated as a ground for termination in the contract. On the other hand, money is impersonal and there is no reason why the designer should not be able to assign the right to receive money.

Bankruptcy or Insolvency. If the Client shall become insolvent or if a petition in bankruptcy is filed against the Client or a Receiver or Trustee is appointed for any of the Client's assets or property, or if a lien or attachment is obtained against any of the Client's assets, this Agreement shall immediately terminate and the Client shall return to the Designer all of the Designer's work which is in the Client's possession and grant, convey, and transfer all rights in the work back to the Designer.

This provision seeks to lessen the impact on the designer of a client's bankruptcy. While the designer may lose fees, at least the work and rights may be returned. Such a provision should also appear in a publishing or licensing contract. However, the bankruptcy law may impede the provision's effectiveness.

Complete Understanding. This Agreement constitutes the entire and complete understanding between the parties hereto, and no obligation, undertaking, warranty, representation, or covenant of any kind or nature has been made by either party to the other to induce the making of this Agreement, except as is expressly set forth herein.

This provision is intended to prevent either party from later claiming that any promises or obligations exist except those shown in the written contract. A shorter way to say this is, "This Agreement constitutes the entire understanding between the parties hereto."

Cumulative Rights. All rights, remedies, obligations, undertakings, warranties, representations, and covenants contained herein shall be cumulative and none of them shall be in limitation of any other right, remedy, obligation, undertaking, warranty, representation, or covenant of either party.

This means that a benefit or obligation under one provision will not be made less because of a different benefit or obligation under another provision of the contract.

Death or Disability. In the event of the Designer's death or an incapacity of the Designer making completion of the work impossible, this Agreement shall terminate.

A provision of this kind leaves a great deal to be determined. Will payments already made be kept by the designer or the designer's estate? And who will own the work in whatever stage of completion has been reached? These issues are best resolved when the contract is negotiated.

Force Majeure. If either party hereto is unable to perform any of its obligations hereunder by reason of fire or other casualty, strike, act or order of a public authority, act of God, or other cause beyond the control of such party, then such party shall be excused from such performance during the pendency of such cause. In the event such inability to perform shall continue longer than ____ days, either party may terminate this Agreement by giving written notice to the other party.

This provision covers events beyond the control of the parties, such as a tidal wave or a war. Certainly the time to perform the contract should be extended in such an event. There may be an issue as to how long an extension will be allowed. Also, if work has commenced and some payments have been made, the contract should cover what happens in the event of termination. Must the payments be returned? And who owns the partially completed work?

Governing Law. This Agreement shall be governed by the laws of the State of _____.

Usually the designer would want the laws of his or her own state to govern the agreement.

Liquidated Damages. In the event of the failure of XYZ Corporation to deliver by the due date, the agreed upon damages shall be $_____ for each day after the due date until delivery takes place, provided the amount of damages shall not exceed $_____.

Liquidated damages are an attempt to anticipate in the contract what damages will be caused by a breach of the contract. Such liquidated damages must be reasonable. If they are not, they will be considered a penalty and unenforceable.

Modification. This Agreement cannot be changed, modified, or discharged, in whole or in part, except by an instrument in writing, signed by the party against whom enforcement of any change, modification, or discharge is sought.

This requires that a change in the contract must at least be written and signed by the party against whom the change will be enforced. This provision should be compared to that for amendments which requires any modification to be in writing and signed by both parties. At the least, however, this provision explicitly avoids a claim that an oral modification has been made of a written contract. Courts will almost invariably give greater weight to a written document than to testimony about oral agreements.

Notices and Changes of Address. All notices shall be sent to the Designer at the following address: _____ and to the Purchaser at the following address: _____. Each party shall be given written notification of any change of address prior to the date of said change.

Contracts often require the giving of notice. This provision facilitates giving notice by providing correct addresses and requiring notification of any change of address.

Successors and Assigns. This Agreement shall be binding upon and inure to the benefit of the parties hereto and their respective heirs, executors, administrators, successors, and assigns.

This makes the contract binding on anyone who takes the place of one of the parties, whether due to death or simply an assignment of the contract. With commissioned works, death or disability of the designer can raise complex questions about completion and ownership of the art. The issues must be resolved in the contract. Note the standard provision on assignment in fact does not allow assignment, but that provision could always be modified in the original contract or by a later written, signed amendment to the contract.

Time. Time is of the essence.

This requires each party to perform exactly to whatever time commitments they have made or be in breach of the contract. It is not a wise provision for the designer to agree to, since being a few days late in performance could cause the loss of all benefits under the contract.

Waivers. No waiver by either party of any of the terms or conditions of this Agreement shall be deemed or construed to be a waiver of such term or condition for the future, or of any subsequent breach thereof.

This means that if one party waives a right under the contract, that party has not waived the right forever and can demand that the other party perform at the next opportunity. So the designer who allowed a client not to pay on time would still have the right to demand payment. And if the client breached the contract in some other way, such as not returning original art, the fact the designer allowed this once would not prevent the designer from suing for such a breach in the future.

Warranty and Indemnity. The Designer hereby warrants that he or she is the sole creator of the Work and owns all rights granted under this Agreement. The Designer agrees to indemnify and hold harmless the Client from any and all claims, demands, payments, expenses, legal fees or other costs based on an actual breach of the foregoing warranties.

This provision protects one party against damaging actions that may have been taken by the other party. Often, one party will warrant that something is true and then indemnify and hold the other party harmless in the event that it is not true. For example, a designer selling an illustration may be asked to warrant that the illustration is not plagiarized. Or the designer may ask an illustrator to warrant this to the designer. If, in fact, the illustration has been plagiarized, this would breach the warranty. The party breaching the warranty would be obligated to protect the other party who has been injured by the warranty not being true.

Volunteer Lawyers for the Arts
There are now volunteer lawyers for the arts across the nation. These groups provide free assistance to designers below certain income levels and can be a valuable source of information. To find the location of the closest volunteer lawyers for the arts group, one of the groups listed here can be contacted:

California: California Lawyers for the Arts, Fort Mason Center, Building C, Room 255, San Francisco, California 94123, (415) 775-7200; and 1641 18th Street, Santa Monica, California 90404, (310) 998-5590; www.calawyersforthearts.org.

Illinois: Lawyers for the Creative Arts, 213 West Institute Place, Suite 403, Chicago, Illinois 60610, (312) 649-4111; www.law-arts.org.

New York: Volunteer Lawyers for the Arts, 1 East 53rd Street, Sixth Floor, New York, New York 10022, (212) 319-2787; www.vlany.org.

A helpful handbook covering the legal issues which designers face is *Legal Guide for the Visual Artist* by Tad Crawford (published by Allworth Press).

Graphic Arts Organizations
Belonging to an organization with fellow professionals can be an important step in learning proper business practices and advancing the designer's career. The following organizations are well worth joining:

The Graphic Artists Guild (GAG), 32 Broadway, Suite 114, New York, New York 10004, (212) 791-3400; www.graphicartsguild.org. The Guild represents professional artists active in illustration, graphic design, textile and needle-art design, computer graphics, and cartooning. Its purposes include: to promote ethical and financial standards, to gain recognition for the graphic arts as a profession, to educate members in business skills, and to lobby for artists' rights legislation. Programs include: group health insurance, newsletters, publication of the *Graphic Artists Guild Handbook of Pricing and Ethical Guidelines*, legal and accounting referrals, and artist-to-artist networking and information sharing. The Guild has local chapters across the country.

The American Institute of Graphic Arts (AIGA), 164 Fifth Avenue, New York, New York 10010, (212) 807-1990; www.aiga.org. Founded in 1914, AIGA promotes excellence in, and the advancement of, graphic design. AIGA sponsors competitions, exhibitions, publications (including an annual, a quarterly journal, a code of ethics, professional practice guidelines, and a sales tax document), educational activities, and projects in the public interest. AIGA has chapters in a number of cities.

Art Directors Club, Inc. (ADC), 106 West 29th Street, New York, New York 10001; www.adcglobal.org. Established in 1920, the Art Directors Club is an international nonprofit membership organization for creative professionals, encompassing advertising, graphic design, new media, photography, illustration, typography, broadcast design, publication design, and packaging. Programs include publication of the *Art Director's Annual,* a hardcover compendium of the year's best work compiled from winning entries in the Art Directors Annual Awards. The ADC also maintains a Hall of Fame, ongoing gallery exhibitions, speaker events, student competitions, portfolio reviews, scholarships, and high school career workshops. Many other cities also have art directors clubs.

The Society for Environmental Graphic Design (SEGD), 100 Vermont Avenue, NW, Suite 400, Washington, D.C. 20005. An international nonprofit organization founded in 1973, SEGD promotes public awareness and professional development in the field of environmental graphic design—the planning, design, and execution of graphic elements and systems that identify, direct, inform, interpret, and visually enhance the built environment. The network of members includes graphic designers, exhibit designers, architects, interior designers, landscape architects, educators, researchers, artisans, and manufacturers. Benefits include access to the members area of their website, which contains a salary survey, a free download of *SEGD Green Paper,* a glossary, and more; member rates on educational events, teleconferences, research reports, and white papers; SEGDTalk, the online forum for SEGD members; a free subscription to the award-winning *eg* magazine; *Messages,* the monthly e-newsletter full of member news, industry trends, and articles; an online member directory; discounted job listings and free résumé postings in the SEGD Job Bank; admittance to the SEGD Conference, the premier educational event for professionals working in environmental graphic design and related fields; participation in local chapter events; and AIA accreditation for all educational events.

Society of Publication Designers (SPD), 27 Union Square West, Suite 207, New York, New York 10003; www.spd.org. Begun in 1964, the SPD was formed to acknowledge the role of the art director/designer in the creation and development of the printed page. The art director as journalist brings a visual intelligence to the editorial mission to clarify and enhance the written word. Activities include an annual exhibition and competition, a monthly newsletter, special programs, lectures, and the publication of an annual book of the best publication design.

Using the Checklists

Having reviewed the basics of dealing with the business and legal forms, it is time to move on to the forms themselves and the checklists which will make the forms most useful.

These checklists focus on the key points to be observed when using the forms. On the organizational forms, the boxes can be checked when the different aspects of the use of the form have been considered. For the contracts, the checklists cover all the points which may be negotiated, whether or not they are in the contract. When, in fact, a point is covered in the contract already, the appropriate paragraph is indicated in the checklist. These checklists are especially valuable when reviewing a contract offered to the designer by someone else.

For the contracts, if the designer is providing the form, the boxes can be checked to make certain all the important points are covered. If the designer is reviewing someone else's form, checking the boxes will show which points they have covered and which points may have to be altered or added. By using the paragraph numbers in the checklist, the other party's provision can be quickly compared with a provision that would favor the designer. Each checklist for a contract concludes with the suggestion that the standard provisions be reviewed to see if any should be added to what the form provides. Of course, the designer does not have to include every point on the checklist in a contract, but being aware of these points will be helpful.

The Code of Fair Practice for the Graphic Communications Industry

The Code of Fair Practice is currently subscribed to by the Graphic Artists Guild and the New York Society of Illustrators. The intention of the Code is to uphold existing law and tradition and to help define an ethical standard for business practice in the graphic communications industry. Drafted in 1948, the Code was conceived to promote equity for those engaged in creating, selling, buying, and using graphic arts. The Code has been used successfully since its formulation by thousands of industry professionals to create equitable relationships in the business of selling and buying art. Each artist should individually decide whether to enter art contests or design competitions, provide free services, work on speculation, or work on a contingent basis. Each artist should independently decide how to price work.

Relations Between Artists and Buyers

The word "artist" should be understood to include creative people in the field of visual communications such as illustration, graphic design, photography, film, and television. This code provides the graphic communications industry with an accepted standard of ethics and professional conduct. It presents guidelines for the voluntary conduct of persons in the industry which may be modified by written agreement between the parties.

ARTICLE 1. Negotiations between an artist or the artist's representative and a client shall be conducted only through an authorized buyer.

ARTICLE 2. Orders or agreements between an artist or artist's representative and a buyer should be in writing and shall include the specific rights which are being transferred, the specific fee arrangement agreed to by the parties, delivery date, and a summarized description of the work.

ARTICLE 3. All changes or additions not due to the fault of the artist or artist's representative should be billed to the buyer as an additional and separate charge.

ARTICLE 4. There should be no charges to the buyer for revisions or retakes made necessary by errors on the part of the artist or the artist's representative.

ARTICLE 5. If work commissioned by a buyer is postponed or canceled, a "kill-fee" should be negotiated based on time allotted, effort expended, and expenses incurred. In addition, other lost work shall be considered.

ARTICLE 6. Completed work shall be promptly paid for in full, and the artwork shall be returned promptly to the artist. Payment due the artist shall not be contingent upon third-party approval or payment.

ARTICLE 7. Alterations shall not be made without consulting the artist. Where alterations or retakes are necessary, the artist shall be given the opportunity of making such changes.

ARTICLE 8. The artist shall notify the buyer of any anticipated delay in delivery. Should the artist fail to keep the contract through unreasonable delay or non-conformance with agreed specifications, it will be considered a breach of contract by the artist. Should the agreed timetable be delayed due to the buyer's failure, the artist should endeavor to adhere as closely as possible to the original schedule as other commitments permit.

ARTICLE 9. Whenever practical, the buyer of artwork shall provide the artist with samples of the reproduced artwork for self-promotion purposes.

ARTICLE 10. There shall be no undisclosed rebates, discounts, gifts, or bonuses requested by or given to buyers by the artist or representative.

ARTICLE 11. Artwork and copyright ownership are vested in the hands of the artist unless agreed to in writing. No works shall be duplicated, archived, or scanned without the artist's prior authorization.

ARTICLE 12. Original artwork, and any material object used to store a computer file containing original artwork, remains the property of the artist unless it is specifically purchased. It is distinct from the purchase of any reproduction rights.* All transactions shall be in writing.

ARTICLE 13. In case of copyright transfers, only specified rights are transferred. All unspecified rights remain vested with the artist. All transactions shall be in writing.

ARTICLE 14. Commissioned artwork is not to be considered as "work for hire" unless agreed to in writing before work begins.

ARTICLE 15. When the price of work is based on limited use and later such work is used more extensively, the artist shall receive additional payment.

ARTICLE 16. Art or photography should not be copied for any use, including client presentation or "comping," without the artist's prior authorization. If exploratory work, comprehensives, or preliminary photographs from an assignment are subsequently chosen for reproduction, the artist's permission shall be secured and the artist shall receive fair additional payment.

ARTICLE 17. If exploratory work, comprehensives, or photographs are bought from an artist with the intention or possibility that another artist will be assigned to do the finished work, this shall be in writing at the time of placing the order.

ARTICLE 18. Electronic rights are separate from traditional media rights and shall be separately negotiated. In the absence of a total copyright transfer or a work-for-hire agreement, the right to reproduce artwork in media not yet discovered is subject to negotiation.

ARTICLE 19. All published illustrations and photographs should be accompanied by a line crediting the artist by name, unless otherwise agreed to in writing.

ARTICLE 20. The right of an illustrator to sign work and to have the signature appear in all reproductions should remain intact.

ARTICLE 21. There shall be no plagiarism of any artwork.

ARTICLE 22. If an artist is specifically requested to produce any artwork during unreasonable working hours, fair additional remuneration shall be paid.

ARTICLE 23. All artwork or photography submitted as samples to a buyer should bear the name of the artist or artists responsible for the work. An artist shall not claim authorship of another's work.

ARTICLE 24. All companies that receive artist portfolios, samples, etc. shall be responsible for the return of the portfolio to the artist in the same condition as received.

ARTICLE 25. An artist entering into an agreement with a representative for exclusive representation shall not accept an order from nor permit work to be shown by any other representative. Any agreement which is not intended to be exclusive should set forth the exact restrictions agreed upon between the parties.

ARTICLE 26. Severance of an association between artist and representative should be agreed to in writing. The agreement should take into consideration the length of time the parties have worked together as well as the representative's financial contribution to any ongoing advertising or promotion. No representative should continue to show an artist's samples after the termination of an association.

ARTICLE 27. Examples of an artist's work furnished to a representative or submitted to a prospective buyer shall remain the property of the artist, should not be duplicated without the artist's authorization, and shall be returned promptly to the artist in good condition.

ARTICLE 28.** Interpretation of the Code for the purposes of arbitration shall be in the hands of the Joint Ethics Committee or other body designated to resolve the dispute, and is subject to changes and additions at the discretion of the parent organizations through their appointed representatives on the Committee. Arbitration by the Joint Ethics Committee or other designated body shall be binding among the parties, and decisions may be entered for judgment and execution.

ARTICLE 29. Work on speculation; Contests. Artists and designers who accept speculative assignments (whether directly from a client or by entering a contest or competition) risk losing anticipated fees, expenses, and the potential opportunity to pursue other, rewarding assignments. Each artist shall decide individually whether to enter art contests or design competitions, provide free services, work on speculation, or work on a contingency basis.

 *Artwork ownership, copyright ownership, and ownership and rights transferred after January 1, 1978, are to be in compliance with the Federal Copyright Revision Act of 1976.

**The original Article 28 has been deleted and replaced by Article 29.

(Note that AIGA also has the "AIGA Standards of Professional Practice," the "AIGA Position on Spec Work," and the series of pamphlets titled AIGA Design Business and Ethics available on its website: www.aiga.org.)

Project Plan and Budget
 • **Estimate Form for Client**
 • **Preliminary Budget and Schedule**
 • **Budget and Schedule Review**

FORM 1

The inclusion or deletion of appropriate column headings makes this a form that can serve many purposes. In the earliest stages of planning an assignment, it can serve as a Preliminary Budget and Schedule, used by the designer to help determine fee amounts, production costs, and the approximate amount of time needed for each phase of the job. By breaking down every aspect of the project into its separate components, the designer can more easily determine how the complexity and scale of the job will affect each task.

When used as an Estimate Form for Clients, it outlines, item by item, how much the project will cost and how long it will take to do individual tasks. It is particularly useful to include the language indicated at the bottom of this form to assure that the client recognizes that this is an estimate and not a contract.

As a Budget and Schedule Review, this form may be used internally to track how much time and money have already been expended on specific job components and how much is left in the budget to complete the job. It may also be shared with the client at periodic intervals, in particular when budgetary problems arise from unexpected additions and changes by the client. It is advisable, however, to use considerable discretion in revealing internal financial information to clients, especially concerning the cost of design and production time when billing is rendered on a flat fee basis. This is when it is useful to "hide" or close those columns or rows that reveal internal rates you do not wish to show.

Filling in the Form
Depending upon its intended use, check the appropriate box for the preferred title of the form. Fill in the client information; the project number, name, and description; the date; and the name of the person creating or revising the form.

For use as either an Estimate Form for Client or as a Preliminary Budget and Schedule, fill in the "allocated" column for time schedule and the "budget" column under the category of cost. Delete or leave blank the columns marked "to-date" and "balance." For use as a Budget and Schedule Review, either internally or for client use, fill in all of the necessary information in the spaces provided.

Using the Form
❏ Long term, complicated projects should be tracked regularly to make sure that time and expenses are not exceeding the amounts budgeted for the assignment.

❏ When adding or deleting columns and rows, make sure to check formulas.

❏ Not every single item has to be accounted for in every communication. For example, if there is a problem in one mechanical area that needs to be brought to the client's attention, it is sufficient to lump together the total amount for design development on one line and focus on the specific production problem. *As with any form, avoid compulsively filling out every item regardless of whether it is useful or necessary.*

❏ To avoid confusion, delete items under scope of work which are not applicable to the project.

❏ Move items listed under "miscellaneous" to the appropriate place above if those items will be provided in-house.

❏ The term "in-house" refers to the use of the designer's equipment for production. There are some existing standard prices for certain kinds of items. For example, photocopies are routinely billed to clients at an average of 15 cents per copy. Color copies, scans, and other computer-generated items produced in-studio are billed to clients at approximately the same rate that it costs to produce them at a commercial copier store. Rather than having to track varying sheet sizes and billing them at different rates per size, an average size can be determined with a fixed cost per sheet for all color copies regardless of their size. Beware, however, if a job uses only one size sheet and adjust billing accordingly. Be prepared to show backup.

❏ Production materials generated by in-house computers can translate into considerable savings for clients. While savings should be passed along, there are significant costs to owning (or renting/leasing), operating, servicing, and supplying the necessary equipment. One approach is to charge separately for the time that the production artist spends on generating such material with a mark-up on his or her hourly rate to include the expenses of the equipment. Another approach is to calculate the total cost of the equipment, including finance payments, servicing, and supplies (except paper, which will be charged separately as copies), and divide the total sum by the approximate volume of use for the same period of time used to calculate the cost of the equipment. The result is a per-page charge. A third approach is to include all equipment costs as part of the overhead applied to hourly rates. A mark-up should always be included in these calculations to account for internal administrative time and a profit. It is not unethical to make a profit on in-house

equipment when there is still savings being passed along to the client. Such material would otherwise have to be purchased and marked-up, resulting in a much higher cost to the client.

Multimedia

To estimate and track different kinds of productions (for example, one that incorporates multimedia) simply swap out and add terms that are appropriate. As with print projects, begin with *concept development, strategizing,* and *thematic research* to establish the basic thinking and direction for the project.

In multimedia, a *navigation flowchart* serves as a "sketch" to illustrate where all of the elements in the production will appear. *Storyboarding* is also useful in these formats.

Design development in multimedia *applications* (the term often used in referring to a production), usually includes the following:

❏ *Graphical User Interface (GUI—pronounced "gooey") Design*
The "Look and Feel" of each screen, including typefaces, colors, and overall layout and the design of buttons, pictures, and text.

❏ *Prototyping*
A multimedia "dummy" of the application. Prototypes, like comprehensives, are often used for usability and/or focus group testing.

❏ *Content Acquisition*
Assets to be used in the application must be gathered and/or created. An asset may be any visual element or aural expression that can be put into digital form. Conversion from source media into digital formats is also referred to as *audio, video, and camera capture* or *digitization.*

❏ *Authoring / Scripting / Engineering for Functionality*
Programming that is required to integrate and make functional every element of the application including buttons, hot spots, assets, databases, and search engines.

❏ Other steps
- Compression (audio/video/other large files)
- Soft launch
- Testing and debugging
- Launch
- On-going site updates and maintenance
- Site evaluation / usage tracking reports
- Other fulfillment for e-commerce
- Marketing

Project Plan and Budget

CLIENT

Name _____

Address (Meetings) _____

Phone _____

Address (Billing) _____

Phone _____

Cell _____

Fax _____

Other Contact Information _____

ESTIMATING FORMAT   ASSUMPTION: RATES ARE PER   ☐ HOUR   ☐ DAY   ☐ WEEK

	LABOR			
	Principal	**Creative Director**	**Designer**	**Other**
RATES	$	$	$	$
Concept Development	Time (Hours × Days × Weeks)			
Initial Client Meetings				
Concept Planning				
Research (Audit and Competitive Analysis)				
Preliminary Sketches				
Comprehensives				
Concept Presentation Meeting				
Preliminary Budget/Schedule Estimates				
Revisions				
Project Management/Miscellaneous				
Subtotal—Hours				
Subtotal—Cost				
Design Development	Time (Hours × Days × Weeks)			
Logo Design				
Typography				
Color Palette				
Systems Design				
Layouts—Collateral Application				
Layouts—Collateral Application				
Layouts—Collateral Application				
Layouts—Collateral Application				
Layouts—Collateral Application				
Layouts—Collateral Application				
Layouts—Collateral Application				
Layouts—Collateral Application				
Presentation Preparation				
Budget/Schedule Revisions				
Design Presentation Meeting				
Revisions				
Project Management/Miscellaneous				
Subtotal—Hours				
Subtotal—Cost				

☐ Estimate Form for Client
☐ Preliminary Budget and Schedule
☐ Budget and Schedule Status Review

Date —————————————
By —————————————

PROJECT

Job Number —————————————
Job Name —————————————
Description —————————————

ESTIMATE FACTORS			COST			SCHEDULE		
Total Labor	F/L Fees	Materials	Budget	To-Date	Balance	Allocated	To-Date	Balance

ESTIMATING FORMAT   ASSUMPTION: RATES ARE PER ☐ HOUR ☐ DAY ☐ WEEK

		LABOR			
		Principal	**Creative Director**	**Designer**	**Other**
	RATES	$	$	$	$
Production		Time (Hours × Days × Weeks)			
Final Artwork—Logo/Logotype					
Final Artwork—Typography, Color Separations					
Retouching					
Artwork—Collateral Application					
Artwork—Collateral Application					
Artwork—Collateral Application					
Artwork—Collateral Application					
Artwork—Collateral Application					
Artwork—Collateral Application					
Artwork—Collateral Application					
Artwork—Collateral Application					
Presentation Preparation					
Budget/Schedule Revisions					
Design Presentation Meeting					
Revisions					
Project Management/Miscellaneous					
	Subtotal—Hours				
	Subtotal—Cost				
Implementation		Time (Hours × Days × Weeks)			
Printing Supervision					
Fabrication					
Installation					
Project Management		Time (Hours × Days × Weeks)			
	Subtotal—Hours				
	Subtotal—Cost				
Miscellaneous		Description			
Audio/Visual Services					
Charts and Graphs					
Color Copies					
Color Transfers/Other Color Processes					
Copywriting/Editing					
Courier Services					
Fabrication					
Illustration/Other Rendering					
Insurance					
Language Translation					
Local Messengers					
Modelmaking/Prototypes					
Models					
Photographic and A/V Supplies					
Photographic Prints					
Photography					

ESTIMATE FACTORS			COST			SCHEDULE		
Total Labor	F/L Fees	Materials	Budget	To-Date	Balance	Allocated	To-Date	Balance
	Amount	Markup	Budget	To-Date	Balance	Allocated	To-Date	Balance

ESTIMATING FORMAT   ASSUMPTION: RATES ARE PER   ☐ HOUR   ☐ DAY   ☐ WEEK

		LABOR		
	Principal	**Creative Director**	**Designer**	**Other**
RATES	$	$	$	$
Miscellaneous (cont'd)	Time (Hours × Days × Weeks)			
Photoprocesses/Copies				
Portable Media (Disks, CDs, etc.)				
Printing				
Props				
Reproduction				
Research and Database Services				
Research Materials				
Scanning				
Shipping and Handling				
Special Supplies/Materials				
Stock Photo/Art Fees				
Stylist				
Telecommunications				
Travel—Air				
Travel—Ground				
Travel—Hotel and Lodging				
Travel—Meals				
Subtotal				
Project Total Hours				
Project Total Cost				

ESTIMATE FACTORS			COST			SCHEDULE		
Total Labor	F/L Fees	Materials	Budget	To-Date	Balance	Allocated	To-Date	Balance

Proposal Form

In assigning new work, one of the most significant factors in the client's selection process is the designer's proposal. Reputation, recommendations, astute marketing, and self-promotion all play an important part in capturing a client's attention, but key among the final deciding elements in winning the assignment is a well-organized, clearly written, concise, and reasonable proposal.

Proposals are often used by clients to compare fees of several designers being considered for an assignment. A ballpark proposal basically needs to let the client know how much would be charged for the prospective work. Such proposals winnow out which designers are to be seriously considered, at which point a more extensive proposal is usually requested. While ballpark proposals need not be extensive, they should include a brief description of the assignment, fee amounts, schedule, and expense policy. Schedules and specific terms can be generalized, but it should be stated that this is a preliminary proposal and that, if accepted, additional items such as specific fee amounts, time schedules, a schedule of payment, and terms will be forthcoming.

In a competitive situation price is not always the sole determining factor in assigning work. It is more significant to be within the range of given price quotes than to be dramatically lower or higher. An extreme departure from the general range of price quotes signals a lack of understanding of the assignment, desperation, or indifference. If information provided by the client is vague or incomplete, it is especially necessary to include a brief phrase indicating that the proposal is predicated on available information and that any additions or changes will have an impact on the final cost of the project. For example, inexperienced clients tend not to understand how many alternate concepts they are entitled to for a basic fee. For nonvisual or new clients, it is useful to specify the number of concepts that are to be provided, followed by a price quote for additional concepts should they be necessary.

The most important pieces of information that need to be conveyed are (1) an understanding of the assignment by means of a brief description; (2) methodology, or an outline of the working process; (3) fees and expense policy (billables, schedule of payment, mark-ups, etc.); (4) time schedule; and (5) basic terms (copyright, credit, changes, termination, etc.). While not every proposal needs to include all of these points, the more informative the proposal, the stronger its impact. Proposals can be standardized, such as the example included here, or they may be written in composition style.

Large projects will require more information in each area. It may be useful to list the names and credentials of the proposed design team. A very lengthy proposal might call for the inclusion of an "executive summary" to give at least a cursory overview to readers who are inclined to flip directly to the budget page. Regardless of length or depth of detail, the proposal should be treated as part of the designer's marketing program.

Some designers construct their proposals so that if they are accepted the client merely needs to return a signed copy and the proposal then becomes a letter of agreement. In such instances, it is very important to include a specific list of terms governing the assignment. Items such as the number of concepts, billing for extras and changes, transfer of rights, credit, sales tax, liability, and termination fees all have to be addressed. However, for a straight proposal most designers limit the terms to a few basic essentials on the premise that too many unfavorable terms for a client will automatically put the designer out of the running. At the very least, it is important to mention the number of concepts that will be provided for the stated fee, cost of additional work, if necessary, and information about termination. Should the proposal be accepted, a more detailed list of terms may be worked out in a final letter of agreement or contract, such as the Project Confirmation Form that appears in this book.

Filling in the Form

Provide the date and name of the person responsible for the contents of the proposal. Fill in all of the client, project, and fee information. In the "fee information" area, specify how the design fee is being calculated. You can specify which expenses are reimbursable by the client and the amount (if any) of the markup. List specifically those expenses that will be billed at cost. Describe the scope of work in the area indicated.

In the "work plan" section, indicate costs and time for each phase of the proposed project. Under "budget," fill in the expected total cost of each item. For "schedule," either give proposed start and finish dates or expected length of time without start and finish dates. Total the "budget" column and show either overall project start and finish dates or the total amount of work time the project will require, regardless of start and finish dates.

In the "terms and conditions" section, fill in or delete the blanks, as appropriate.

Using the Form

❏ Under "fee information," you can either indicate the basis of the project budget (that is, whether it is based on a flat fee, hourly rates, reimbursable expenses, or some combination of the three), or you can use this area to fill in the total amounts.

❏ In "scope of work," try to be as specific as possible about the nature and number of deliverables—provide enough information to indicate the level of complexity of the proposed project.

❏ Design services are customarily billed on a phase-by-phase basis. In the event this is a flat-fee project, you may still want to break out the design fee into these phases. In case the project is canceled, it will be easier to collect the appropriate fee for completed work phases.

❏ For each relevant item under the "work plan detail," include special notes, such as known or preferred vendors or any other specific indicators that help identify the source of the costs.

❏ Make sure to completely fill in all of the "terms and conditions" information indicated, and add any you are accustomed to requiring. Also, delete any items that are irrelevant to your operation.

❏ The designer should close the form with his or her signature and date and include a cover letter with the proposal. The cover letter can serve many purposes. It can add a personal touch to a proposal that appears as an outline; it may include promotional information that highlights specific reasons why the designer is the best choice for the assignment; it may also serve to remind the client of the origins of the relationship if that would be favorable. Use the following checklist for cover letters:

• Every detail, including the letter's appearance, must be perfect. Make sure the name, title, and address of the contact is correct in form and spelling.

• Sound personable, but not too familiar. Use first names in the salutation only if you have previously spoken to each other.

• Mention the source of information about the contact or prospective assignment, the context in which the initial contact, if any, was made, or the person, if known to the contact, who recommended the contact be made.

• Keep the cover letter brief, simple, and straightforward. One page is ideal.

• If scheduling is an issue, indicate availability as well as any constraints.

• Sign off with a phrase that leads to the possibility of a dialogue, such as: "I would be pleased to discuss this proposal further," "Let me know if I can provide you with any additional material or information," or "If you have any questions or concerns, please let me know so that we may discuss them."

• All correspondence should be on letterhead which includes the designer's name, address, and telephone/fax numbers.

❑ Review the negotiation checklist for the Project Confirmation Form, which might be used to reach final agreement if the Proposal Form is not signed by the client. Note the different statement of some points in the Project Confirmation Form and consider incorporating additional provisions into the terms of the Proposal Form.

Checklist for How to Write Composition Style Proposals

❑ In an introductory paragraph itemize what is to be designed and, if appropriate, mention the source of information about the project. This description need not include all technical specifications, but should include the type of product (logo, brochure, packaging, etc.), size, number of colors and pages, and other descriptive characteristics.

❑ Under the heading of "scope of work" list the phases of the project's development, such as competitive research, sketches, design development, layouts, mechanical production, and printing supervision. If the prospective client is not familiar with the design process, it is helpful to list phase by phase what the designer will do and at what points the client will be presented with material.

❑ For the "time schedule" paragraph, give, if possible, an estimate of the length of time each stage will take. State clearly that this estimate is predicated on the client's timely provision of information and approvals at each stage.

❑ For the "fees and expense policy" paragraph either provide an overall flat fee to cover the assignment and then break that number down into a series of payments; or provide a fee amount for each phase of the job's development and let that be the basis for the payment schedule. Indicate any additional costs that may not be included in the fee, such as reimbursable expenses, author's alterations, and other client-directed changes.

❑ The expenses of photography, illustration, copywriting, printing, fabrication, and travel are also generally not included in the designer's fee and should be specified as such. Offer estimates of approximate costs, if possible, and indicate mark-ups wherever they apply.

❑ Termination fees must be specified as a standard part of every agreement. Termination (also known as "kill fee") refers to the discontinuation of an assignment by either the client or the designer. Some designers require advance payment for each stage of work to be started and specify that this amount is the kill fee in the event the assignment is stopped at any time during this stage of work. With this kind of a schedule of payment the designer is always financially at an advantage and need not resort to withholding work if payments are behind schedule.

❑ Another way of organizing all of this information is to include fees and time schedules along with the descriptions for each separate stage of work. In this format, there should be a separate paragraph for the payment schedule and another for information about reimbursable expenses.

Proposal Form

Date _____

By _____

CLIENT INFORMATION

Name _____

Address _____

Phone _____

Address (Billing) _____

Phone _____

Cell _____

Fax _____

Other Contact Information _____

PROJECT

Name _____

Location _____

FEE INFORMATION

Fee _____

Hourly Rates _____

Expenses—Billable (with markup) _____

Expenses—Billable (without markup) _____

Expenses—Travel _____

SCOPE OF WORK

WORK PLAN

	START-END DATES	BUDGET	DURATION
Concept Development		$	
Design Development			
Production			
Project Implementation			
Total			

DETAIL

	NOTES	BUDGET	SCHEDULE
Meetings		$	
Visual Audits (Internal/External)			
Research/Strategy			
Comps			
Layouts—Collaterals			
Stationery			
Brochure			
Folder			
Poster			
Signage			
POS/POP			
Other			
Logos/Logotypes			
Typography			
Color Palette			
Photography			
Shoot Art Direction			
Photographer			
Stylist			
Models/Props			
Photoprocesses			
Retouching			
Illustration			
Other Art (Stock)			
Copywriting			
Editing			
Proofreading			
Mechanical Production			
Artwork—Final			
Scanning			
Templates			
Mechanicals			
Style Guide			
Color Separation			
Pre-Press			
Specs (paper, ink, etc.)			
Bids—Printing/Other			
Bluelines, Proofs			
Printing Supervision			
Printing			
Fabrication			
Installation			

	NOTES	BUDGET	SCHEDULE
Miscellaneous		$	
Travel			
Messengers			
Courier Services			
Telecommunications			
TOTAL			

All information in this proposal is subject to the Terms and Conditions listed herein.

TERMS AND CONDITIONS

Sketches and Comps Fee quoted includes _____ preliminary concepts / sketches; additional concepts / sketches are $ _____ each.

Final Artwork Fee quoted includes one set of final mechanical artwork. Changes to final artwork will be provided at an additional cost based on the extent and complexity of the changes, at $ ___ per hour or a mutually agreed upon fee, TBD.

Rights Upon full payment of all fees and costs, the following rights to the use of the designs and/or artwork transfer to Client, as noted:

Credit Unless otherwise agreed, Designer shall be accorded a credit line on all published, printed material, to read as follows:

Overtime Fees quoted are based upon work performed during the course of regular working hours (based on a _____ hour week). Overtime, rush, holiday, and weekend work necessitated by Client's directive is billed in addition to the fees quoted at $ _____ per hour or a mutually agreed upon fee, TBD.

Change Orders Work change orders will be issued for additional work and changes requested after approvals or commencement of work. WCO's include a description of the change/addition requested, estimated additional costs, and changes to work schedules/project completion. Client's signature is required on WCO's to proceed with changes/additions.

Billable Items In addition to the fees and costs estimated herein, costs incurred for outside services (TBD), messengers, and courier services are billable (at cost __; with a markup of __ percent). Wherever applicable, state and local sales taxes will be included in Billable Items. Travel expenses are billed additionally, at cost.

Purchasing All purchases made on client's behalf will be billed to client. In all cases, such prices will reflect a markup of ___%. Charges for sales tax, insurance, storage, and shipping and handling are additional to the price of each purchase. In the event client purchases materials, services, or any items other than those specified by the designer, the designer is not liable for the cost, quality, workmanship, condition, or appearance of such items.

Schedule of Payment Hourly Rate: Regular billing periods (bimonthly, monthly) based on hours consumed or periodic approval points. Fee Billing: _____ percent upon project commencement, _____ percent following completion of concept development, _____ percent upon completion of design development, _____ percent upon completion of production, _____ percent upon completion of implementation. Invoices are payable upon receipt.

Termination Policy Client and Designer may terminate project based upon mutually agreeable terms to be determined in writing, either prior to signing of this proposal or within the final Client-Designer Contract.

Term of Proposal The information contained in this proposal is valid for 30 days. Proposals approved and signed by the Client are binding upon the Designer and Client beginning on the date of Client's signature.

If the information in this Proposal meets with Client's approval, Client's signature below authorizes Designer to begin work. Kindly return a signed copy of this Proposal/Agreement to Designer's office.

Designer Signature _____ Print Designer Name _____ Date _____

Client Signature _____ Print Client Name _____ Date _____

Credit Reference Form

New and unknown clients are naturally a welcome challenge to every design firm. They may bring stimulating opportunities for interesting design solutions. They may develop into long-term artistically and financially rewarding relationships. They may also bring financial havoc. Whether a client is simply new or entirely unknown, a serious look at the newcomer's financial history would be a prudent first step toward deciding whether or not to spend the time and effort needed to produce an excellent proposal.

In the case of a new but not unknown client, a call or two to the vendors or individuals known to have business relationships with the client might produce the necessary information.

In the case of an entirely unknown prospective client, the only way to obtain financial information is to ask the prospect for a list of credit references. Designers are often reluctant to go to this extent to protect their interests; however, they should remember that they have to furnish the same information to obtain credit with vendors and suppliers. Large or small, suppliers rarely open accounts with designers without first verifying their credit worthiness.

It is not enough simply to ask the client to fill out this form. It is up to the designer to actually contact the references and ask about the prospect's credit status. Some credit agencies may require a fee for this service. Generally, neither banks nor individuals will commit to stating the exact dollar worth of the prospect (which in any case is not the issue). However, they are able to provide information about the prospect's cycle of payments and general financial history. Be prompt in starting your credit inquiries, since the references may take some time to respond or require a written request. At the same time the client may want to move ahead.

In the event the prospective client is unable to furnish any credit history and you still choose to take the assignment, the only recourse in protecting yourself is to require that the client pay at least one-half, if not the entire, fee in advance. Reimbursables should be billed with regular frequency (weekly or bi-monthly), and payments should be required within a specified number of days. It is also advisable to make arrangements for large out-of-pocket expenses to be paid in advance.

Filling in the Form

Fill in the name of the company, its address, telephone number, and the name of the contact at the company who is the liaison on the account. Fill in the date. Under "company" the company's representative should provide the specific information being requested concerning years in business, number of employees, number of locations, type of business, and its Federal identification number (EIN). Individuals are asked to provide the name of their employer (if not self-employed, or self-employed but not incorporated), its address and telephone number, years of employment, status of home ownership, and the number of years at their current address. The client fills in the names, addresses, telephone numbers, account numbers, and/or contact names of those references he or she prefers to list. An authorized representative of the client signs and dates the form on the bottom, below the statement granting the designer permission to run a credit check. The "notes" column is reserved for the designer to jot down information as it is relayed through phone conversations. If responses are in written form, positive or negative responses can be indicated in the "notes" column and a copy of the letter attached to this form.

Using the Form

The most important questions to ask when checking the prospect's credit are:

❏ How long has the reference done business with the prospect?

❏ What type of business relationship has the reference had with the prospect?

❏ Has the reference ever extended credit to the prospect?

❏ If credit has been extended, what was the maximum amount of the credit?

❏ How many days does the prospect take to pay bills?

❏ Does the prospect pay all invoices in full as presented, or does it pay on account (in small but regular payments over a drawn out period of time)?

❏ Ask if the reference would have any reservation about extending credit to the prospect in the amount of the billing being proposed for the project in question.

Credit Reference Form

Individual or Company Name _____   Date _____

Billing Address _____   Phone _____

_____   Fax _____

_____   Contact Name _____

Companies   **Individuals**

Years in business _____   Employer Name _____

Number of employees _____   Address _____

Number of locations _____   Telephone _____

Business type _____   Years with current employer _____

Private _____   Home: own / rent _____

Incorporated _____   Years at current home address _____

Partnership _____

Federal ID Number _____

Credit Agencies (Name and Address)	Telephone Number	Fax Number	Reference Number	Notes
1.				
2.				

Banks (Name and Address)	Telephone Number	Fax Number	Account Number	Contact
1.				
Notes				
2.				
Notes				

Trade References (Name and Address)	Telephone Number	Fax Number	Account Number	Contact
1.				
Notes				
2.				
Notes				

Personal References (Name and Address)	Telephone Number	Fax Number		Notes
1.				
2.				

By the signature below, authorization and permission is granted to contact the references listed above for the purpose of verifying available credit information about the company and/or individual named above.

_____   By _____   Date _____

Company Name   Authorized Signatory

Job Index

What is the start up procedure for any new job? Immediately after an agreement has been reached (presumably in writing) between the client and designer concerning scope of work, fees, and terms, the designer can consider the job in-house and begin work. At this point, a few simple procedures will effectively organize any job and allow the tracking of its financial and scheduling history.

The first step in opening a studio job is to assign it the job number which will be used to identify every aspect and component of the assignment. The job number is also referred to as the project number, particularly in client communications. *The Job Index is the source of all job numbers.* It is a chronological list of every job, past and present, in the studio and is the simplest and clearest way of knowing what jobs are in-house, who is doing them, how long they have been going on, and whether or not they have been billed.

The "job number" list can begin with any number initially, but then must follow consecu-

tively thereafter. Job numbers may be keyed to the year, such as "14-001," but regardless of how the numerical order is determined, it is best to keep it uncomplicated and as brief as possible since it will have many applications. Always keep the numbers in sequence. Do not fill in the numbers in advance since some assignments may need additional space. For jobs with several distinct subparts which need to be tracked separately for billing purposes, use one job number for the overall name of the assignment/client and use subnumbers or letters to indicate the different parts of the job (also keep separate job sheets for such subnumbers or letters). See example A.

If jobs are unrelated, but have the same client and came in-house at the same time, use separate job numbers. See example B.

Filling in the Form

In the "date opened" column fill in the date the job is officially assigned to the studio. Upon the

Example A

Date	Client	Job Name	Project Lead	Job #
5/17/13	Aztec House	Restaurant —logo	GL	2201-A
"	" "	—menus	DF	2201-B
"	" "	—signage	JK	2201-C
"	" "	—ads	GL	2201-D

Example B

Date	Client	Job Name	Project Lead	Job #
6/30/13	Atlantis Magazine	Supplement—Oct.	SZ	2219
"	" "	Arts Section—Nov.	GL	2220
"	" "	Cover Illus—Dec.	JB	2221

project's completion, fill in the finished date for "date closed." Also, list invoice numbers of the project's billings. Under "client" fill in the company name of the client. Under "job name" indicate briefly what the assignment is, for example: "Toy catalogue—Spring"; "Sinatra Album—front & back"; or "The Joy of Baking—recipe cards."

Under "project lead" fill in the initials of the designer who will have primary responsibility for the assignment. Then fill in the job number.

Using the Form

❑ Use job numbers on job sheets, time sheets, purchase orders, billable invoices, and for logging in-house charges. The job number is the link to all job-related costs and materials.

❑ Post the jobs sheet where employees can easily refer to it and use job numbers consistently. It greatly simplifies record-keeping.

❑ Open a job file in your computer for artwork and correspondence. Open a job bag for each new job to keep physical job-related materials in one place. Label the envelope to show the job number, client, and job names, as well as the date the job was opened.

❑ Open a job file to store hard copies of agreements, work orders, receipts, and back-up copies of billable invoices. It is useful to clip all correspondence and nonbillable papers to the inside of the front cover of the file folder (chronological order, most recent on top). Since designers are frequently required to show back-up for reimbursable expenses such as typography, photoprocesses, printing, messengers, travel, and so on, the file folder is a convenient place to gather back-up copies of these billables.

❑ As soon as a bill has been posted to its job sheet (form 5), pull one of the copies of the bill (if it comes in duplicate), or make an extra copy of bills that don't, and place the copy in this job file. When it is time to bill out the job, all of the necessary back-up copies will be in this file—along with hard copies of all correspondence relating to the assignment. When the job is completed and billed, simply file the folder in either chronological, alphabetical, or subject order for future reference. Quite often it is helpful to be able to check back to earlier proposals and contracts when estimating or negotiating new jobs.

Job Index

Date Opened	Date Closed	Client	Job Name	Project Lead	Job #

Job Sheet

Cost accounting, or keeping track of time and costs expended on a project, is essential to maintaining a regular and accurate billing system. The job sheet is the detailed record of all time and costs incurred during the course of an assignment. It is useful to record time and costs regardless of any fee arrangement since even miscellaneous unbillable time and expenses have an impact on profits when all real costs are fully known. Items such as special supplies, research time, and very long and frequent client meetings not originally calculated into the fee may significantly diminish what might have seemed to be an acceptably profitable job. The advantage of knowing all costs, including extras, is the possibility of more astutely negotiating time and fees of prospective assignments, or perhaps renegotiating a current one.

Job sheets can be used to analyze the following information:

Time. This category can be further notated to indicate specific aspects or phases of jobs. For example, in a packaging assignment with several components, it may be necessary or useful to know how much time was spent on design development, comping, and mechanicals, or how much time it took to do various individual packages.

Billable costs. Graphic designers can expect to bill and often mark up the cost of photography, photoprocesses, retouching, and other outside production services. Special supplies, prototypes, couriers, even postage and toll calls may be billable depending upon the arrangement with the client. All of these items and their mark-up rate are to be negotiated before the deal is finalized. Indicate with an "NB" to the right of the "total" column those items which are nonbillable.

Profitability. In some instances a designer may be working for an hourly fee, in which case accurate records are indispensable. However, when on a flat fee basis, it is still essential to be able to determine whether the fee was adequate for the time spent doing the work. To examine profitability, subtract total actual costs from the total amount billed for the job (not including the tax), for example:

Flat Fee minus Nonreimbursable Project Costs* = Gross Profit
$7,000.00 minus $2,000.00   = 5,000.00

Gross Profit   minus   Overhead Allocation = Net Profit
$5,000.00 minus $3,000.00   = $2,000.00

*Nonreimbursable project costs include the labor and expenses expended to do the job, not covered by out-of-pocket reimbursables.

Overhead refers to the general cost of running the design studio. These include the costs of rent, leases, insurance, utilities, cleaning, maintenance, general supplies, and so on. None of these items are billable to specific assignments, but, along with salaries and profit, they must be figured into the fee structure of every assignment. The overhead factor must also be calculated into the hourly rates used when billing is based on time rather than on a flat fee. To calculate overhead expenses, add up all of the monthly business costs (which are not billable as reimbursable expenses) and divide this total figure by the number of jobs in the studio per month; the resulting number is the dollar amount which every job has to produce to cover the minimum cost of running the business.

For example:

Per Month

Rent	$2,000
Equipment & Supplies	$ 800
Utilities	$ 500
Insurance	$ 300
Accounting & Legal	$ 100
Marketing & Promotion	$ 300
Payroll (inc. taxes & benefits)	$5,000
Total	$9,000

This designer must produce $9,000 worth of revenue every month, just to stay in business. If this designer averages five assignments per month, approximately $1,800 of every assignment's monthly revenue goes directly to paying for overhead. Naturally, higher-paying jobs cover the lower-paying ones, but somehow the final numbers have to average the basic minimum amount needed to cover the essential expenses of the business. To calculate the minimum hourly rate needed to cover overhead expenses, divide the monthly overhead costs by the number of working hours in the month, for example:

$$\$9,000 \div 160 = \$56.25$$

$56.25 is the minimum hourly rate the designer can charge in order to meet his or her monthly expenses, including his or her salary. If there are other salaries in the business which are not billable to jobs, these salaries must also be considered as part of the overhead. Remember, however, that this calculation assumes all project costs are reimbursable and *does not account for profit*.

Calculating profit into fees and hourly rates is not an exact science. Generally, designers add an additional 20 percent to 100 percent into the overhead figure, for example:

$$\frac{\begin{array}{r} \$56.25 \text{ (minimum hourly rate)} \\ \times .20 \text{ (percent profit desired)} \end{array}}{\$ 11.25 + \$56.25 = \$67.50 \text{ (total hourly rate)}}$$

Naturally, any hourly rate has to have a reasonable relation to what other professionals are charging for similar work and what the market will bear—that is, how strongly the client wants to work with the designer. Flexibility is important in determining fees and hourly rates.

Filling in the Form: Page One

In the "Information" section, enter the job number, its name and location, as well as the client contact information indicated. Note different billing and shipping addresses, if necessary. Referral source information is useful in determining the effectiveness of your marketing or sales efforts. If the referral was a former client, it should signal a valuable source of future references, as well as a special note of acknowledgement to that client. Project team information is important to note, in that it is a quick reference for the person preparing periodic cost accounts and billing.

The "dates" section is useful for cost accounting in several ways. First, if a project is billable at specific stages or completion dates, it is necessary to keep track of these dates. Second, since project deliverables are predicated upon specific approvals, it is important to be able to show the client a record of missed sign-off dates that affect deliverable dates. Additionally, a clear record of dates is very useful in understanding those areas of the project that were particularly efficient or inefficient and applying this knowledge to future project plans.

The "billing" area of this form is the place to note the terms of the fees to be charged; whether fee plus costs, time plus materials, markups, discounts, and any other specific details of the fee agreement. Keep a record of billings under "invoice date," "invoice number," and "invoice amount" for a quick review of the project's billing history. It's handy to have all billing information available on one sheet. The "work change orders" section is particularly important to keep up to date. It is a summary of the work changes approved by the client and spells out the amounts of additional (or reduced) billing, as well as changes in deliverable dates. A quick summary on this sheet will eliminate time wasted looking through stacks of paperwork.

Using the Form

Start a Job Sheet as soon as a job number has been assigned to the project from the Jobs Index (which can be a worksheet in your electronic project file).

Posting to page 2 "cost account" should take place after time sheets have been collected and approved for payroll and when job-related bills are being paid. Indicating job numbers on time sheets and payable invoices makes it easier to post these items to individual job sheets.

Messenger, courier, and other service logs should have a jobs index nearby for easy reference to job numbers. When you receive bills for these services, it will be easy to assign these expenses to projects.

When a time-plus-cost-based project is ready for billing, using the information on page 2, side 1, tally all related items separately and post the totals onto page 1, side 2. For example, add messengers and other outside costs separately. Add up project personnel time and/or total cost (if freelancer or contractor) separately. For billing, either itemize each cost type separately or combine under general headings by project areas or tasks. Remember to factor markups as appropriate.

For example:

Stock photography (out-of-house)

$300
300
300
300
—————
$1,200 x 20% = 240 (markup)

$1,200
240
—————
$1,440   (total cost of out-of-house stock photography including markup to client)

John Designer (Freelance)

10 hours
5 hours
4 hours
11 hours
—————
30 hours

30 hours x $40 (hourly rate) = $1,200 (cost to studio)

$40 x 2.5 (markup factor) = $100/hour

$100 x 30 (hours) = $3,000 (cost to client)

You may or may not choose to show these calculations on your invoices, depending on the agreement you have with your client. Generally, markups are rolled into total numbers, although some designers clearly delineate them.

Filling in the Form: Page Two

The "summary of costs" is a comprehensive view of the project's estimated and actual job costs. Labor and materials expenses are shown separately. You may wish to total both labor and materials expenses for each line item. Use this summary as a worksheet when calculating the total costs of the completed project. You can add additional "actual" columns for interim summaries for partial billing, but do include a final total column.

Filling in the Form: Page Three and Continuing on Supplementary Pages

Uncomplicated, short-term assignments may only need a couple of these supplementary pages. When projects are complex and involve a great variety and frequency of services, or continue for long periods of time, there may be many supplementary pages to list the ongoing time and costs. This form allows for the listing of billables, line by line. The date that the item is posted on this sheet goes in the "date" column. "item" is the name of either the person (staff or freelance) or the vendor/supplier. For staff, put the number of billable hours under "hrs/rate"; there is no need to show their rates here, since you have already included that in the project team section on page one. For freelancers, you can either indicate their hours and rates in this column, or put their invoice fee under "total labor." Under "description," fill in the invoice number and date; in the case of a staff person, fill in the name, the date of the time sheet or the week-ending date and the project code.

The "outside services and material expenses" column is for invoices received that separate labor from expenses. For example, a researcher might submit an invoice like this:

Competitive industry research services:
18 hours @ $40.00/hour
Subtotal: $720.00

Expenses:
Library Reference Room Fees $ 12.00
Books $ 75.00
Transportation (NYC/Boston/NYC) $195.00
Subtotal: $282.00

Total: $1,002.00

For jobs that require periodic billing for fees and costs, draw a bold line or skip a space under the last item included in each separate invoice, and jot down the invoice number by this line, so that it will be easy to see where to start tallying for the next invoice.

Electronic Costs

While computers can generate type, retouch images, make line art, color separations and film, among other tasks, they do so without the visible evidence of purchase orders and backup invoices from outside vendors. Estimate and track time spent on these tasks and either bill them as production items or include these costs in the design fee.

Job Sheet

INFORMATION

Job Number _____

Job Name _____

Location _____

Client

Name _____

Address _____

Phone _____

Cell _____

Fax _____

Bill To _____

_____

_____

Ship To _____

_____

_____

P.O. # _____

Referral Source

Name _____

Address _____

Phone _____

Sales/Marketing Source _____

Project Team Name

Principal _____

Design Director _____

Senior Project Designer _____

Designer _____

Design Assistant _____

CADD _____

Consultant _____

Other _____

Billing Rate

_____

_____

_____

_____

_____

_____

_____

_____

DATES

	Target Date	Actual Date	Notes
Contract Start	_____	_____	_____
Client Intake Meeting(s)	_____	_____	_____
Concept Development Start			
Presentation (1)	_____	_____	_____
Presentation (2)	_____	_____	_____
Concept Development Sign-Off	_____	_____	_____

	Target Date	Actual Date	Notes
Design Development Start			
Presentation (1)	_____	_____	_____
Presentation (2)	_____	_____	_____
Design Development Sign-Off	_____	_____	_____
Production Start			
Revisions (1)	_____	_____	_____
Revisions (2)	_____	_____	_____
Production Sign-Off	_____	_____	_____
Project Implementation			
Printing	_____	_____	_____
Fabrication	_____	_____	_____
Installation—Site Supervision	_____	_____	_____
Final Project Completion Items			
Walk-Through and Punch List	_____	_____	_____
Punch List Completion	_____	_____	_____

BILLING

Fee Information

Fee Amount _____

Time and Materials _____

Tax Percent _____

Invoice Date(s) _____ Invoice Number(s) _____ Invoice Amount(s) _____

WORK CHANGE ORDER(S)

Date _____ Order Number _____ Item _____ Hrs/Rate _____ Expense _____ Total _____

SUMMARY OF COSTS

Item	Estimated Labor	Estimated Outside Services & Materials Expense	Estimated Total	Notes	Actual Labor	Actual Outside Services & Materials Expense	Actual Total
Concept Development	_____	_____	_____	_____	_____	_____	_____
Design Development	_____	_____	_____	_____	_____	_____	_____
Production	_____	_____	_____	_____	_____	_____	_____
Project Implementation	_____	_____	_____	_____	_____	_____	_____
Project Total (By Phases)	_____	_____	_____	_____	_____	_____	_____
Project Details							
Meetings	_____	_____	_____	_____	_____	_____	_____
Visual Audit	_____	_____	_____	_____	_____	_____	_____
Research/Strategy	_____	_____	_____	_____	_____	_____	_____
Comps	_____	_____	_____	_____	_____	_____	_____
Layouts—Collaterals							
Stationery	_____	_____	_____	_____	_____	_____	_____
Brochure	_____	_____	_____	_____	_____	_____	_____

Item	Estimated Labor	Estimated Outside Services & Materials Expense	Estimated Total	Notes	Actual Labor	Actual Outside Services & Materials Expense	Actual Total
Folder							
Poster							
Signage							
POS/POP							
Other							
Logo(s)/Logotype(s)							
Typography							
Color Palette							
Photography							
Shoot Art Direction							
Photographer							
Stylist							
Models/Props							
Photoprocesses							
Retouching							
Illustration							
Other Art (Stock)							
Copywriting							
Editing							
Proofreading							
Mechanical Production							
Artwork—Final							
Scanning							
Templates							
Mechanicals							
Style Guide							
Color Separation							
Pre-Press							
Specs (paper, ink, etc.)							
Bids—Printing/Other							
Bluelines, Proofs							
Printing Supervision							
Printing							
Fabrication							
Installation							
Miscellaneous							
Travel							
Messengers							
Courier Services							
Telecommunications							
Project Total (By Details)							

COST ACCOUNT

Date	Item	Hrs/Rate	Description	Total Labor	Outside Services & Materials Expenses	Billable/Nonbillable

Time Sheet

Regardless of whether assignments are billed on a flat fee or hourly rate basis, it is essential to know exactly how much time is spent by all staff members on every assignment; additionally, it is useful to know how nonbillable time is being used. Naturally, it is important to have an accurate record for jobs billed by the hour, mostly to ensure that all billable time is reimbursed, and partly in the event the client requests an audit of time-keeping records. While it is not customary to attach staff members' time sheets to client invoices, many project agreements contain language entitling the client to review the designer's records pertaining to the client's specific assignment.

Time should also be accounted for on projects that are billed on a flat fee basis. Working backwards, the fee itself is generally based on an approximation of the amount of time to be spent on the project, with a mark up to include profit and overhead expenses (nonbillable costs such as rent, utilities, insurances, etc., are discussed under the Job Sheet section). To approximate the time to be spent, the designer needs to think the assignment through its technical stages . . . how many pages . . . how many colors . . . how big . . . how complex . . . will there need to be outside services such as illustration and photo retouching? . . . does the client have a tendency to conduct numerous and lengthy meetings? . . . etc. Naturally, there are other factors in determining prices, such as the intrinsic value of the finished piece (usually keyed to its uses, volume of reproduction, and breadth of its distribution), the market for which it is being produced, as well as the size and financial resources of the client; all of these factors are more or less fixed and known in the earliest stages of the project. Time is the variable in determining fees and the most important key to profitability on a flat-fee-based assignment. The more exact the understanding is of the technical production and frequency of client contact required, the more accurate the estimation of the time that will be required. As a safety device, also called a contingency charge, some designers customarily add 15 percent to whatever number of hours they estimate will be needed to complete the assignment.

Filling in the Form

Each staff member fills in his name, the current month, dates covered by the time sheet (usually covering a week's activities), and the year. Fill in the "Project Number" column so that whoever is posting time sheets to job sheets does not have to refer to the Jobs Index every time a job name appears. Mid- to large-scale design firms now set up these tracking documents on their Intranets and can automate the transfer of data from time sheets to job sheets. You could also set up job sheets for non-project types of activities, to capture time spent on general administration, marketing, maintenance, sick days, etc.

Fill in the "job name" as listed on the Jobs Index. Specify activities using codes under the headings of "phase code," "activity code," and "detail code." Indicate the number of hours worked on each job every day. It is important to note the "Total Billable" time, because project agreements may vary with regard to which activities are billable and which are not.

The "Notes" column can be used to indicate the percentage of billable versus nonbillable hours spent, as shown in the sample form. Or it can be used to show other calculations, such as regular versus overtime hours, marketing versus project time, or other kinds of staff time information that the design firm would like to track.

The staff or project supervisor should sign or initial the "Approved" space. Whoever is responsible for transferring time sheet information to job sheets should indicate the posting date next to "Date Posted."

Using the Form

The coding system shown here is a suggested format that follows the system suggested throughout the business forms part of this book, including the estimate and job sheet forms. You may decide to either simplify, show greater detail, or use other coding symbols of your choice.

The advantage of this kind of breakout of phases, activities, and details in separate columns is that, in Excel, you can sort information by columns and analyze staff members' time spent on various activities.

For the most part, design firm employees do not get paid overtime. The reason you should track it anyway is that on hourly jobs, while you are billing the total time worked (regardless of whether it is regular or overtime), you are incurring additional costs for staff that is working overtime. These costs include overhead items, such as utilities, and variable costs, such as food and transportation for late-night work sessions. Knowing how much overtime is incurred is also helpful in determining if a staff person may be entitled to some additional time off, or "comp" time, particularly if the overtime is incurred to meet client demands rather than for poor working habits.

Everyone who is required to fill out a time sheet—and for the sake of billing, principals and other senior personnel need to be accountable—should fill out their time sheet daily. It is often hard to remember exactly how much time is spent on specific activities when the firm is busy and people are rushing to get work done.

Time sheets should be checked and signed by project leads or senior designers, as appropriate to the management style of your firm. Principals and senior staff usually turn over their time sheets directly to the person who does the posting.

Time sheets should be posted weekly, so that no more than a few days are needed to prepare billing when an assignment is complete or ready for the next phase of billing.

Also, some clients like to get weekly time accounts of their project's activities.

Time Sheet

Name _____

Month _____

Dates _____

Year _____

		CODES					
Job Number	Job Name	Phase	Activity	Detail	Monday	Tuesday	Wednesday
Totals							

Approved _____

Date Posted _____

Phase Codes	Phases	Activity Codes	Activities	Detail Codes	Detail Items
1	Concept	A	Art Direction	00	Not a Detail Item
2	Design	B	Budget/Schedule/Proposal	01	Website
3	Production	C	Client Relations (Attendance at Meetings/Presentations)	02	Corporate Identity
4	Implementation	D	Designing/Drawing	03	Brochure
		N	Press Supervision	04	Product Packaging
		P	Presentation Preparation	05	Poster
		R	Research	06	Signage
		S	Production	07	POS/POP
		T	Travel	08	Style Guide
		W	Copywriting/Editing/Proofing	09	Other

Nonbillable Codes

GA, General Administration; MN, Maintenance; PM, Promotion/Marketing; VA, Vacation; HD, Holidays; SK, Sick Days; EA, Excused Absences (Jury Duty, Family Leave, etc.)

Thursday	Friday	Saturday	Sunday	Total	Total Billable	Notes

Studio Production Schedule

It is characteristic of the graphic design profession that work must be produced on deadline schedules. One of the designer's most serious concerns is the ability to complete assignments on time. In order to calculate the blocks of time needed to meet deadlines, the designer should work out a studio production schedule after receiving the details of a new assignment. Most commonly, designers calculate production schedules by working backward from the final due date for delivering the assignment. This form is a simplified version of the very detailed Preliminary Budget and Schedule which appears in this book.

Filling in the Form

Fill in all the known due dates. Block out the amount of time, using specific dates, needed to complete each activity listed. Estimate the dates when specifications, copy, approvals, and other material will be needed from the client. Let the client know that the designer's ability to meet deadlines is predicated upon the client providing the necessary information, material, and approvals on time. Under "to/from" indicate, unless self-explanatory, in which direction material is moving, or more specifically, the names of vendors or freelancers who are responsible for providing material. Fill in the actual date items are completed and delivered.

Using the Form

❑ Designers may choose to attach a copy of the studio production schedule to the agreement or contract for the assignment in order to assure that the necessary information and approvals from the client are delivered on time, thus enabling the designer to meet his or her deadlines. In the event the client is negligent in providing necessary material, a record of the actual dates of such deliveries may help substantiate the designer's problems with delivering the job on time or need for additional compensation.

❑ A production schedule is good for planning later stages of jobs when the designer is dependent upon others for completing the assignment. There are several benefits to contacting prospective illustrators and photographers in the planning stages of a project: it gives the designer time to review the necessary portfolios; the prospective talent has an opportunity to come in on the conceptual stage and may possibly contribute additional insight or useful suggestions; and, finally, the selected talent is able to allocate the appropriate time necessary to produce the work. Printers also appreciate being able to schedule print runs in advance and may be more cooperative in finding the exact papers or other special materials specified.

Studio Production Schedule

CLIENT

Name _____

PROJECT

Job Name _____

Job Number _____

Phase/Item	Start	End	Due Dates	To	From	Date Completed
Concept Development						
Preliminary Meetings						
Materials Due From Client (Specs/Copy)						
Research/Strategy						
Visual Audit (Client and/or Industry/Competitive)						
Presentation Preparation						
Concept Presentation						
Revisions						
Client Sign-Off						
Design Development						
Artwork Creation (Logos, etc.)						
Layouts—Collaterals						
Stationery						
Brochure						
Folder						
Poster						
Signage						
POS/POP						
Other						
Other						
Other						

Phase/Item	Start	End	Due Dates	To	From	Date Completed
Photography						
Illustration						
Other Art						
Copy (Writing, Editing, Proofreading)						
Presentation Preparation						
Design Development Presentation						
Revisions						
Client Sign-Off						
Production						
Final Artwork (Logos, Charts, etc.)						
Scanning						
Templates						
Application Files						
Style Guide						
Specs						
Bids						
Final Art and Copy to Client						
Revisions						
Client Sign-Off						
Project Implementation						
Bluelines, Proofs						
Printing Supervision						
Shipping & Delivery						
Fabrication						
Installation						
Samples						
Case Study						

Project Status Report

Designers use project status reports for long term and complicated projects, where they are invaluable in keeping clients informed. The report includes information about what is presently going on, who is waiting for what, from whom, and when. Used regularly, these reports help smooth communications between designer and client and may also be helpful in keeping subcontractors tuned into the rhythm and direction of the project. For short term, less complex assignments, project status reports can be used to prod a client out of a stalled situation. This report can also be particularly useful to non-visual or inexperienced clients because it gives them a clear picture of what is expected to happen and in what order. Using standard professional terminology (such as comps, copy, mechanicals, proofs, and so on) also allows the client to become familiar with the language as well as the process of graphic design. Finally, a status report helps to identify those individuals who have responsibility to carry out specific tasks. It is a clear, but non-confrontational way of getting people to respond to specific issues and needs.

Filling in the Form

In the "to" and "copies" areas, fill in the name of the person(s) who will be receiving this report, or the corporate name of the client if it is to be circulated widely. Fill in the name of the project; list the names of additional people who will be receiving a copy of this report, the job number, and the date of the report. (This format may also be used for summarizing the minutes of meetings, in which case the date of the meeting should be indicated as well.)

There are two ways to use this form: (1) For short specific tasks that correspond to the list of phases, check mark the applicable phases, and fill in the items and other information in the spaces provided; (2) if the need is to discuss one

or two topics in greater length and detail, check the phase appropriate to the discussion and use the entire space available on the sheet to outline the points to be made.

Using the Form

❑ Someone on the design team should take notes during client meetings. These may simply be key phrases informally jotted down, or they may be standard, outline-style notes. Whatever the form, the ability to articulate the client's needs and ideas briefly, along with a written record of critical decisions, serves as a great advantage in conceptualizing and moving a project along.

❑ When it is useful to keep subcontractors (such as freelance artists, vendors, and manufacturers) appraised of project developments, this form can be addressed either directly to them, or they can be included in the general distribution of copies. Very often, subcontractors are either directly affected by specific changes on a project or they simply need to know whether the work is proceeding according to schedule.

❑ Most assignments have critical deadlines and it is important for everyone involved to know how their contribution fits into the overall scheme. It cannot be overstated that clear, timely, and accurate communications are essential to the success of group projects.

Project Status Report

To _____ Job Number_____ Date _____

Copies _____ Job Name _____

Phase	Item	Status	Action Required	From	To	Date Due
Concept Development						
Design Development						
Production/Pre-Press						
Project Implementation (Printing/Fabrication)						
Other						

Work Change Order Form

In the course of virtually any kind of assignment, it is almost inevitable that clients will request some kind of changes. Whether changes are required in the conceptual stage, during design development, layout, or even during the printing or fabrication process, it is very important to document these changes. First, to verify the exact nature of the change, and second, to justify any additional billing that the extra work necessitates. Such changes are sometimes referred to as "author's alterations" (also known as AA's) and are always billed as extras.

A brief and simple form is easier for clients to read, sign, and return than addenda to contracts, or even letters outlining the new client instructions. While it is desirable to have clients return these forms signed and dated to indicate approval, when they do not, the language printed on the bottom of this form is intended to protect the designer from an unresponsive client.

Filling in the Form

Fill in all the information concerning client name, project name, job number, work change order number, and the date. Indicate the stage of work during which this particular change is being requested. Specify under "work change description" what aspect of the work is being changed. If lengthy copy changes have been required, attach a copy of such changes to this sheet. Indicate the estimated additional time and/or cost it will take to make these changes. Specify the number of days during which the client may correct the form. Make sure to have the form signed by the client and returned. Attach specifications, if they are longer than the space permits.

Using the Form

❏ Keep track of all additional time and costs incurred by changes in the project's scope or specifications. If the client questions additional charges, these work change orders serve as proof that additional work took place either at the client's behest or with the client's approval for changes initiated by the designer.

❏ Keep this form in the job file. Jot down a brief summary of work change orders on the project's job sheet, page 1, side 2.

Work Change Order Form

Client _____   Change Order Number _____

Project _____   Date _____

Work Change Requested By _____   Job Number _____

Phase

Concept Development ❑

Design Development ❑

Production ❑

Project Implementation ❑

Other ❑

Work Change Description	Cost Change	Schedule Change
_____	_____	_____
_____	_____	_____
_____	_____	_____
_____	_____	_____
_____	_____	_____

This is not an invoice. Revised specifications on work in progress represents information that is either different from that which the original project budget and schedule were based upon, or follows after client's approval to the stage of work in which this (these) item(s) appear(s). Changes in time and cost quoted here may be approximate, unless otherwise noted. Your signature below will constitute authorization to proceed with the change(s) noted above. Kindly return a signed and dated copy of this form to: _____. The information contained in this work change order is assumed to be correct and acceptable to client unless designer is otherwise notified in writing within ____ days of the date of this document.

Authorized Signature _____

Print Name _____

Date _____

Estimate Request Form

Whenever clients and designers prefer to have a variety of choices in the selection of outside services (such as photoprocesses, illustration/photography, prepress, fabrication, and so on), it becomes necessary to request bids from eligible and appropriate suppliers. To avoid confusion in evaluating these bids, it is useful to provide the competing suppliers with exactly the same description of the work to be performed. This form may also be used to back up a verbal quote when the supplier has been selected without preliminary bidding. Although it is clearly a quotation of approximate fees and costs, the estimate request helps to control significant variations in vendor billings.

Filling in the Form

Fill in the name of the client and project, the date, the job number, the name of the person requesting the estimate, and his or her contact numbers. Fill in the name, address, and telephone number of the vendor/supplier. Fill in the item number as a simple list. Fill in "specifications/description" in as great a detail as possible; include as much information as necessary to accurately estimate the work to be done. Fill in the delivery or due date. Leave blank the spaces for estimate, subtotal, tax, shipping/delivery, total, and deposit required. The vendor/supplier should sign the estimate next to "quotation by" and fill in the date.

Using the Form

❏ When requesting bids, fill in the heading and the specifications/description part of the form; make as many copies as needed to distribute to the prospective bidders (plus one for the designer's files); and then fill in the "to" section with the name of each individual bidder on each separate copy of the form.

This way it is certain that everyone has exactly the same instructions on which to base their bids.

❏ If necessary, send a copy of all estimate requests to the client. Include information which will have an effect on the bid, even though it is not exactly related to the job; for example, if there are complicated shipping requirements, or if the assignment will require the vendor to travel, or any other service that will be in addition to the basic required work.

❏ Keep this form in the job file. Jot down a brief summary of bidding estimates on the project's job sheet, page 1, side 2.

Estimate Request Form

Client _____

Project Name _____

Job Number _____

Date _____

Requested By _____

Phone _____

Fax _____

Email _____

Supplier Name _____

Address _____

Phone _____

Fax _____

Email _____

SPECIFICATIONS/DESCRIPTION

Item Number	Specifications/Description	Delivery Date	Estimate Quote	Shipping/ Tax/etc.	Total
_____	_____	_____	_____	_____	_____
_____	_____	_____	_____	_____	_____
_____	_____	_____	_____	_____	_____
_____	_____	_____	_____	_____	_____
_____	_____	_____	_____	_____	_____
_____	_____	_____	_____	_____	_____
_____	_____	_____	_____	_____	_____
_____	_____	_____	_____	_____	_____
_____	_____	_____	_____	_____	_____

Delivery Date _____

Notes _____

Supplier Signature

_____

Print Supplier Name

_____

Subtotal _____

Shipping/Handling _____

Tax _____

Total Estimate _____

Deposit Required _____

Date _____

This is not a purchase order. The information contained in this form is to provide a basis for estimating the cost of the services requested. It is understood that while the estimated costs are approximate, final billing will be adjusted according to specific instructions provided in a purchase order or contract. Kindly fill in the information requested in the shaded area under Estimate, sign, date and return a copy of this form by _____ .

Thank you.

Purchase Order

The purchase order serves as a written notice to vendors, manufacturers, and other suppliers, including freelance artists, to begin work on a specific assignment or to deliver goods. Many vendors will not proceed without a written purchase order. For the design studio, the purchase order form is handy in two ways. First, it is a record of when goods are ordered, from whom, and when they are expected to be delivered. Second, when invoices are being checked, purchase orders are useful for verifying precisely what was ordered. In the event the supplier is in error, the purchase order serves as verification of the original order. Additionally, if prices are included on the purchase order form, the designer is quickly able to justify and post the invoice incurred by the order.

As with job numbers and invoice numbers, purchase orders start with any number and then continue in chronological order. It is very helpful, but not absolutely necessary, to have forms with preprinted numbers. It is, however, essential to make the forms either in duplicate or triplicate. If not using computer-generated forms, pressure sensitive paper, carbons, or photocopying will serve this purpose. At the very least, the designer will need to send the original copy to the vendor and keep a copy for him or herself. Studios with separate bookkeeping departments would need a third copy for the bookkeeper's records.

Filling in the Form

Write in the number of the purchase order, date of the order, the client and project names, and the project number (job number). Fill in the name of the vendor, the address if it is a new or unknown supplier, and the name of the contact or sales representative at the vendor's place of business. In the space for "schedule" fill in the date the job must be received in the designer's hands and check the appropriate level of urgency. "Overtime" refers to nonbusiness hours, weekends, and holidays. In the space under "specifications" fill in the instructions for the work to be done or the goods to be delivered. Give quantities, sizes, dimensions, and any other specific information necessary to communicate exactly what is expected. If ordering from a catalogue, give item numbers, catalogue page numbers, descriptions, and so on. Be absolutely precise. In the space for "shipping address" fill in the name and address of where the goods are to be delivered. The designer should compute the subtotal and total, if costs are known in advance. In the space for "bill to" fill in the name and address of where the supplier is to send his or her invoice if other than the designer. Print or clearly sign the order and fill in the telephone and extension number where the designer can be reached for questions.

Using the Form

❏ Purchase order forms should be on letterhead or some other form of stationery that clearly shows the name of the designer, the name of the firm, its address, and its telephone number.

❏ Remember that both rush and overtime will incur additional costs. It is best to check what these will be in advance. Markups for rush and overtime orders can be as much as 100 percent and more. Overtime refers to work that must be completed overnight, on weekends, or on holidays.

❏ Provide a sketch, if necessary, to convey a full understanding of the order. The more detailed and descriptive an order, the less chance there is of having to accept and pay for mistakes.

❏ Most suppliers prefer to bill the designer directly and usually are not pleased to have to bill a third party. This is a detail that should be worked out in advance. The supplier may require a deposit, as well as bank and business references before acceding this point.

❏ Copies of completed purchase order forms should be kept all together in one place, in a document folder on your computer or as hard copies in a loose-leaf ring binder, in numerical order (most recent number used on top); in addition, keep another copy in the job file together with all the other paperwork for the project.

❏ If the designer chooses to use purchase order forms to contract freelance work, he or she must remember to include information pertaining to copyright, usage, and credit lines that the freelance artist may require. Also, it is useful to require the freelancer's social security number so that Form 1099 can be completed (as required by the Internal Revenue Service for any payments of $600 or more to independent contractors).

❏ Be certain that the rights which the designer obtains from freelance artists or photographers are at least as great as the rights which the designer must transfer to the client.

❏ If the designer must oversee and pay for printing, consider using the Contract with Printer form that appears in this book. It seeks to protect the designer from the many problems that may arise, including the issue of client satisfaction with the printed piece.

Purchase Order

Job Number _____ P.O. Number _____

Date _____

Vendor _____ Phone _____

Address _____ Fax _____

Contact _____ Email _____

Schedule   Delivery Due: _____   ❑ Regular   ❑ Rush   ❑ Overtime (holiday, weekends, etc.)

SPECIFICATIONS

Item Number	Description	Quantity	Unit Price	Other	Total

NOTES _____

_____

_____

_____

_____

Subtotal	_____
Shipping/Handling	_____
Tax	_____
Total	_____
Deposit	_____
Balance Due	_____

Ship to: _____

_____

_____

Bill to: _____

_____

_____

Ordered by

Signature _____ Phone _____

Print name _____ Fax _____

Requisition Form

Small design studios rarely make use of internal requisition forms. Larger studios tend to have more of a need for them since there is greater efficiency in ordering supplies and distributing them from a central source. Further efficiency is achieved by not duplicating orders, being able to take advantage of discounts on larger orders, and minimizing loss and disappearance of supplies. This form is flexible in that it acknowledges different types of supply orders according to their source. These forms can either be distributed to all staff members, or they can be held by one person in each department.

Filling in the Form

The person who is requesting supplies fills in his or her name, telephone extension number, and the date of the order. Using the "source codes" indicated on the form, identify each item by the appropriate code and give the information requested for that code number. Check mark whether the items are needed urgently or within the regular time frame for such orders. Provide job numbers wherever applicable.

Using the Form

❑ For billable items, the job number is immediately applied to purchase orders as well as to order forms, thereby simplifying the task of posting when the invoice for the order arrives.

❑ It is helpful to have an up-to-date selection of art and office supply catalogues that are easily accessible to anyone wishing to place an order.

Requisition Form

Name _____

Telephone Extension_____ Date _____

Delivery

❑ Regular

❑ Rush

Source Codes

1. Catalogue (Include name of catalogue, page number, item number, brief description, quantities, and unit prices)

2. Internal Supplies (Include name of item, description including sizes and colors, and quantities)

3. Other (Include name of source, address and telephone number, a description of the item including sizes, colors, quantities, and unit price)

Source Code	Description	Unit Price	Total	Job Number

Payables Index

The payables index is used to track incoming invoices, whether or not they are related to billable jobs. It is handy for checking monthly statements and determining whether or not bills have been approved. It also contains all of the necessary information to relocate lost bills. Incoming invoices should be gathered on a daily or bi-weekly basis (depending upon the volume of payable bills). After recording the required information to the payables index, distribute the bills to those who will be approving them. (A closed-sided manilla file folder with each person's name on the tab is handy for this purpose.)

Filling in the Form

Under "date received" fill in the date the bill came into the studio. Under "vendor/supplier" write in the name of the company or individual printed on the bill. Indicate the total amount of the bill under "amount." Write in the invoice number and the date of the invoice. "Attention" refers to the person in the studio who is responsible for approving this particular bill. When the invoice is returned, write the date it was returned in the "approved" column. Job-related bills are now ready for posting to job sheets "posted," after which they can be paid and filed; bills not related to jobs can be paid and filed directly.

Using the Form

❏ Every bill for expenses incurred for any specific job, or the studio in general, should be looked over by the art director, designer, or other individual who ordered the corresponding material or services. (Generally, job captains on large assignments have the responsibility of reviewing such invoices.)

Any person responsible for reviewing invoices should indicate the following on each invoice:

❏ If the invoice is related to a job, indicate the job number on the invoice even if it is not a billable expense, but incurred by the needs of the project. Indicate with an "NB" those job-related bills that are not billable to the client as a charge-back, also known as an OOPs (out-of-pocket) expense.

❏ If the bill is for a studio expense and not related to any specific job, simply indicate "studio" on the bill. Likewise, marketing expenses.

❏ The person approving the bill should place their initials on it.

❏ Indicate the date the bill is approved.

❏ If the bill is for more than one job, divide the sum appropriately and indicate the amounts applicable to the separate jobs.

❏ If the bill is incorrect, this is the time to make adjustments with the vendor. Ask the vendor to reissue a correct bill, if possible, rather than making the corrections by hand.

❏ File a copy of all billable invoices in file folders identified on the outside by individual job numbers. Every job should have this "back up" file to collect copies of all reimbursable expenses (which are then sent to the client when the job is billed to substantiate these expenses). This file can be the same as the one described in the Job Sheet section of this book.

Payables Index

Date Received	Vendor/Supplier	Amount	Invoice #	Amount Due	Attention	Approved	Posted

Transmittal Form

The transmittal form is most frequently used as a cover letter for enclosures, attachments, and any other kind of material being disseminated within or outside of the studio. The advantage of having one multi-use transmittal form is that it eliminates the need to create individually written letters every time material needs to be circulated. Also, the information on the form is comprehensive, thereby uniformly communicating the necessary facts about the accompanying material. Create an electronic template with your letterhead and make sure the firm's name, address, telephone, and fax numbers are clearly legible.

Filling in the Form

Fill in the name of the recipient, his or her company name, the job number if applicable, the name of the person sending the material and the names of additional people who will also be receiving a copy of this form. Next to "for" check the reason for sending the enclosed or accompanying material. Next to "via" check the means by which this communication is being sent. For "enclosed" check mark the nature of the attachment or enclosure. Under "media," check if the enclosure is hardcopy or digital. If digital, the file name is a useful guide to the recipient. For "disposition" indicate whether the material is to be returned, kept, or distributed. Use the space left for "remarks" for additional messages.

Using the Form

❏ Under "remarks" state that ownership of the artwork and all rights are reserved to the artist, unless otherwise specified.

❏ Keep copies of all transmittals in the job file.

❏ If the transmittal is not job-related, keep copies in either an electronic document file or a loose-leaf, ring-bound notebook with the most recent copy on top.

❏ If material of great value is being transmitted (such as original photographic transparencies), obtain adequate insurance to cover loss and damage.

❏ If the material transmitted is valuable, indicate who is responsible for loss or damage—including during shipment.

Transmittal Form

To —————————————————— From ——————————————————

Company —————————————— Date ——————————————————

Phone ———————————————— Job Number ————————————————

Email ———————————————— Fax ——————————————————

Copies to: ——————————————

For: —————————————————————————————————————

❑ Review ❑ Files ❑ Information

❑ Approval ❑ Distribution ❑ As Requested

Via: —————————————————————————————————————

❑ Email ❑ Fax (Number of pages, including transmittal) ——————

❑ Messenger ❑ Pouch ❑ Interoffice

❑ Courier Service ——————————————————————

❑ Freight Forwarder ——————————————————————

❑ US Mail (regular) ❑ US Mail (express)

Enclosed/Attached: ——————————————————————————

❑ Document ❑ Comps ❑ Promotion Package

❑ Artwork ❑ Mechanicals ❑ Article/Book

❑ Pre-Press Materials ❑ Other

——————————————————————————————————

——————————————————————————————————

Media: ————————————————————————————————

❑ Digital

❑ Hard Copy **Type** **File Name(s)**

❑ USB Drive ——————————

❑ DVD ——————————

❑ Other ——————————

Disposition: ———————————————————————————————

❑ Kindly Reply ❑ Return ❑ Keep ❑ Distribute

Remarks: ——————————————————————————————

——————————————————————————————————

——————————————————————————————————

Artwork Log and Digital File Management

This form is used to track the whereabouts of artwork sent out by the studio. Artwork includes digital and/or hardcopy of original art, sketches, mechanicals, transparencies, prototypes, models, and so on. The form is also intended to serve as a permanent record of the location of artwork stored within the studio. It is not uncommon for designers to be responsible for the storage of mechanicals, particularly for corporate identity and other projects involving stationery, in which case it is important to be able to locate materials quickly when they are needed for reorders and changes.

Digital File Management

There are several issues concerning the management of digital files. Most important, when there are many rounds of concept development, iterations of designs and revisions, it is absolutely critical that a consistent file naming system is in place to separate iterations from final art—and also to identify presentations, proposals, budgets and schedules, and so on.

At the time that a job is being opened (with a job number and job sheet, etc.), it is a good idea to set up computer files as well. Most jobs should have some of the following files: Proposals, Presentations, Contracts, Correspondence, Budgets and Schedules, Concept Development (with, perhaps, different files for different concepts), Final Art, Imagery, and Guidelines, among others.

Document Naming

Every studio should have a document naming convention and stick with it. It is a good idea for documents to have the name of the client or job, the title of the document, and any other identifier that the studio will find useful when trying to

access a file, especially if its creator is not available. Examples:

- ❑ "Journal_prop_v3.PPT" and "Journal_prop_final.PPT"

- ❑ "Journal_contract_rev1.doc" and "Journal_contract_final.doc"

- ❑ "Journal_logo_v2.tif," "Journal_logo_bw.tif," and "Journal_logo_4c.tif"

Filling in the Form

Fill in the date and time the artwork is being sent; the job number to which it relates, the name and address of its destination, and a very brief description (such as "original art," "sketches," "mechanicals," and "models," or, in the case of an electronic file, the name and directory location of the file). For "via" indicate how the work is being sent (for example, UPS, messenger, name of courier service). If applicable, indicate the date the work is due back in the studio. When the work is returned, note the date and where it is to be found the next time it is needed ("location").

Using the Form

- ❑ This form either can be used by individual designers, or can be located in or near the studio's traffic area and filled in by individual staff members; or, it can be the responsibility of one person in the studio—perhaps the receptionist—in which case all staff members need to remember to transmit the necessary information to this person. In large firms, individual departments maintain their own log files.

Artwork Log

Date	Time	Job #	To	Description	Via	Due Back	Returned	Location

Billing Index

One of the most critical pieces of information for any business is the amount and schedule of expected income. The billing index is the list of all monies billed to clients for on-going or completed work.

While bookkeepers and accountants are familiar with "accounts receivables" and keep a separate ledger of all outgoing invoices, it is helpful on the studio level to be able to quickly and easily check when jobs have been billed, whether or not they have been paid, and how long bills have been outstanding (not paid).

The billing index is also the source of all invoice numbers. *Invoice numbers are to billing what job numbers are to cost accounting.* An invoice number is an identifying "tag" that serves to keep track of invoices within both the designer's and the client's bookkeeping systems. When assigning invoice numbers, begin with any number and then follow consecutively thereafter. It is best not to link invoice numbers to job numbers or purchase order numbers. An uncomplicated, independent, sequential list of numbers is less likely to create confusion for both manual and computerized billing systems. To allow for varying space needs, do not fill in the numbers in advance.

Filling in the Form

Fill in the date that will appear on the invoice under "date." Fill in the invoice number and the job number relating to the assignment being billed. For "billed to" fill in the name of the client as it appears on the jobs index. With two to three words identify the job, or use the job name as it appears on the jobs master index. Fill in the fee, total expenses, other costs, and tax, if applicable, in the designated columns. Fill in the total amount of the invoice. The "paid" column is filled in with the date and the check number when the payment is received.

Using the Form

❏ The billing index is used for invoicing regular fees and costs on studio jobs, consulting fees, re-use fees for reproduction rights to artwork, and any other kind of item for which the studio should be paid or reimbursed.

❏ Use this index concurrently in preparing invoices. First, determine the fee or rates due, tally up all the billables from the job sheet and assign a number to the invoice from the billing index. Write up the invoice and fill in the rest of the information indicated on the billing index.

Billing Index

Date	Invoice #	Job #	Billed To	Job Name	Fee	Expenses	Other	Tax	Total	Paid

Invoice Forms

Billing is the financial pipeline of the graphic design studio. Considering that the turnaround time for payment can be anywhere from thirty to ninety days and more, it is imperative that billing be done quickly and regularly. Whenever possible, establish a payment schedule even for small assignments. At the least, arrange for an advance payment against the total fee with the balance and reimbursable expenses to be due upon completion of the work. If the job is based on one-time payment, it should be billed as quickly as possible.

Two different sample invoice forms are reprinted here. Although the information contained in each is nearly identical, the second is more detailed than the first, and is intended to be a template. The first form (form 17) would probably be most appropriate for simple, very straightforward jobs. The second is meant to capture all the details of a more complex assignment. The billing index is the running log and source of all invoice numbers. Of course, the forms on CD-ROM allow easy customization and outputting as needed.

Filling in Form 17

Fill in the date of the invoice, its number (from the billing index), and the project number (same as the job number). Fill in the full corporate name of the client and its address. "Att" may be either the contact on the assignment, the name of the client's purchasing agent, or simply "accounts payable." If a purchase order has been issued by the client, fill in that number. State the name of the assignment next to "project title."

The easiest way to write the "description" of services for an invoice is to copy or summarize with a list in the same language used in the assignment's proposal, letter of agreement, or contract. If the agreement contains a schedule of payment, the invoice can be a direct copy of that

schedule. If there is an overall flat fee, list the services performed by the studio, but do not assign dollar amounts to each service, just summarize the list with an all encompassing phrase, such as, "Design and Production Fee." The rest of the invoice is actually a summary of all the billables (reimbursables) listed on the job sheet for the assignment. If the time spent by individual staff members is separate from the overall fee arrangement, a simple statement may suffice.

For example:

Staff Time...$____

Some clients may require a more detailed accounting, such as:

Staff Design Time (1/5/04-2/7/04)..............$____

Or:

Staff Design Time (1/5/04-2/7/04; 287 hrs) $____

Or:

John Designer
(1/5/04-2/7/04) 121 hrs @ $____/hr..............$____

Jane Designer
(1/5/04-1/9/04) 27 hrs @ $____/hr................$____

Al Production
(1/5/04-2/7/04) 139 hrs @ $____/hr..............$____

It is best to check in advance what the client's preference is in notating this kind of information.

A separate list of reimbursable expenses follows the description and fees section. Subtotal all the items, indicate if the invoice is subject to tax, show the amount, and fill in the total for the entire bill. In the "terms" section, if not payable upon receipt, indicate the number of days in which the studio expects to receive payment from the client, as per the project agreement.

Indicate the disposition of the original artwork and the expected time frame of its return. Indicate the specific rights which the client is entitled to. For example: "Product packaging"; "First time reproduction in North America, hard cover version"; "Television advertising"; "All rights, except for television advertising."

Filling in Form 18

Fill in the date of the invoice, its number (from the Billing Index), and the project number (same as job number). Fill in the full corporate name of the client and its address. "Att" may be either the contact on the assignment, the name of the client's purchasing agent, or simply "accounts payable." If a purchase order has been issued by the client for the assignment, fill in that number. State the name of the assignment next to "project name."

Under "project phase" check-mark the phases covered by the fee. In the space next to it, fill in the fee amount. List personnel, hours, rates, and total if charging for staff separately.

For "reimbursable expenses" check all of the applicable items, indicate either hourly rates, cost-per-diem, or mark-ups and the total amount of the individual item. The space underneath is for any necessary additional information. Fill in the subtotals, the applicable tax, if any, and the grand total. Also, fill in the information needed to complete the "terms" section, as for form 17.

Using the Forms

❑ One of the inevitable snags in producing bills quickly is that suppliers and freelancers often do not submit their bills in time to be approved and posted to the job sheet. This results in incomplete back-up information. First, it is necessary to urge all outside providers to be timely in their billing, and second, it may be necessary to bill a job in stages. The studio can issue a bill for the fee or billable time and all available costs with a note on the invoice, clearly written and in an obvious location, saying, "Additional production costs to follow." When all such costs have been received, approved, and posted, a second invoice can follow, notated under "description":

Additional production costs, as per our invoice #_____, date _____.

❑ When mark ups are arranged in advance, the hourly rates shown on the invoice should automatically reflect the marked-up rate. Some studios prefer to standardize hourly rates by having tiers of different rates for different types and levels of work. For example:

Senior Design Staff	$_____ per hour
Junior Design Staff	$_____ per hour
Production Staff	$_____ per hour

While this system is easier to compute and notate, it should be carefully evaluated so that the resulting dollar amounts actually cover the full cost of each individual within his or her tier.

❑ If markups are specified for production expenses in the assignment agreement, the invoice should automatically reflect the marked-up rate. It is not necessary to itemize every markup computation; it is recommended, however, that the back up material for each separate item be stapled together with an adding machine tape showing both the tally of the attached bills, and the markup computation. This is a courtesy to the client's bookkeeper, and it is also helpful in moving invoices along.

Invoice 1

Date _____

Invoice Number _____

Job Number _____

To _____

_____

_____

Attention _____

Purchase Order Number _____

Work Change Order Number(s) _____

Project Name _____

Description	Amount
_____	_____
_____	_____
_____	_____
_____	_____
_____	_____
_____	_____
_____	_____

Subtotal $ _____

Shipping/Handling _____

Tax _____

Total $ _____

Terms: Invoices are payable upon receipt.

Design documents including, but not limited to, sketches/comps, designs, illustrations, photography, models, and all other design documents are the exclusive property of Designer. Exclusive copyright of these materials is reserved by the Designer; upon full payment of all fees and costs, Client is granted the right to use the designs contained in these materials as per project contract or as specified below. Rights transferred are limited to:

_____

All others rights remain the exclusive property of the designer.

Invoice 2

To _____

_____

Attention _____

Project Name _____

Date _____

Invoice Number _____

Job Number _____

Purchase Order Number _____

Work Change Order Number (s) _____

Project Phase

❏ Concept Development

❏ Design Development

❏ Production

❏ Project Implementation

Fee

_____

_____

_____

_____

Fee Subtotal $ _____

Personnel	Hours	Rate	Total

Personnel Subtotal $ _____

Reimbursable Expenses	Amount	Description	Markup	Total
Audio/Visual Services				
Charts and Graphs				
Color Copies				
Copywriting/Editing				
Courier Services/Shipping				
Digital Prints				
Fabrication				
Illustration/Other Rendering				
Language Translation				
Local Messengers				
Modelmaking/Prototypes				
Photographic & A/V Supplies				
Photography				
Portable Media (USB Drives, DVDs, etc.)				
Printing				
Proofreading				
Reproduction				
Research and Database Services				
Research Materials				
Scanning				
Special Supplies/Materials				
Telecommunications				
Other				

Reimbursable Expenses Subtotal $ _____

Travel				
Airfare				
Ground Transportation				
Hotel and Lodging				
Meals				
Other Travel Expenses				

Travel Subtotal $ _____

Tax $ _____

Total $ _____

Terms: Invoices are payable upon receipt.

Design documents including, but not limited to, sketches, comps, designs, illustrations, photography, models, and all other design documents are the exclusive property of Designer. Exclusive copyright of these materials is reserved by the Designer; upon full payment of all fees and costs, Client is granted the right to use the designs contained in these materials specified in project contract only. All other rights remain the exclusive property of the designer.

Monthly Billing Statement and Collection Letter

Designers may request that clients pay invoices within any reasonable amount of time, but in reality it is more likely that clients will pay according to their own payment cycles. However, once payment for an invoice is overdue (anywhere from ten to sixty days, depending on the specific time frame established within the agreement for the assignment), the designer has two options. He or she can call the client contact, mention the possibility of an oversight, and ask the contact to look into the matter. Or, the designer can send the client a billing statement such as form 19. Such statements are routinely sent by all vendors and creditors and are merely a summary of the amounts due for payment.

In the unfortunate event that there is no response to the first statement or call, another call can be placed to the client contact or the client's bookkeeper. If this does not yield satisfaction within a very short time, a second notice should be sent. It can be a copy of the first statement with a stamped or hand written note saying "Second Notice." For a new or unknown client, a lack of response to the statement may necessitate one more contact before sending a final notice.

A final notice, such as form 20, is the last direct communication the designer sends to the client. The letter should be sent in a way that the client has to sign a receipt acknowledging its delivery: messenger, telegram, registered mail, or some other courier service would all serve this purpose.

Filling in the Forms

Fill in the date; the corporate name of the client; its address; and the name of the contact on the assignment or the head of accounts payable next to "attention." If the problem concerns one specific assignment, next to "reference" fill in the name of the project, its job number, and the client's purchase order number, if any. If several assignments are involved, state the overall name of the account, if any. List the unpaid invoices. Fill in the name and phone number of the party whom the client should contact and have that person sign the form.

Using the Forms

❏ There is no guaranteed way of avoiding the problem of collecting payment. It is therefore important to have all the financial details of an assignment arranged in advance and in writing. Ideally, a copy should be returned to the designer with the client's signature. It is also important to bill promptly and regularly.

❏ Establishing advance payments and a schedule of payments is also extremely useful. It is better to spot financial problems while the designer still has some leverage (such as possession of final artwork).

❏ The last recourse is to turn the account over for collection either by a reputable agency or attorney. This may involve paying 25 to 40 percent of the money collected as a collection fee. Keep in mind that collection agencies can only ask for money. They are not licensed to practice law and cannot bring lawsuits. If the client is unlikely to pay, retaining an attorney for an hourly fee might be the best approach.

❏ For amounts of less than a few thousand dollars, depending upon locale, small claims court may be a viable option. Local court offices provide information about filing claims.

❏ Tenacity is important to the success of collecting, but in some cases it may be necessary to be flexible in accepting partial payment with a revised payment schedule.

Statement

Date _____

To _____

_____

_____

_____

Attention _____

Reference _____

_____

_____

Please be advised that payment for the following has not been received as of the date of this statement.

Date of Invoice	Invoice Number	Invoice Amount Due	Service Charge
_____	_____	_____	_____
_____	_____	_____	_____
_____	_____	_____	_____
_____	_____	_____	_____

Total Due _____

Your prompt attention and earliest payment would be greatly appreciated. Please contact us if you have questions about this statement. Please note that invoices not paid according to terms are subject to a 1½ percent monthly service charge.

Contact _____

Telephone Number _____

Fax Number _____

Email Address _____

Final Notice

Date _____

To _____

_____

_____

_____

Attention _____

Reference _____

_____

_____

This account is now seriously in arrears. We have repeatedly requested payment and have neither received payment nor have we been contacted with an explanation.

We must collect immediately, and, if payment is not received within _____ days of the date of this notice, we have no choice but to turn this account over for collection. Be aware that this process may result in additional legal and court costs to you and may damage your credit rating.

It is not too late to contact us:

Contact _____

Telephone Number _____

Fax Number _____

Email Address _____

Marketing Checklists:
Calls Log
Qualifying Checklist

Logic would dictate that talent, experience, sensible business practices, and the ability to manage people and endless project details are all key prerequisites to a successful design practice. In fact, these are useful attributes, but without the constant pursuit and flow of new projects, no independent firm can stay in business. Even an in-house design studio has to maintain a level of productivity that justifies its existence within a larger organization. Every design firm should have a realistic and well-thought-out plan to promote its capabilities. There have to be funds for some reasonable expenditure on marketing materials, including, stationery, brochures, photography, and a website. It also requires the investment of time by both principals and staff members.

Firms that are founded by two or more partners are usually at an advantage in this area, because it is very likely that one of the partners is well suited to the marketing and promotion needs of the business. It is also possible that a sole proprietor is someone with a strong vision and force of personality that is able to drive the business in directions that will reap new sources of work. Given the advantage of personality, vision, and drive, with a plan and regular procedures, the chances for long-term success are much greater. If there is not someone within the firm that can devote the time and resources needed to develop such a plan, it may be necessary to hire a marketing consultant. Be sure to select someone who either understands your business very well, or has extensive experience and proven success in those markets in which you wish to develop a presence.

With all the promotion tactics and techniques that are available (see Using the Forms, below), the most immediate and most valuable source of new work can be found in your client list—past and present. Word-of-mouth, personal introductions, and references are the cheapest and most reliable sources of new business that

exist. There is no more credible recommendation than from former or current clients. Endeavor to understand their design needs and their personal choices, and help them realize their vision by delivering the best quality possible for the price. Do all you can to mitigate problems, and be flexible and creative in solving them. Do all that can be done, within reason, to make clients feel that they have received the best possible design services that you can offer.

Filling in the Forms
The first part of this form is the Calls Log, form 21. This form can be copied and repeated endlessly as a separate log, or it can be combined with the second part, the Qualifying Checklist. The Qualifying Checklist can stand on its own or, as noted, be attached to the individual Calls Log that generated the need for further information.

Calls Log
Fill in the date of the call and who made the call (next to "by"). Jot down the name and title of the contact that was reached and any comments that may be useful to follow-up. Under "results/next steps," check the appropriate box and the recommended date for the action to be taken. Make sure to follow through, either personally or transmit the needed information to the person who is supposed to follow up.

Qualifying Checklist
Fill in the date the form is being generated and who is filling in the form (next to "by"). Fill in all of the information about the prospective client, including company and contact name, address, and all contact information, such as phone, cell, and fax numbers, and email address. For project information, check the type of job (add items, as needed). Also indicate, if known, when the project might start and/or is

proposed to be completed under "proposed schedule." Check the known history, and list possible competitors. Include any special remarks and other information under "notes." Finally, check the applicable "results/next steps" and the dates they should be taken.

Using the Forms

Here is a brief outline of the steps, questions, and actions involved in developing a marketing plan:

Self-Assessment

❏ **Mission:** Why are we in business? What do we hope to accomplish? What do we want to be known for?

❏ **Strengths:** What kinds of special skills and unique experiences do we have? Are we in a highly specialized niche?

❏ **Experience:** Develop a case history sheet for every significant project.

❏ **Capabilities:** What is the range of skills we have? At what relative levels?

❏ **Capacity:** How much work can we do well at one time?

❏ **Client list:** Develop a client list that has the dates, names, and notes for all projects worked on with each client.

❏ **Competitors:** Who are the closest competitors in our market? How do they promote themselves?

Market Assessment

❏ Using resources such as newspapers, trade and government journals, local newsletters, industry reference guides, and trade association resources, study possible sources of work in:

- Niche markets—specific trades and industries
- Local area—look for areas of growth
- Regional area—look for areas that are underserved

Action Plans

❏ Identity and Visibility

- Develop logo, stationery, business cards, brochures, signage, leave-behinds, website, and other image materials that give a clear message of the firm's professionalism and expertise
- Enter completed work in competitions
- Participate in showcase events—charity-sponsored, trade shows, and other opportunities to raise visibility in the community, trades, and local industry
- Appear/speak at lectures and industry and trade events
- Serve on design juries
- Write articles and send pictures to local newspapers, newsletters, and consumer, trade, and industry magazines
- Send press releases to announce special events
- Hire a public relations firm
- Consider paid inserts in a design directory

❏ Lead Generation

- Former clients—reference list and quotes that may be used as endorsements
- Industry and trade contacts—reference list and quotes that may be used as endorsements
- Develop/buy call and mail lists—cull qualified leads into a database
- Institute regular system of cold calling and follow-up
- Institute regular mailings and follow-up

❏ Lead Qualification and Pursuit

- Cull warm leads and institute process for follow through
- Have boilerplates ready of initial estimates and proposals for quick response to RFPs (requests for proposal)
- Develop presentation materials and skills
- Selling and closing—study the art of persuasion

Marketing Checklist

CALLS LOG

Date _____   By _____
Contact: Phone _____
Name _____
Title _____

NOTES

_____
_____

Results/Next Steps:

❏ No Lead   ❏ Will call   ❏ Call back   ❏ Research   ❏ Send materials   ❏ Appointment
              Date _____   Date _____   Date _____   Date _____   Date _____

Date _____   By _____
Contact: Phone _____
Name _____
Title _____

NOTES

_____
_____

Results/Next Steps:

❏ No Lead   ❏ Will call   ❏ Call back   ❏ Research   ❏ Send materials   ❏ Appointment
              Date _____   Date _____   Date _____   Date _____   Date _____

Date _____   By _____
Contact: Phone _____
Name _____
Title _____

NOTES

_____
_____

Results/Next Steps:

❏ No Lead   ❏ Will call   ❏ Call back   ❏ Research   ❏ Send materials   ❏ Appointment
              Date _____   Date _____   Date _____   Date _____   Date _____

Marketing Checklist

QUALIFYING CHECKLIST

Date _____   By _____

PROSPECT INFORMATION

Company _____   Phone _____

Contact Name _____   Cell _____

Address _____   Fax _____

_____   Email _____

Source of Lead _____

PROJECT

Name _____   ❏ Identity

Description _____   ❏ Packaging

_____   ❏ Web Design

Estimated Fee _____

% Opportunity _____

Proposed Schedule
    ❏ Q1   ❏ Q2   ❏ Q3   ❏ Q4

CLIENT HISTORY   COMPETITION

❏ No prior contact   ❏ _____

❏ Aware of firm   ❏ _____

❏ Knows firm well   ❏ _____

❏ Other   ❏ _____

NOTES

_____

_____

_____

Results/Next Steps:

❏ Call back   ❏ Send materials   ❏ Research   ❏ Send letter   ❏ Proposal   ❏ Appointment

    Date _____   Date _____   Date _____   Date _____   Date _____

Project Confirmation Agreement

The project confirmation form serves as a contract to be used when the client is ready to move forward on a project based on a proposal or estimate. While the client can make a contract simply by signing a proposal, such as Form 2 in this book, the project confirmation form offers a more detailed and formal understanding between the parties.

Ideally, the client will review a proposal and request whatever changes are necessary. Then the designer will fill in the project confirmation form to conform to what the parties have agreed and both parties will sign to make a binding contract. By signing such a form before the commencement of an assignment, the parties resolve many of the issues likely to cause disputes. Since the goal with any client is to create a long-term relationship, the avoidance of needless disputes is a very positive step.

Filling in the Form

Fill in the date and the names and addresses for the client and the designer. In Paragraph 1 describe the project in detail, attaching an additional sheet to the form if needed. Specify the number of sketches and designs, any other specifications, the form in which the job will be delivered if not as physical mechanicals (such as files on a computer disk), any other services to be rendered by the designer, the client's purchase order number, and the designer's job number. In Paragraph 2, fill in how many days it will take to go from starting work to sketches and from approval of sketches to finished designs. In Paragraph 3 give the limitations on the rights granted, specify whether the client's rights are exclusive or nonexclusive, and whether any electronic rights are granted. In Paragraph 5 state the fee. In Paragraph 7 fill in the markup for expenses and the amount of any advance to be paid against expenses. In Paragraph 8 give a monthly

interest rate for late payments. Fill in Paragraph 9 if advances on the fee are to be paid. Check the boxes in Paragraphs 11 and 12 to indicate whether copyright notice or authorship credit will be given in the name of the designer. State in Paragraph 13 the percentages of the total fee that will be paid for cancellation at various stages of work. In Paragraph 14 fill in a value for the original design and any other originals, such as illustrations or photographs. In Paragraph 16 specify who will arbitrate disputes, where this will be done, and give the maximum amount which can be sued for in small claims court. In Paragraph 17 give the state whose laws will govern the contract. Both parties should then sign the contract.

Negotiation Checklist

❏ Describe the assignment in as much detail as possible, attaching another sheet to the contract if necessary (in which case the project description would refer to the attached sheet). (Paragraph 1)

❏ Give a due date for sketches, which can be expressed as a number of days after the client's approval to start work. (Paragraph 2)

❏ If the client is to provide reference materials, the due date should be expressed as a number of days after the designer's receipt of these materials. (Paragraph 2)

❏ The due date for delivery can be expressed as a number of days after the client's approval of sketches. (Paragraph 2)

❏ Time should not be of the essence.

❏ State that illness or other delays beyond the control of the designer will extend the due date, but only up to a limited number of days.

❏ State that the grant of rights takes place when the designer is paid in full. (Paragraph 3)

❏ Limit the grant of rights to the final form of the designs, so rights in sketches or other work products are not transferred. (Paragraph 3)

❏ Specify whether the client's usage rights will be exclusive or nonexclusive. (Paragraph 3)

❏ Limit the exclusivity to the particular use the client will make of the designs, such as for product packaging, a point of purchase ad, a direct mail brochure, and so on. This lets the designer benefit from other future uses which the client might make of the designs.

❏ Name the product or publication for which the designs are being prepared. (Paragraph 3)

❏ State the language of permitted usage.

❏ Give a geographic limitation, such as local, regional, the United States, North America, and so on. (Paragraph 3)

❏ Limit the time period of use. (Paragraph 3)

❏ Other limitations might include the number of uses, the number of printings (or quantity printed), and the size of the work when reproduced. The concept behind such limitations is that fees are based in part on usage.

❏ For contributions to magazines, such as when the designer might do an illustration, the sale of first North American serial rights is common. This gives the magazine the right to be the first magazine to make a one-time use of the illustration in North America. This could be limited to first United States serial rights. If no agreement about rights is made for a magazine contribution, the copyright law provides that the magazine has a nonexclusive right to use the illustration as many times as it wishes in issues of the magazine but can make no other uses.

❏ Retain electronic rights or make any grant of electronic rights subject to all the limitations as to type of use, language, product or publication, territory, time period, exclusivity or nonexclusivity, and other limitations. (Paragraph 3)

❏ All rights not granted to the client should be reserved to the designer, including rights in sketches and any other preliminary materials. (Paragraph 4)

❏ If the client insists on all rights or work for hire, offer instead a provision stating, "Designer shall not permit any uses of the Designs which compete with or impair the use of the Designs by the Client." If necessary to reassure the client, this might also state, "The Designer shall submit any proposed uses to the Client for approval, which shall not be unreasonably withheld."

❏ In the face of a demand for all rights or work for hire, advise the client that fees are based in part on rights of usage. The fee for all rights or work for hire should be substantially higher than for limited usage.

❏ If the work is highly specific to one client, selling all rights for a higher fee would be more acceptable than for a work likely to have resale value for the designer.

❏ If the client demands a "buyout," find out how the client defines this. It can mean the purchase of all rights in the copyright; it may be work for hire; and it may or may not involve purchasing the physical design as well as the copyright.

❏ Do not allow the client to transfer or assign usage rights without the consent of the designer, since the client may benefit from re-use fees that more appropriately belong to the designer.

❏ The fee must be specified. For a lengthy or complex project, a schedule of fees coordinated to stages of completion might be attached to the form. (Paragraph 5)

❏ The obligation of the client to pay sales tax should be included. Many states charge sales tax if a physical object (such as a mechanical board) is sold to or altered by the client. This is in contrast to sales of reproduction rights which are often not subject to sales tax. The laws vary widely from state to state. The designer must check the law in his or her state, since the failure to collect and pay sales tax can result in substantial liability. (Paragraph 5)

❏ If additional usage rights are sought by the client, additional fees should be agreed upon and paid. (Paragraph 6)

❏ If it is likely a certain type of additional usage will be made, the amount of the re-use fee can be specified. Or the re-use fee can be expressed as a percentage of the original fee.

❏ The client's obligation to reimburse expenses to the designer should be specified to avoid misunderstandings. (Paragraph 7)

❏ If expenses will be marked up, this should be stated. The rationale for marking up expenses is the use of the designer's funds until reimbursement and the extra paperwork. If expenses are modest, however, some designers prefer to cover them in the fee. (Paragraph 7)

❏ If expenses will be significant, provide for an advance against expenses. (Paragraph 7)

❏ Specify that any advance against expenses is nonrefundable unless, of course, the expenses are not incurred. (Paragraph 7)

❏ For substantial expenses, such as printing, illustration, or photography, consider whether the client should contract and pay directly for such expenses. If the client does contract directly, can the designer still justify a markup in view of the designer's supervision of the supplier?

❏ If the client insists on a binding budget for expenses, provide for some flexibility, such as a 10 percent variance, or for the client to approve items which exceed the variance.

❏ Require payment within thirty days of delivery of the finished art. (Paragraph 8)

❏ State that interest will be charged for late payments, but be certain the interest rate is not usurious. (Paragraph 8)

❏ Deal with the issue of payment for work-in-progress which is postponed but not cancelled. A pro rata billing might be appropriate. (Paragraph 8)

❏ Specify advances to be paid against the fee, either on signing the contract, on approval of sketches, or at both times. A schedule of payments is especially important for an extensive job. (Paragraph 9)

❏ State that any advances against the fee are nonrefundable. This is not done in Paragraph 9 because of the interplay with the cancellation provision in Paragraph 13.

❏ Revisions can be a problem. Certainly the designer should be given the first opportunity to make revisions. (Paragraph 10)

❏ If revisions are as a result of designer error, no additional fee should be charged. However, if the client changes the nature of the assignment, additional fees must be charged for revisions. (Paragraph 10)

❏ Consider limiting the amount of time the designer must spend on revisions, whether or not the revisions are the fault of the designer.

❏ If the client ultimately has revisions done by someone else, the designer should reserve the right to have his or her name removed from the designs. (Paragraph 10)

❏ With respect to revisions or the assignment itself, additional charges might be specified for work which must be rushed and requires unusual hours or other stresses.

❏ Any revisions or changes in the assignment should be documented in writing, if possible, since there may later be a question as to whether the changes were approved and whether they came within the initial description of the project. This can be done by using the Work Change Order Form. (Paragraphs 10 and 17; see form 9)

❏ State whether copyright notice will appear in the designer's name. (Paragraph 11)

❏ State whether the designer will receive name credit that will accompany the design. (Paragraph 12)

❏ Specify the type size for authorship credit and the placement of that credit.

❏ If authorship credit should be given but is omitted, require the payment of an additional fee.

❏ Fees for cancellation at different stages of the assignment must be specified. This very much depends on the nature of the project. For example, sketches may take very little time or they may come close to the finished designs. In the event of cancellation, the designer must also be reimbursed for expenses incurred. (Paragraph 13)

❏ State that the designer shall own all rights in the work in the event of cancellation. (Paragraph 13)

❏ Specify a time for payment of cancellation fees, such as within thirty days of the earlier of client's stopping work or the delivery of the finished designs. (Paragraph 13)

❏ Never work on speculation, which is a situation in which no fees will be paid in the event of cancellation or a failure to use the work.

❏ State that the client owns the final electronic files, but that the designer owns any preliminary concepts or materials as well as any original art or photography. (Paragraph 14)

❏ If preliminary concepts are used by the client, a fee should be charged.

❏ If physical art or photography is to be sold, a separate price should be specified.

❏ Require the client to return physical art or photography within thirty days of use. (Paragraph 14)

❏ Specify a safe method for the return of any physical art or photography. (Paragraph 14)

❏ Indicate a value for the art or photography, which can serve as a basis for damages if the client does not take reasonable care of it.

❏ If removable electronic storage media are to be delivered to the client, specify whether such media must be returned. If the client can keep the media or make copies of the files, consider limiting the use of the media to "archival purposes only." (Paragraph 14).

❏ Raise the standard of care which the client must give originals, such as making the client strictly liable for loss or damage while in the client's possession or even in transit.

❏ Require the client to insure any physical art or photography at the value specified for it. Remember that lost art can result in very large lawsuits and the designer may be found to be liable for the value of what has been lost. The designer should also consider insuring such original work while in the designer's possession.

❏ Try not to give a warranty and indemnity provision, in which the designer states the work is not a copyright infringement and not libelous and agrees to pay for the client's damages and attorney's fees if this is not true.

❏ If the client insists on a warranty and indemnity provision, try to be covered under any publisher's liability insurance policy owned by the client and ask the client to pay the cost of covering the deductible.

❏ Require the client to indemnify the designer to cover a situation in which the client wants certain materials to be included in the designs but does not request that the designer obtain needed copyright permissions or privacy

releases or uses the designs in a way that exceeds the uses allowed by the permissions or releases. (Paragraph 15)

❏ Provide for arbitration, except for amounts which can be sued for in small claims court. (Paragraph 16)

❏ Compare the standard provisions in the introductory pages with Paragraph 17.

Project Confirmation Agreement

AGREEMENT as of the _____ day of _____, 20 _____, between _____,
located at _____ (hereinafter referred to as the "Client")
and _____, located at _____
(hereinafter referred to as the "Designer") with respect to the creation of a certain design or designs (hereinafter referred to as the "Designs").

WHEREAS, Designer is a professional designer of good standing;

WHEREAS, Client wishes the Designer to create certain Designs described more fully herein; and

WHEREAS, Designer wishes to create such Designs;

NOW, THEREFORE, in consideration of the foregoing premises and the mutual covenants hereinafter set forth and other valuable considerations, the parties hereto agree as follows:

1. **Description.** The Designer agrees to create the Designs in accordance with the following specifications:
   Project description_____
   Number of finished designs_____
   Other specifications_____
   The Designs shall be delivered in the form of one set of finished ❑ camera-ready mechanicals ❑ electronic mechanicals, more fully described as_____
   Other services to be rendered by Designer_____
   _____
   Client purchase order number_____Job number_____

2. **Due Date.** The Designer agrees to deliver sketches within _____ days after the later of the signing of this Agreement or, if the Client is to provide reference, layouts, or specifications, after the Client has provided same to the Designer. The Designs shall be delivered _____ days after the approval of sketches by the Client.

3. **Grant of Rights.** Upon receipt of full payment, Designer grants to the Client the following rights in the Designs:
   For use as_____
   For the product or publication named_____
   In the following territory_____
   For the following time period_____
   Other limitations_____
   With respect to the usage shown above, the Client shall have ❑ exclusive ❑ nonexclusive rights.
   This grant of rights does not include electronic rights, unless specified to the contrary here _____
   _____, in which event the usage restrictions shown above shall be applicable. For purposes of this agreement, electronic rights are defined as rights in the digitized form of works that can be encoded, stored, and retrieved from such media as computer disks, CD-ROM, computer databases, and network servers.

4. **Reservation of Rights.** All rights not expressly granted hereunder are reserved to the Designer, including but not limited to all rights in sketches, comps, or other preliminary materials created by the Designer.

5. **Fee.** Client agrees to pay the following purchase price: $_____ for the usage rights granted. Client agrees to pay sales tax, if required.

6. **Additional Usage.** If Client wishes to make any additional uses of the Designs, Client agrees to seek permission from the Designer and make such payments as are agreed to between the parties at that time.

7. **Expenses.** Client agrees to reimburse the Designer for all expenses of production as well as related expenses including but not limited to illustration, photography, travel, models, props, messengers, and telephone. These expenses shall be marked up _____ percent by the Designer when billed to the Client. At the time of signing this Agreement, Client shall pay Designer $_____ as a nonrefundable advance against expenses. If the advance exceeds expenses incurred, the credit balance shall be used to reduce the fee payable or, if the fee has been fully paid, shall be reimbursed to Client.

8. **Payment.** Client agrees to pay the Designer within thirty days of the date of Designer's billing, which shall be dated as of the date of delivery of the Designs. In the event that work is postponed at the request of the Client, the Designer shall have the right to bill pro rata for work completed through the date of that request, while reserving all other rights under this Agreement. Overdue payments shall be subject to interest charges of _____ percent monthly.

9. **Advances.** At the time of signing this Agreement, Client shall pay Designer ____ percent of the fee as an advance against the total fee. Upon approval of sketches Client shall pay Designer ____ percent of the fee as an advance against the total fee.

10. **Revisions.** The Designer shall be given the first opportunity to make any revisions requested by the Client. If the revisions are not due to any fault on the part of the Designer, an additional fee shall be charged. If the Designer objects to any revisions to be made by the Client, the Designer shall have the right to have his or her name removed from the published Designs.

11. **Copyright Notice.** Copyright notice in the name of the Designer ❏ shall ❏ shall not accompany the Designs when reproduced.

12. **Authorship Credit.** Authorship credit in the name of the Designer ❏ shall ❏ shall not accompany the Designs when reproduced.

13. **Cancellation.** In the event of cancellation by the Client, the following cancellation payment shall be paid by the Client: **(A)** Cancellation prior to the Designs being turned in: ____ percent of the fee; **(B)** Cancellation due to the Designs being unsatisfactory: ____ percent of fee; and **(C)** Cancellation for any other reason after the Designs are turned in: ____ percent of fee. In the event of cancellation, the Designer shall own all rights in the Designs. The billing upon cancellation shall be payable within thirty days of the Client's notification to stop work or the delivery of the Designs, whichever occurs sooner.

14. **Ownership and Return of Designs.** Upon Designer's receipt of full payment, the final electronic files delivered to the Client shall become the property of the Client. The ownership of removable electronic storage media and of original artwork, including but not limited to physical and electronic concepts and any other materials created in the process of making the Designs as well as illustrations or photographs, shall remain with the Designer. Any such physical materials delivered by Designer to Client with the electronic files shall be returned to the Designer by bonded messenger, air freight, or registered mail within thirty days of the Client's completing its use of the final electronic files. The parties agree that the value of original design, art, or photography is $_____, and these originals are described as follows

_____

15. **Releases.** The Client agrees to indemnify and hold harmless the Designer against any and all claims, costs, and expenses, including attorney's fees, due to materials included in the Designs at the request of the Client for which no copyright permission or privacy release was requested or uses which exceed the uses allowed pursuant to a permission or release.

16. **Arbitration.** All disputes arising under this Agreement shall be submitted to binding arbitration before _____ in the following location _____ and settled in accordance with the rules of the American Arbitration Association. Judgment upon the arbitration award may be entered in any court having jurisdiction thereof. Disputes in which the amount at issue is less than $_____ shall not be subject to this arbitration provision.

17. **Miscellany.** This Agreement shall be binding upon the parties hereto, their heirs, successors, assigns, and personal representatives. This Agreement constitutes the entire understanding between the parties. Its terms can be modified only by an instrument in writing signed by both parties, except that the Client may authorize expenses or revisions orally. A waiver of a breach of any of the provisions of this Agreement shall not be construed as a continuing waiver of other breaches of the same or other provisions hereof. This Agreement shall be governed by the laws of the State of _____.

IN WITNESS WHEREOF, the parties hereto have signed this Agreement as of the date first set forth above.

Designer_____ Client_____
          Company Name   Company Name

By_____   By_____
          Authorized Signatory, Title   Authorized Signatory, Title

Website Design Agreement

The engagement of graphic designers in the creation of websites has expanded from a trickle to a torrent that is unlikely to ever crest. While the quality of websites may vary greatly, each site offers the opportunity for an imaginative design solution. Whether businesses operate from new web-based paradigms or enhance their traditional activities by web initiatives, the web can be an important profit center for designers.

Form 24, Website Design Agreement, addresses the wide variety of tasks that the designer may undertake in the creation of a website. The designer starts by creating a prototype that gives the look and feel of the website's graphic user interface (GUI), showing dummies for the home page and other crucial web pages and developing a flow chart. After the client approves the prototype, the designer may engineer the functional website or the client may have this work done in-house or by other suppliers. If the designer creates the functional website, it will have to be tested and debugged before being placed on the client's web server. Finally, the client may retain the designer in an ongoing capacity to maintain and update the website.

Each of these tasks requires a different fee. Limits must be placed on the scope of the work in each phase for which the designer is retained, so that the fee will be commensurate with the amount of work. Since the continuing maintenance of the site will be difficult to gauge as to the amount of work, the designer will be wise to specify an hourly fee or some other compensation based on the quantity of work to be done.

Rights will have to be negotiated. At the least, the client will need exclusive web world rights with respect to the design of the website. If the client asks for more than this, the designer should weigh what the client intends to do with the extra rights and how this may affect any permissions (such as for illustration and photogra-

phy) that the designer is to obtain for the site. In addition, the designer should seek to be protected by the client from lawsuits that third parties may bring based on the content or use of the website. Since most or all of the assets (text, images, etc.) for the website will be supplied by the client, the designer should be willing to protect the confidentiality of these assets. At the same time, the designer should charge additional fees if extra work must be done to put these assets into proper electronic format or if revisions are asked for that exceed the agreed-upon scope of the work.

The Website Design Agreement essentially transforms form 23, the Project Confirmation Agreement, so that it is focused on and sufficiently flexible to be used for web design. Therefore, form 23 should be reviewed in conjunction with the use of form 24.

Filling in the Form

Fill in the date and the names and addresses for the client and the designer. In Paragraph 1, check the boxes indicating which phases of the work the designer will undertake—prototype, website delivery and testing, and website maintenance. Under "prototype," check the boxes as to the elements of the prototype and describe these elements more fully as indicated, giving the number of subsection web pages and the number of additional sample web pages. For "website development and testing," give a limit on the number of web pages to be created for the fee and indicate how the website will be delivered if it will not be uploaded to the client's web server. If "website maintenance" is checked, describe more fully what the designer will do. Fill in the due dates in Paragraph 2. Limit the grant of rights by filling in the blanks in Paragraph 3. Specify fees and installment payments in Paragraph 5. If the designer is to do web maintenance, indicate the manner in which compensation will be computed. In Paragraph 7 specify any markup for expenses. In Paragraph 8 indicate when invoices must be paid and the charge for late payments. In Paragraph 10 describe how additional compensation for revisions will be calculated. If the designer is to receive some form of copyright notice, perhaps for the website design, fill in the blank in Paragraph 11. In Paragraph 12 indicate where the designer's authorship credit will appear on the website. Specify in Paragraph 13 any special provisions regarding cancellation. In Paragraph 14 give a time for the client to deliver assets to the designer. In Paragraph 16 give the name and location of the arbitrating body and, if the designer can use the local small claims court, fill in the maximum amount that can be sued for in small claims court. If the designer cannot use the local small claims court, strike the last sentence of Paragraph 16. In Paragraph 17 indicate the state whose laws will govern the agreement. Both parties should then sign the agreement.

Negotiation Checklist

❏ Include a brief description of the project. (Project Description)

❏ Review the negotiation checklist for form 23, the Project Confirmation Agreement. The negotiation checklist for form 24 is designed to supplement the issues raised in the checklist for form 23.

❏ The designer must carefully determine the scope of the work, which may only involve the creation of a prototype of the website or may extend to delivery of a functional website, including testing and debugging, and perhaps ongoing site maintenance. (Para - graph 1)

❏ Ascertain that the client has registered the domain name with InterNIC Registration Services and, if this has not been done, agree as to who will perform this task.

❏ In describing the prototype, indicate how many subsection and additional sample web pages will be required and describe the additional sample web pages and any special features such as might be achieved using sample web pages and any special multimedia features, if any. (Paragraph 1)

❏ If a functional website is to be developed by the designer, place limitations on the amount of work to be done for the initial fee. (Paragraphs 1 and 5)

❏ If the designer is to do website maintenance, give a full description of what the designer will provide. (Paragraph 1)

❏ If the website is to operate off a data base, consider how this will affect the amount of work to be done and the fee, then customize the agreement accordingly.

❏ Specify due dates for the various phases of the work that the designer agrees to undertake. (Paragraph 2)

❏ Indicate that the client's failure to provide assets or other actions causing delay will increase the designer's time for performance. (Paragraph 2)

❏ Limit the grant of rights to world website usage rights only. (Paragraph 3)

❏ If the client demands rights that exceed world website usage rights, consider the impact of this on any rights that the designer must obtain for site elements such as photography and illustration as well as the possibility of uncompensated reuse of the website design by the client for a different company, project, or product. (Paragraph 3)

❏ Break out the fees for each phase of the website. (Paragraph 5)

❏ When appropriate, such as for the prototype and website delivery phases, require installment payments and specify when installments will be due. (Paragraph 5)

❏ Require additional fees for work exceeding the anticipated scope of the project. (Paragraph 5)

❏ If web maintenance is included in the agreement, decide how compensation for this shall be computed and allow for renegotiation after the passage of a specified time period. (Paragraph 5)

❏ Bill for electronic storage media that the client does not return. (Paragraph 7)

❏ Negotiate for an advance against expenses, especially if the expenses are substantial. (Paragraph 9)

❏ Determine how payment shall be calculated for revisions that are not due to the fault of the designer. (Paragraph 10)

❏ Consider whether the designer might seek copyright notice in the designer's name for the website design. (Paragraph 11)

❏ Allow for the inclusion of copyright notices that may be required in permissions obtained by the designer from suppliers such as photographers and illustrators. (Paragraph 11)

❏ Specify where on the website the designer will receive authorship credit and, if possible, give the designer's email address and, perhaps, a hyperlink to the designer's website. (Paragraph 12)

❏ Indicate any special provisions regarding cancellation. (Paragraph 13)

❏ Require the client to deliver ready-to-use assets in electronic format and provide for additional compensation if the designer must do additional work to correct such assets or place them into electronic format. (Paragraph 14)

❏ Agree to keep confidential all assets supplied by the client and only use such assets in creation of the website. (Paragraph 14)

❏ Have the client warrant that it has the rights to use all assets that it provides to the designer. (Paragraph 15)

❏ Require the client to indemnify and hold harmless the designer from third party lawsuits arising in connection with the website, whether based on assets supplied by the client or obtained by the designer in accordance with the client's instructions. (Paragraph 15)

❏ Make the warranty and indemnity broad enough to protect the designer against lawsuits of any kind, such as a trademark infringement lawsuit based on inappropriate metatags or an unfair competition lawsuit based on parasites that link to and frame the contents of other sites. (Paragraph 15)

❏ In the event that the designer is to be involved in the selection of and integration with an ecommerce provider, this can be added to Paragraph 5 with respect to both duties and fees.

❏ If the designer is to provide webhosting services for the client, the duties and fees should be included in the agreement.

❏ Compare the standard provisions in the introductory web pages with Paragraph 17.

Website Design Agreement

Agreement as of the _____ day of _____, 20 ___, between _____ (hereinafter referred to as the "Client"), located at _____ and _____ (hereinafter referred to as the "Designer"), located at _____ with respect to the creation and licensing of a website (hereinafter referred to as the "Website").

WHEREAS, Designer is a professional designer with experience in the design of websites; and

WHEREAS, the Client wishes to develop a Website in furtherance of the Client's activities; and

WHEREAS, Designer wishes to create such a Website for Client;

NOW, THEREFORE, in consideration of the foregoing premises and the mutual covenants hereinafter set forth and other valuable considerations, the parties hereto agree as follows:

1. **Scope of Work**. The Designer agrees to perform the following work with respect to the Website as indicated by the checked boxes:

   ❏ **Prototype**. Designer shall provide Client with an initial prototype for approval, which shall consist of:

     ❏ home page, described as _____
     _____
     _____

     ❏ ____ subsection web pages, described as _____
     _____
     _____

     ❏ ____ additional sample web pages, described as _____
     _____
     _____
     _____
     _____
     _____

     ❏ navigational flow chart

     ❏ special features, described as _____
     _____
     _____
     _____
     _____
     _____

   The web pages shall show the look and feel of the Website, including type style, colors, navigational devices, illustrative/photographic styles, buttons, and related design elements.

❏ **Website Delivery and Testing.** Upon Client's approval of the initial prototype and receipt of the necessary assets (including but not limited to text, visual, and sound elements) from the Client, the Designer shall create a fully functional Website consisting of ____ web pages and reasonably conforming to the initial prototype. If the assets provided by Client cause the Website to exceed ____ web pages, the due date specified in Paragraph 2 and fee specified in Paragraph 5 shall be adjusted as provided in those paragraphs. After creation of the functional Website, the Designer shall test the Website in a Beta version. In consultation with the Client, the Designer shall make necessary corrections in the functionality before uploading the final version of the Website to the Client's web server or otherwise delivering the final version to the Client as follows

_____

_____

_____

❏ **Website Maintenance.** Designer shall maintain the Website and incorporate new assets as Client gives such assets to the Designer. The maintenance process is more fully described as _____

_____

_____

2. **Due Dates.** The Designer shall meet the following due dates:

❏ **Prototype.** The initial prototype shall be presented to the Client on or before _____, 20___.

❏ **Website Delivery and Testing.** The functional Website shall be provided in a Beta version to the Client within ____ days of Client's approval of the prototype and receipt of the necessary assets from Client. If the quantity of assets delivered by Client causes the Website to exceed ____ web pages, the deadline for Website Delivery shall be extended by ____ days for every ____ additional web pages. After consultation with Client, the Designer shall make any corrections and upload or deliver the final version of the Website within ____ days of receipt of Client's corrections.

❏ **Website Maintenance.** Designer shall incorporate new assets into the Website as agreed between the parties at the time of receipt by Designer of said assets.

The Designer's time for performance shall be extended by any delays caused by the Client, including but not limited to delays arising from the failure to deliver assets or advise the Designer as to corrections.

3. **Grant of Rights.** Upon receipt of full payment, Designer shall grant to the Client exclusive world website usage rights for the business, nonprofit organization, project, product, or publication named _____ for the following time period _____. The Client shall be the owner of the Website but shall have the right to use the Website design for this particular Website only. In addition, the Client shall have the right to use assets supplied by the Designer only for the Website. The html files, images files, animations, JAVA scripts, CGI programs, and related assets supplied by the Designer may not be used by the Client apart from their use on the Website. The Designer retains the right to make portfolio use of the Website or parts thereof after the Website has been placed on Client's web server.

4. **Reservation of Rights.** All rights not expressly granted shall be reserved to the Designer.

5. **Fee.** Client agrees to pay the following fees:

❏ **Prototype.** A fee of $_____ shall be paid for the prototype, ____ percent on the signing of this Agreement, ____ percent when half the prototype is completed, and ____ percent when the prototype is provided to the Client.

❏ **Website Delivery and Testing.** A fee of $_____ shall be paid for Website Delivery and Testing, ____ percent on commencement, ____ percent when half the work is completed, and ____ percent on the uploading or delivery of the final version. Alternatively, the fee may be paid in installments as follows _____

_____

If the quantity of assets delivered by Client causes the Website to exceed ____ web pages, the fee for Website Delivery and Testing shall be increased by $_____ for every ____ additional web pages.

❏ **Web Maintenance.** A fee of $_____ shall be paid for web maintenance. The fee shall be $____ per hour or shall be computed as follows _____

_____.

These compensation provisions for web maintenance shall be in effect for ____ months after the date of this Agreement and then shall be subject to renegotiation.

6. **Additional Usage.** If Client wishes to make any additional uses, Client shall seek permission from the Designer and pay an additional fee to be agreed upon.

7. **Expenses.** Client agrees to reimburse the Designer for all expenses of production as well as related expenses including but not limited to illustration, photography, travel, messengers, telephone, and unreturned electronic storage media. These expenses shall be marked up _____ percent by the Designer when billed to the Client to cover overhead and carrying expenses.

8. **Payment.** Designer shall invoice Client as fees are due and Client shall pay within ____ days of receipt of each invoice. Overdue payments shall be subject to interest charges of _____ percent monthly.

9. **Advances Against Expenses.** At the time of signing this Agreement, Client shall pay Designer $_____ as a non-refundable advance against expenses. If the advance exceeds expenses incurred, the credit balance shall be used to reduce the fee payable or, if the fee has been fully paid, shall be reimbursed to Client.

10. **Revisions.** The Designer shall be given the first opportunity to make any revisions requested by the Client. If the revisions are not due to any fault on the part of the Designer, additional compensation shall be paid as follows

_____.

11. **Copyright Notice.** Copyright notice for the Website shall appear in the name of the Client, unless specified to the contrary _____. Other copyright notices, such as for photography, illustration, and music, shall be included as required in the relevant releases.

12. **Authorship Credit.** Authorship credit in the name of the Designer shall appear on the Website in the following location _____ along with the Designer's email address. If Client alters the Website design, the Designer shall have the right to have Designer's name removed from the Website.

13. **Cancellation.** In the event of cancellation by the Client, the Client shall pay all expenses incurred by the Designer as well as fees based on the degree of completion of the Website. Special provisions regarding cancellation are as follows _____

_____

14. **Client Responsibilities and Confidentiality.** Any and all assets that Client is to supply for the Website shall be delivered to the Designer by _____, 20___, in electronic format (delivered on removable storage media or

transmitted via the Internet), and such supplied assets shall be in final form and ready for Website use. Client shall proofread and edit such assets prior to delivery to Designer, and any additional work due to corrections of such assets, file conversions, or scanning of text or images shall be billed additionally to the fee specified in Paragraph 5. The Designer agrees that any asset supplied by Client, whether for the Website or in relation to the business purposes for its development, shall be treated as confidential and neither disclosed to third parties nor used in any way other than for the development of the Website. At the completion of work, the Designer shall return to Client the assets supplied by Client.

15. Releases. The Client warrants that it has the right to enter into this Agreement and that Client owns or has obtained appropriate Website usage rights for any assets supplied by the Client to the Designer. The Client shall indemnify and hold harmless the Designer and its subcontractors against any and all claims, lawsuits, costs, and expenses, including reasonable attorney's fees, arising in connection with the Website. This indemnification shall extend to assets obtained by the Designer on the Client's behalf if the Designer has secured either exclusive or nonexclusive world Website usage rights.

16. Arbitration. All disputes shall be submitted to binding arbitration before _____ in the following location _____ and settled in accordance with the rules of the American Arbitration Association. Judgment upon the arbitration award may be entered in any court having jurisdiction thereof. Disputes in which the amount at issue is less than $_____ shall not be subject to this arbitration provision.

17. Miscellany. Neither this Agreement nor any rights or obligations hereunder shall be assigned by either of the parties, except that the Designer shall have the right to assign monies due hereunder. Both Client and any party on whose behalf Client has entered into this Agreement shall be bound by this Agreement and shall be jointly and severally liable for full performance hereunder, including but not limited to payments of monies due to the Designer. The terms and conditions of this Agreement shall be binding upon the parties, their heirs, successors, assigns, and personal representatives. This Agreement constitutes the entire understanding between the parties; its terms can be modified only by an instrument in writing signed by both parties, except that the Client may authorize additional fees and expenses orally. A waiver of a breach of any of this Agreement's provisions shall not be construed as a continuing waiver of other breaches of the same or other provisions hereof. The relationship between the Client and Designer shall be governed by the laws of the State of _____.

IN WITNESS WHEREOF, the parties hereto have signed this Agreement as of the date first set forth above.

Designer _____   Client _____
                Company Name   Company Name

By_____   By_____
          Authorized Signatory, Title   Authorized Signatory, Title

Contract with Illustrator or Photographer

Many design projects require illustration or photography. These images must satisfy not only the designer, but the client as well. While images occasionally may be obtained from stock libraries, it is more likely that the designer will assign a freelance illustrator or photographer to create the needed images. To ensure a greater likelihood of satisfaction, the specifications for the images must be as clear and detailed as possible.

Of course, there must be agreement as to the fee and what is purchased for the fee. Most illustrators and photographers seek to sell only limited rights. If greater rights are purchased, they ask for a higher fee. If the designer is sensitive to this, the best approach may be to ask for limited rights. This should avoid paying for usage rights that are never exploited.

On the other hand, the designer must obtain all of the rights which his or her client needs. In the first instance, the designer must consider what rights will be transferred to the client. Rights can be limited in many ways, including the duration of use, geographic area of use, type of product or publication, title of the product or publication, and whether the use is exclusive or nonexclusive.

The designer may find a lesson in the approach of the illustrator or photographer. Design may have reuse value for the client, even in cases when it has no resale value to third parties. For example, a designer might do a logo for the letterhead of a local business. If the business becomes international and the logo receives innumerable other applications, should the designer receive any payment beyond the initial fee? This will depend on the contractual arrangement between the designer and client.

A client may want all rights. This would mean the client could use the work in any conceivable way. However, on questioning the client, it often develops that the client does not need all rights.

Rather, the client wants to prevent competitors from using the illustration or photography (and, of course, the design). Another approach would be for the designer to promise by contract that no use will be made of the design in certain markets without first obtaining the written consent of the client. Or to agree that the client has exclusive rights in those markets where the client faces competitors, but that the client will not unreasonably withhold from the designer (or illustrator or photographer) the right to resell the image or design in a noncompetitive way.

In any case, the designer must act as an intermediary—and, perhaps, as a mediator of sorts—between the demands of the client and the desire of the illustrator or photographer to retain rights and earn more money for greater usage.

Expenses can be a significant aspect of the cost of illustration and, especially, photography. The designer has to know the likely range of these expenses, perhaps by setting a maximum budget to be spent. If the designer requires changes, revisions, or reshoots, this will also add to the expense. Here the designer has to be careful not to be caught in a squeeze between a client with a limited budget and an image cost which exceeds that budget because of changes.

In fact, there is a fundamental issue about payment. Fees and expenses for photographers or illustrators can be substantial. Should the designer become liable for such sums at all? This same issue is present in printing contracts. While designers often pay illustrators or photographers, if the costs are very large it may be better to have the client pay directly. The designer will also have to decide whether to charge a markup on illustration or photography, especially if the client does pay the fee directly.

The illustrator or photographer must also work on schedule. Failure to do this should be a reason for the designer to terminate the contract.

A number of professional references will aid the designer in dealing with photographers or illustrators. These include *Pricing and Ethical Guidelines* (Graphic Artists Guild, distributed by North Light Books), *Pricing Photography, Licensing Art and Design*, and *Legal Guide for the Visual Artist*.

Filling in the Form

Fill in the date and the names and addresses for the illustrator or photographer and the designer. In Paragraph 1 give the project title and description, a description of the images to be created, specifications for the images, and any other services the illustrator or photographer will perform. In Paragraph 2 specify the amount of time the illustrator or photographer has to complete the assignment, including any procedures to review work in progress. In Paragraph 3 fill in the nature of the use, the name of the product or publication, and any limitations on the geographic extent or duration of the grant of rights. In Paragraph 4 fill in the amount of the fee, including a computation method if the fee is variable. In Paragraph 5 fill in the maximum amount which the illustrator or photographer is allowed to bill for expenses. In Paragraph 7 indicate how revisions or reshoots will be charged for by the illustrator or photographer. In Paragraph 8 indicate whether or not the illustrator or photographer shall receive authorship credit. In Paragraph 10 fill in which party will own the images delivered as well as any preliminary or other materials (such as outtakes). In Paragraph 13 fill in who will arbitrate, the place of arbitration, and the maximum amount which can be sued for in small claims court. State the term in Paragraph 15. In Paragraph 16 specify which state's laws will govern the contract. Both parties should then sign the contract.

Negotiation Checklist

❏ Describe the assignment in whatever detail is required, attaching another sheet to the contract if necessary. It is very important to determine exactly what the illustrator or photographer is agreeing to do, including any services beyond creating the images (such as proofing). (Paragraph 1)

❏ Give specifications in detail, such as black and white or color (and number of colors, if appropriate), number of images, form in which the images are to be delivered, and whatever else is known at the time of signing the agreement. (Paragraph 1)

❏ Approve the work in progress at as many stages as possible. (Paragraph 2)

❏ Give a due date for the work to be completed, as well as due dates for each approval stage. (Paragraph 2)

❏ If the designer is to provide reference materials, the due date can be stated as a number of days after the illustrator or photographer's receipt of these materials. (Paragraph 2)

❏ If even a short delay would cause serious problems, make time of the essence.

❏ State that illness or other delays beyond the control of the illustrator or photographer will extend the due date, but only up to a limited number of days.

❏ Be certain the grant of rights encompasses all the rights needed by the designer and, of course, by the designer's client. (Paragraph 3)

❏ If the project is in electronic as opposed to traditional media, make certain that the necessary electronic rights are obtained. (Paragraph 3)

❏ State that the grant of rights extends to the client or, depending on the designer's contract with the client, gives the designer the right to assign rights to the client. (Paragraph 14)

❏ If it is likely a certain type of additional usage will be made, the amount of the re-use fee can be specified. Or the re-use fee can be expressed as a percentage of the original fee. Or the original fee can be increased and the grant of rights expanded. If the client will want to make a re-use of a unique image on T-shirts, it would be wise to obtain novelty rights in the initial contract. Another approach would be to seek all rights, but illustrators or photographers object to selling rights which may not be used and for which nothing is presumably being paid. In any case, the fact that usage fees must be paid (and permission obtained) for uses beyond the grant of rights should be kept in mind.

❏ Specify the fee. This would also cover any possible variations in the fee, such as a greater fee for the use of more images or for a greater media exposure than originally planned. (Paragraph 4)

❏ Determine whether sales tax must be paid. Many states provide that the sale of a copyright licence does not transfer tangible property and is not taxable (assuming the physical illustrations or photographs are returned to the creator). However, the sales tax laws vary from state to state and must be checked for the particular state involved.

❏ Any expenses which the designer will reimburse to the illustrator or photographer should be specified to avoid misunderstandings. Some illustrators include expenses in their fee (especially if the expenses are minimal), and the designer can certainly ask that this be done, but many illustrators and virtually all photographers bill separately for expenses. (Paragraph 5)

❏ If expenses are to be reimbursed, consider putting a maximum amount on how much will be reimbursed. Any expenses beyond this amount would have to be absorbed by the illustrator or photographer. This makes sense if the cap is based on an estimate provided by the illustrator or photographer. Or, after receiving an itemized estimate of expenses from the illustrator or photographer, the designer may wish to attach this to the contract and state that expenses shall not exceed those estimates by more than 10 percent without the consent of the designer. (Paragraph 5)

❏ Determine whether the illustrator or photographer marks up expenses, such as billing 15 to 20 percent of the expenses as an additional charge. If expenses are going to be marked up, this should be stated. (Paragraph 5)

❏ If expenses will be significant, consider whether an advance against expenses is justified. If an advance against expenses is given, it should certainly have to be repaid if the expenses are never incurred.

❏ State that payment shall be made within a certain number of days after delivery of the finished art, usually within thirty days after such delivery. Obviously this should be after the date when payment will be received from the client, unless the designer is willing to bear the negative cash flow. (Paragraph 6)

❏ Deal with the issue of payment for work-in-progress that is postponed but not cancelled. A pro rata billing might be appropriate to handle this. (Paragraph 6)

❏ The fee for cancellation of the assignment should be specified. The designer should have the right to stop work on the project without being liable for more than the work done to date by the illustrator or photographer, unless special circumstances have caused the illustrator or photographer to have other losses. Such losses might, for example, be caused by cancellation on such short notice that a photographer is unable to schedule other work. (Paragraph 6)

❏ Specify any advances to be paid against the fee. A schedule of payments might be necessary for an extensive job, in which case the designer might also want advances from the client.

❏ Revisions or reshoots can be a problem. The illustrator or photographer should be given the first opportunity to make revisions or reshoots, after which the designer should be able to change to another illustrator or photographer. (Paragraph 7)

❏ If revisions or reshoots are the fault of the illustrator or photographer, no additional fee should be charged. However, if the designer changes the nature of the assignment, additional fees will be payable. Again, if the designer is making changes because of changes by the client, the designer's contract with the client will have to provide for additional payments. (Paragraph 7)

❏ If the illustrator or photographer is to receive authorship credit, the designer may allow the illustrator or photographer to remove his or her name if changes are done by someone else. (Paragraph 7)

❏ With respect to revisions or the assignment itself, the designer should seek to avoid forcing the illustrator or photographer to rush or work unusual hours since the fees for work under such stress may be higher.

❏ Document any changes in the assignment in writing, since there may later be a question as to whether the changes were executed accurately and whether they came within the initial description of the project. Paragraph 16 requires that all modifications to the agreement be written. Form 9, the Work Change Order Form, can be used as necessary to document changes.

❏ State whether the illustrator or photographer will receive name credit with the image. (Paragraph 8)

❏ State if copyright notice for the photographs or illustrations will appear in the name of the photographer or illustrator when the design is published. (Paragraph 9)

❏ Specify who owns the physical art or transparencies. (Paragraph 10)

❏ Unless there is a special reason to obtain ownership of preliminary materials used to create the design, the ownership of these materials would be retained by the illustrator or photographer. This would include the photographer's outtakes. (Paragraph 10)

❏ The illustrator or photographer must obtain releases with respect both to using copyrighted work or, in some cases, using the images of people. Such releases should protect both the designer and the designer's client. (Paragraph 11)

❏ The designer may want a warranty and indemnity provision, in which the illustrator or photographer states the work is not a copyright infringement and not libelous and agrees to pay for the designer's damages and attorney's fees if this is not true. Such a warranty should not extend to materials provided by the designer for insertion in the book. (Paragraph 12)

❑ Include a provision for arbitration, except as to amounts which can be sued for in small claims court. (Paragraph 13)

❑ Allow the illustrator or photographer the right to assign money payable under the contract, unless there is a particular reason not to do so. (Paragraph 14)

❑ Give the designer the right to assign the contract or rights under the contract. The designer will want to assign rights to the client. (Paragraph 14)

❑ Specify a short term for the agreement. (Paragraph 15)

❑ Allow the designer to terminate if the illustrator or photographer does not meet the project's specifications, falls behind schedule, or becomes insolvent. (Paragraph 15)

❑ Compare the standard provisions in the introductory pages with Paragraph 16.

Other provisions that can be added to form 25:

❑ Noncompetition. If the client is concerned about competitors obtaining a similar look, one solution for the designer is to insist on an all rights contract. The illustrator or photographer would have no right to re-use the work at all. A less extreme solution is to have a noncompetition provision, although even this can be objectionable since the illustrator

or photographer cannot risk his or her livelihood by agreeing not to work in a particular style. In any case, a noncompetition provision might read as follows:

Noncompetition. The Supplier agrees not to make or permit any use of the Image or similar images which would compete with or impair the use of the Image by the Designer or its client. The Supplier shall submit any proposed uses of the Images or similar images to the Designer for approval, which approval shall not be unreasonably withheld.

Contract with Illustrator or Photographer

AGREEMENT entered into as of the _____ day of _____, 20 _____, between

_____, located at _____

(hereinafter referred to as the "Supplier") and_____, located

at _____ (hereinafter referred to as the

"Designer") with respect to the creation of certain images (hereinafter referred to as the "Images").

WHEREAS, Supplier is a professional illustrator or photographer of good standing;

WHEREAS, Designer wishes the Supplier to create the Images described more fully herein; and

WHEREAS, Supplier wishes to create such Images pursuant to this Agreement;

NOW, THEREFORE, in consideration of the foregoing premises and the mutual covenants hereinafter set forth and other valuable considerations, the parties hereto agree as follows:

1. **Description.** The Supplier agrees to create the Images in accordance with the following specifications:
   Project title and description of Images _____
   _____
   _____
   Other specifications _____
   _____
   Other services to be rendered by Supplier _____
   _____

2. **Due Date.** The Supplier agrees to deliver the Images within _____ days after the later of the signing of this Agreement or, if the Designer is to provide reference, layouts, or specifications, after the Designer has provided same to the Supplier. If the Designer is to review and approve the work in progress, specify the details here
   _____

3. **Grant of Rights.** Supplier hereby grants to the Designer the following exclusive rights to use the Images:
   For use as_____
   For the product or publication named_____
   These rights shall be worldwide and for the full life of the copyright and any renewals thereof unless specified to the contrary here_____
   This grant of rights includes electronic rights, unless specified to the contrary here _____
   _____. Electronic rights granted shall be subject to the usage restrictions shown above. For purposes of this agreement, electronic rights are defined as rights in the digitized form of works that can be encoded, stored, and retrieved from such media as computer disks, CD-ROM, computer databases, and network servers.

4. **Fee.** Designer agrees to pay the following purchase price: $_____ for the usage rights granted. If the fee is variable, it shall be computed as follows_____
   _____

5. **Expenses.** Designer agrees to reimburse the Supplier for expenses incurred in creating the Images, provided that such expenses shall be itemized and supported by invoices, shall not be marked up, and shall not exceed $_____ in total.

6. **Payment.** Designer agrees to pay the Supplier within thirty days of the date of Supplier's billing, which shall be dated as of the date of delivery of the Images. In the event that work is postponed or cancelled at the request of the Designer, the Supplier shall have the right to bill and be paid pro rata for work completed through the date of that request, but the Designer shall have no further liability hereunder.

7. **Revisions or Reshoots.** The Supplier shall be given the first opportunity to make any revisions or reshoots requested by the Designer. If the revisions or reshoots are not due to any fault on the part of the Supplier, an additional fee shall be charged as follows _____
   If the Supplier objects to any revisions to be made by the Designer, the Supplier shall have the right to have any authorship credit and copyright notice in his or her name removed from the Images.

8. **Authorship Credit.** Authorship credit in the name of the Supplier ❑ shall ❑ shall not accompany the Images when reproduced.

9. **Copyright Notice.** Copyright notice in the name of the Supplier ❑ shall ❑ shall not accompany the Images when reproduced.

10. **Ownership of Physical Images and Storage Media.** The ownership of the physical Images in the form delivered shall be the property of _____. Sketches and any other materials created in the process of making the finished Images shall remain the property of the Supplier, unless indicated to the contrary here _____ Storage media (such as computer disks and CD-ROM) that contain electronic images shall be the property of _____.

11. **Releases.** The Supplier agrees to obtain releases for any art, photography, or other copyrighted materials to be incorporated by the Supplier into the Images.

12. **Warranty and Indemnity.** The Supplier warrants and represents that he or she is the sole creator of the Images and owns all rights granted under this Agreement, that the Images are an original creation (except for materials obtained with the written permission of others or materials from the public domain), that the Images do not infringe any other person's copyrights or rights of literary property, nor do they violate the rights of privacy of, or libel, other persons. The Supplier agrees to indemnify and hold harmless the Designer against any claims, judgments, court costs, attorney's fees, and other expenses arising from any alleged or actual breach of this warranty.

13. **Arbitration.** All disputes arising under this Agreement shall be submitted to binding arbitration before_____ _____ in the following location _____ and settled in accordance with the rules of the American Arbitration Association. Judgment upon the arbitration award may be entered in any court having jurisdiction thereof. Disputes in which the amount at issue is less than $_____ shall not be subject to this arbitration provision.

14. **Assignment.** The Designer shall have the right to assign any or all of its rights and obligations pursuant to this Agreement. The Supplier shall have the right to assign monies due to him or her under the terms of this Agreement, but shall not make any other assignments hereunder.

15. **Term and Termination.** This Agreement shall have a term ending _____ months after payment pursuant to Paragraph 6. The Designer may terminate this Agreement at any time prior to the Supplier's commencement of work and may terminate thereafter if the Supplier fails to adhere to the specifications or schedule for the Images. This Agreement shall also terminate in the event of the Supplier's bankruptcy or insolvency. The rights and obligations of the parties pursuant to Paragraphs 3, 8, 9, 10, 11, 12, 13, and 14 shall survive termination of this Agreement.

16. **Miscellany.** This Agreement constitutes the entire understanding between the parties. Its terms can be modified only by an instrument in writing signed by both parties. A waiver of a breach of any of the provisions of this Agreement shall not be construed as a continuing waiver of other breaches of the same or other provisions hereof. This Agreement shall be binding upon the parties hereto and their respective heirs, successors, assigns, and personal representatives. This Agreement shall be governed by the laws of the State of _____.

IN WITNESS WHEREOF, the parties hereto have signed this Agreement as of the date first set forth above.

Supplier _____   Designer _____
                                                                    Company Name

                                                   By _____
                                                        Authorized Signatory, Title

Contract with Printer

Clients frequently ask designers not only to design a job, but also to deliver finished printed pieces. Perhaps the job is a simple one, such as a two-fold brochure in black and white. Or the job may be complex, involving six-color printing and die-cuts. The basic issues for the designer remain the same: minimizing the risk to the designer's reputation, sanity, and finances while endeavoring to satisfy the client. This section deals with the business and legal ramifications of working with a printer. However, the more the designer learns about the printing process, the greater the likelihood that each job will be a success.

The designer must realistically assess whether he or she is qualified to take the job through the printing process. The production aspects of printing have been dealt with at length in books such as *Pocket Pal* (International Paper Company) and *Getting It Printed* (FW Media). If the designer is not qualified to work with a printer, it might be possible to find an advisor to fill the role of production supervisor. Of course, the printer should be trustworthy enough to ensure proper production techniques and quality, but this is not always the case. Certainly the designer should review samples of the printer's work to see if the quality is satisfactory. However, the designer who is handling the printing is expected by the client to be able to monitor the performance of the printer and make the printer correct the errors that inevitably have to be dealt with in production.

If the designer feels comfortable in agreeing to take the job through the completion of printing, the issue of the scope of the designer's duties must be resolved. Is the designer expected to proof, to be on press, to handle all contacts with the printer, and to make any corrections which are necessary? The scope of duties will be a function of whether the designer or client is most competent in these areas.

If the designer is to handle the printing, a crucial issue is who pays the printer. The designer may want to give a quotation to the client that includes the cost of the printing. This gives the opportunity to make a profit on the printing. In some cases, the profit on the printing can be greater than the design fee.

What happens if, after the job is printed, the client refuses to pay the designer? The designer has a bill from the printer that must be paid. The typical scenario involves a client with (sometimes unreasonably) high standards and a printing job that is "commercially acceptable." This means that the printing is all right, but not of the highest quality. The printer expects the designer to accept the job, yet the designer finds the job is not acceptable to the client. Nor can the designer easily reject the job, since the printer has not made errors that would justify such a rejection.

This nightmare can be avoided in several ways. Some designers simply refuse to handle money in relation to printing. They insist that the client contract directly with the printer, even if the designer is to render services during the printing process. What duties the designer performs are billed to the client on an agreed upon basis, either as a fee, an hourly rate, or a markup. If the designer prefers to pay the printer, the printer must understand and agree to meet a quality standard consistent with the client's expectation (and the designer's agreement with the client).

The first step in dealing with a printer is to request a price quotation. To do this, detailed specifications must be given. It is always wise to seek more than one bid, since prices vary widely. One reason for great price variation is that printers have different equipment. The equipment may make the printer effective for one project but not another, which is reflected in the price. Asking each printer about what they print most efficiently may give helpful insights into selecting the right printer.

Since the specifications initially given to the printer are always subject to change, estimates often include variable costs for different formats, number of pages, type of paper, and the size of the print run. Schedule A can be used as a Request for Printing Quotation or, when the job is ready to print, it can be used as Printing Specifications to accompany form 26. When requesting quotations, always keep the specifications identical for each printer. This may be difficult if, for example, a printer has a standard house paper (which is purchased in large quantities to create a cost savings) and bases its bid on such paper. Of course, the designer is free to supply his or her own paper and ink. If this is to be done, it should be indicated in the quotation request. Also, find out how long a quotation will hold before the printer will insist on rebidding the job (and may increase the price).

Once a printer has given an acceptable printing quotation, the designer wants to know that the job will be of appropriate quality and delivered on time. It is important to check the printer's proofs before allowing the job to be printed. After approval, the printer is free to print in conformity with the approved proofs. Some clients will want the designer or a production specialist on press to watch and approve the print run, especially for color printing.

The printing industry has developed what it calls "trade customs," which are a set of rules intended to govern the relationship of printer to client. Notwithstanding these self-serving rules, the designer can certainly create his or her own contractual arrangement by having the printer sign a contract with explicit terms such as those contained in form 26.

The price will usually be expressed as a certain amount for a certain quantity (such as $7,500 for 7,500 brochures). Trade custom allows for the printer to deliver 10 percent more or less than the agreed upon quantity. These "overs" or "unders" are paid for at the marginal unit cost (which might be $.50 apiece, even if the average unit cost is $1, since the initial cost of the film work and setting up the press are not part of the marginal unit cost). If the designer will not accept either overs or unders, this should be stated in the specifications. In such a case the printer will probably adjust its price upward.

The designer will certainly keep ownership over whatever materials he or she gives to the printer, such as electronic files, mechanicals, or art. If these materials are valuable, they should be insured and returned as soon as possible after printing. A more sensitive issue is ownership of the materials created by the printer in the course of the project. If, for whatever reason, the designer wishes to have a future printing done by a different printer, the designer must have the right to receive any film and separations back from the printer. The best way to accomplish this is to own the film, require the printer to store it without charge, and pay only for delivery charges if the designer decides to move the film to another printer. Printers should agree to this, since the film will never have to be moved if they satisfy the designer. At the same time, the designer should also be aware that the client may expect to own what both the designer and the printer create, so this must be resolved in a way consistent with the understanding between designer and printer.

Printers will seek to limit their liability to the amount paid for the printing job. But what if a job costs $10,000 to print, yet the designer loses a $30,000 fee because the printer never delivers or delivers too late? The printer will also prefer to deliver "F.O.B. printing plant," which means that the printer will load the job at the printing plant without charge but has no responsibility after that. The designer will either arrange to pay shipping and insurance costs to the final destination or ask the printer to ship "C.I.F. Bridgeport, Connecticut," if that is the destination. C.I.F. means that a price quotation covers the cost of the merchandise as well as insurance and freight charges to the destination which are paid by the shipping party (in this case, the printer). If the printer does arrange this, it will no doubt want to bill an extra charge. In any case, the designer must be assured that if the job is lost or damaged in shipment, the insurance funds are available to cover the loss and, if feasible, reprint.

If the designer is not handling the job for the client, the client may still be very appreciative if the designer alerts the client to risks in the printing process. Although form 26 is set up for the designer to contract with and pay the printer, it could as easily be used between the client and the printer.

Filling in the Form

In the Preamble fill in the date and the names and addresses of the parties. In Paragraph 1 check the appropriate box and either fill in the specifications in Paragraph 1 or in Schedule A. For a job with several components to print, more than one copy of Schedule A might be used. In Paragraph 2 specify the delivery date, the place of delivery, and the terms (probably F.O.B. or C.I.F.). In Paragraph 3 restate the number of copies, give the price, indicate the amount of overs and unders which are acceptable, and specify the price per unit for the overs and unders. In Paragraph 4 specify when payment must be made after delivery (usually thirty days for United States printers, although sixty days is sometimes agreed to). In both Paragraph 5 and Paragraph 6 indicate whether the printer must insure the materials and, if so, for how much. In Paragraph 6 also indicate which party will pay the expense of returning the materials. In Paragraph 8 specify the arbitrator, the place of arbitration, and the amount beneath which claims can be brought in small claims court. In Paragraph 9 specify a term for the contract. In Paragraph 10 indicate which state's laws shall govern the contract. Have both parties sign and append Schedule A, if necessary. Detailed instructions on filling out Schedule A are not included here, because the designer should either be expert enough to fill out that schedule or should use the assistance of a skilled production manager.

Negotiation Checklist

❏ Fill out the specifications to attain the printed piece that the designer wants, including quantity, stock, trim size, number of pages, binding (if any), whether proofs (such as blue lines, match prints, or color keys) will be provided, packing, and any other specifications. (Paragraph 1 or Schedule A)

❏ Specify a delivery date. (Paragraph 2)

❏ Specify a delivery location. (Paragraph 2)

❏ Indicate the terms of delivery, such as F.O.B. or C.I.F., and be certain the job is sufficiently insured. (Paragraph 2)

❏ State that the risk of loss is borne by the printer until the job is delivered according to the terms of the contract. (Paragraph 2)

❏ State that time is of the essence. The printer will resist this, since late delivery will be an actionable breach of contract. (Paragraph 2)

❏ Do not allow the printer to limit damages for nondelivery or late delivery to the purchase price of the job.

❏ State the price for the quantity ordered. (Paragraph 3)

❏ Specify whether 10 percent overs or unders is acceptable. (Paragraph 3)

❏ Determine whether any sales or other tax must be paid on the printing, and ascertain whether this tax has been included in the price or will be an additional charge. This can be extremely complex, since out of state sales and sales for resale may not require the payment of tax. If there is any doubt, it should be resolved by checking with the sales tax authorities in the printer's, designer's, and client's states.

❏ State when payment will be made after delivery, which is usually within thirty or sixty days. (Paragraph 4)

❏ Do not give the printer a security interest in the job, which the printer might want until full payment has been made. Such a security interest, when perfected by filing with the appropriate government agencies, would give the printer a right to the printed materials or to any sale proceeds from the materials.

❏ State that all materials supplied by the designer remain the property of the designer and must be returned when no longer needed. (Paragraph 5)

❏ Do not give the printer a security interest in materials supplied by the designer.

❏ Indicate that the printer shall pay the expense of returning the materials supplied by the designer. (Paragraph 5)

❏ State whether materials supplied by the designer shall be insured by the printer and, if so, for how much. (Paragraph 5)

❏ State that all materials created by the printer shall be the property of the designer, must be stored without charge, and must be returned when no longer needed. (Paragraph 5)

❏ Indicate who will pay for the return to the designer of materials created by the printer. (Paragraph 5)

❏ State whether materials created by the printer and owned by the designer will be insured by the printer and, if they are to be insured, for how much. (Paragraph 5)

❏ Decide whether the printer may use other companies to do part of the production process. Printers may have color inserts, binding, shrink-wrapping, or other production done by other companies. If the designer's trust is with a particular printer, this practice may be ill-advised. In any case, the designer should be familiar with the true capabilities of the printer. Jobbing work out may cause production delays. Also, a printer's bid which seems too high may be the result of the printer marking up work to be done by others, instead of doing that work itself.

❏ If the printer requests a provision to extend the delivery date in the event of war, strikes, or similar situations beyond its control, the designer should specify that after some period of time the contract will terminate. This period of time might be relatively brief if the job has not yet been printed.

❏ Require proofs for all parts of the job, and hold the printer responsible for matching these proofs. (Paragraph 7)

❏ Require that the printer meet a quality standard reflected in samples shown by the printer.

❏ Do not allow the printer to make a blanket disclaimer of warranties, since these warranties are to protect the buyer. A warranty is a fact the buyer can rely upon, such as the printer's statement that a certain kind of paper will be used or simply the fact that the printer has title to what is printed and can sell it.

❏ The designer should ascertain any extra expenses, such as charges for changes in the specifications after an order has been placed; charges to use paper and ink provided by the designer; charges for delays caused by the designer's tardiness in reviewing pre-press proofs; charges for press proofing (that is, having someone review sheets and make adjustments while the press is running); charges for samples to be air freighted or for extra covers; charges for storage of unbound sheets or bound books; charges for shipping; and any other charges.

❏ State that disputes shall be arbitrated, but do not allow the printer either to have the arbitration at its sole option or to specify the location as its place of business. (Paragraph 8)

❏ Specify a short contractual term, such as a period of months. (Paragraph 9)

❏ Allow the designer to terminate without charge prior to the printer's commencement of work or if the printer fails to meet the production specifications or the production schedule. (Paragraph 9)

❏ State that the contract will terminate in the event that the printer becomes bankrupt or insolvent. (Paragraph 9)

❏ Specify that the designer's right to materials it supplied or materials the printer created will survive termination of the contract, as will the right to arbitration. (Paragraph 9)

❏ If there is to be any charge for cancellation of an order, make certain such a charge bears a reasonable relationship to expenses actually incurred by the printer for that order.

❏ If work beyond the original specifications is needed, define a method or standard that the printer will use to bill such extra work.

❏ Do not allow the printer to limit the time to inspect the printed materials and complain about defects, since the designer should certainly have a reasonable amount of time to do this. What is reasonable will depend on the use to which the client will put the materials. Of course, defects should be looked for and documented in writing as soon as discovered.

❏ If at all possible, refuse any provision stating that the designer or client warrants the printed materials are not a copyright infringement, libelous, obscene, or otherwise unlawful, and indemnifies the printer if this is not true. Another variation to be avoided would allow the printer to refuse to complete or deliver the job in the event of a breach of such a warranty.

❏ The materials to be provided should be specified in the description, especially if printing charges may be affected. Also, if the printer takes an electronic file, the designer will want to confirm the file meets the printer's specifications.

❏ Review the standard provisions in the introductory pages and compare them with Paragraphs 8 and 10.

Contract with Printer

AGREEMENT entered into as of the _____ day of _____, 20____, between _____ (hereinafter referred to as the "Designer"), located at _____, and _____ (hereinafter referred to as the "Printer"), located at _____, with respect to the printing of certain materials (hereinafter referred to as the "Work").

WHEREAS, the Designer has prepared the Work for publication and wishes to have the Work printed in accordance with the terms of this Agreement; and

WHEREAS, the Printer is in the business of printing and is prepared to meet the specifications and other terms of this Agreement with respect to printing the Work;

NOW, THEREFORE, in consideration of the foregoing premises and the mutual covenants hereinafter set forth and other valuable consideration, the parties hereto agree as follows:

1. **Specifications.** The Printer agrees to print the Work in accordance with ❏ Schedule A or ❏ the following pecifications:

   Title_____

   Description_____

   _____

   _____

   Quantity_____

   Repro Materials_____

   _____

   _____

   Stock_____

   PrePress_____

   Proofs_____

   Binding_____

   Packing_____

   Other specifications_____

   _____

2. **Delivery and Risk of Loss.** Printer agrees to deliver the order on or before _____, 20_____ to the following location _____ and pursuant to the following terms _____. The Printer shall be strictly liable for loss, damage, or theft of the order until delivery has been made as provided in this paragraph. Time is of the essence with respect to the delivery date.

3. **Price.** The price for the quantity specified in Paragraph 1 shall be $_____. Overs and unders shall not be acceptable unless specified to the contrary here _____, in which case the price shall be adjusted at the rate of $_____ per thousand.

4. **Payment.** The price shall be payable within _____ days of delivery.

5. **Ownership and Return of Supplied Materials.** All electronic files, camera-ready copy, artwork, film, separations, and any other materials supplied by the Designer to the Printer shall remain the exclusive property of the Designer and be returned by the Printer at its expense as soon as possible upon the earlier of either the printing of the Work or the Designer's request. The Printer shall be liable for any loss or damage to such materials from the time of

receipt until the time of return receipt by the Designer. The Printer ❏ shall ❏ shall not insure such materials for the benefit of the Designer in the amount of $_____.

6. **Ownership and Return of Commissioned Materials.** All materials created by the Printer for the Designer, including but not limited to flats, plates, or belts, shall become the exclusive property of the Designer and shall be stored without expense by the Printer and be returned at the Designer's request. The expense of such return of materials shall be paid by the ❏ Printer ❏ Designer. The Printer shall be liable for any loss or damage to such materials from the time of creation until the time of return receipt by the Designer. The Printer ❏ shall ❏ shall not insure such materials for the benefit of the Designer in the amount of $_____.

7. **Proofs.** If proofs are requested in the specifications, the Work shall not be printed until such proofs have been approved in writing by the Designer. The finished copies of the Work shall match the quality of the proofs.

8. **Arbitration.** All disputes arising under this Agreement shall be submitted to binding arbitration before _____ _____ at the following location _____ and the arbitration award may be entered for judgment in any court having jurisdiction thereof. Notwithstanding the foregoing, either party may refuse to arbitrate when the dispute is for less than $_____.

9. **Term and Termination.** This Agreement shall have a term ending _____ months after payment pursuant to Paragraph 4. The Designer may terminate this Agreement at any time prior to the Printer's commencement of work and may terminate thereafter if the Printer fails to adhere to the specifications or production schedule for the Work. This Agreement shall also terminate in the event of the Printer's bankruptcy or insolvency. The rights and obligations of the parties pursuant to Paragraphs 5, 6, and 8 shall survive termination of the Agreement.

10. **Miscellany.** This Agreement contains the entire understanding between the parties and may not be modified, amended, or changed except by an instrument in writing signed by both parties. A waiver of any breach of any of the provisions of this Agreement shall not be construed as a continuing waiver of other breaches of the same or other provisions hereof. This Agreement shall be binding upon the parties hereto and their respective heirs, successors, assigns, and personal representatives. This Agreement shall be interpreted under the laws of the State of _____.

IN WITNESS WHEREOF, the parties have signed this Agreement as of the date first set forth above.

Printer_____   Designer_____
　　　　　　　Company Name　　　　　　　　　　　　　　　　　　Company Name

By_____   By_____
　　　　Authorized Signatory, Title　　　　　　　　　　　Authorized Signatory, Title

Schedule A   ❏ **Request for Printing Quotation**   ❏ **Printing Specifications**

Printer _____   Designer _____

Address _____   Address _____

_____   _____

Contact Person _____   Contact Person _____

Phone _____   Phone _____

Job Name _____   Job Number _____

Description _____   Date for Quotation _____

_____   Date Job to Printer _____

_____   Date Job Needed _____

Quantity: 1) _____   2) _____   3) _____ ❏ Additional _____

Size: Flat Trim_____ x _____   Folded/ Bound to _____ x _____

Number of Pages _____   ❏ Self Cover   ❏ Plus Cover   ❏ Cover Bleed

Design includes: ❏ Page Bleeds #_____   ❏ Screen Tints #_____   ❏ Reverses #_____

Halftones Print: ❏ Halftone (black) # _____   ❏ Duotone (black plus PMS _____) #_____

Size of Halftones _____

Color Requirements:

Cover: ❏ 4 Color Process ❏ Spot Colors PMS #s_____ plus Black

Inside: ❏ Full Color ❏ Spot Color PMS #s _____ ❏ Color Signatures only #_____

Color Separations: ❏ transparencies #_____ ❏ reflective art #_____ ❏ film provided by client

Original art will be supplied as separated electronic files, or ____ b&w and ____ color images must be scanned.

Resolution of finished separations _____

Coatings:	Varnish	Spot Varnish	UV Coating	Film Lam	Gloss	Matte
Cover	❏	❏	❏	❏	❏	❏
Inside	❏	❏	❏	❏	❏	❏

Special instructions _____

_____

_____

Electronic Files:

File name(s) for print output _____

Software used and version _____

Included: ❑ fonts ❑ images files ❑ hard copy print out ❑ color proof

Mechanicals: (if supplied)

Color breaks shown: ❑ on acetate overlays ❑ on tissues ❑ # of pieces of separate line art _____

Paper Stock: Name Weight Grade Finish Color

Cover _____ _____ _____ _____ _____

Inside _____ _____ _____ _____ _____

Insert / Other _____ _____ _____ _____ _____

❑ Send samples of paper ❑ Make book dummy

Other Printing Specifications:

❑ Special Inks _____

❑ Die Cutting ❑ Embossing ❑ Engraving ❑ Foil Stamping ❑ Thermography ❑ Serial Numbering

❑ Other _____

_____

Proofs: ❑ Digital ❑ Blues ❑ Color Keys ❑ Chromalins ❑ Pictro Proof ❑ Press Proofs

Details _____

Bindery: ❑ Hard Bound ❑ Perfect Bound ❑ Spiral Bound ❑ Ring Binder ❑ Saddle Stitch

❑ Score ❑ Perforate ❑ Fold ❑ Drill ❑ Punch ❑ Round Corners ❑ Tip In

Details _____

Packing: ❑ Rubber/String/Paper Band in #_____ ❑ Shrink Wrap in #_____ ❑ Bulk in Cartons

❑ Maximum weight per carton _____lbs ❑ Skids ❑ Pallets ❑ Other _____

Shipping:

Deliver To _____

_____

_____

❑ Truck ❑ Rail ❑ Sea ❑ Air ❑ Drop Ship ❑ UPS/Other _____

❑ Customer pick up ❑ Separate shipping costs ❑ Send cheapest way ❑ Other _____

Shipment terms _____ ❑ Insure for _____ percent of printing cost

Miscellaneous instructions: _____

_____

_____

_____

Designer–Sales Agent Contract

Many designers are also illustrators. Form 27 is a contract for use with an agent when the designer is acting as an illustrator. However, designers may legitimately wonder why the practice of having a sales agent does not play a greater role in the field of design. Most designers, when questioned, will say that they obtain work by word of mouth. They do not advertise, do direct mail, or make cold calls to potential clients. Of course, every design firm has its own website and many are active in social media, which is certainly a form of promotional outreach. However, many designers feel that appearing to seek work is undignified. Whether such an attitude can survive, especially for new designers seeking to establish their businesses, is an issue that each designer will have to face.

Larger design firms may use an employee to develop business through a combination of overtures to potential clients, websites, social media, promotional pieces, press releases, articles written by or about principals of the firm, and participation in organizations where a designer might meet either clients or peers. Many owners of firms feel that they must be solely responsible for generating business. If an unusual situation were to arise in which an agent were used for the sale of design, form 27 would provide a framework to create a contract. Of course, each provision would have to be carefully examined. For example, the designer is used to doing billing and servicing accounts. So there would be little reason to give the agent any commission on accounts not obtained directly by the agent. The mix of fees, expenses, and overhead costs would have to be carefully analyzed, but it is unlikely that the designer would pay as high a rate of commission to an agent as an illustrator pays. Whether such arrangements will come into existence depends in part on the willingness of clients to deal with someone other than the designer.

In any case, an agent who sells illustration can be of great value to a designer. Instead of seeking illustration assignments, the designer can devote more time to his or her creativity and to seeking design work. The cost to the designer is the agent's commission, which is usually 25 percent, but the hope is that the agent will enable the designer to earn more. The agent may have better contacts and be able to secure a better quality of client and more remunerative assignments.

The agent should not be given markets in which the agent cannot effectively sell. For example, an agent in New York may not be able to sell in Los Angeles or London. Nor should the agent be given exclusivity in markets in which the designer may want to sell or want to have other agents sell. The most important exclusion here is that the agent should not have any rights to commissions with respect to design work. If the agent, by chance, obtains a design assignment, a different fee structure should be used to compensate the agent.

The length of the contract should not be overly long, or should be subject to a right of termination on notice, because if the agent fails to sell the designer must take over sales or find another agent. The agent's promise to use best efforts is almost impossible to enforce.

Promotion is an important aspect of the agent's work for the designer. The designer will have to provide sufficient samples for the agent to work effectively. Beyond this, direct mail campaigns and paid advertising in the promotional directories may gain clients. The sharing of such promotional expenses must be agreed to between the designer and agent.

One sticky issue can be house accounts, which are clients of the designer not obtained by the agent. Both the definition of house accounts and the commission paid to the agent on such accounts must be negotiated. Clearly the designer must not allow design clients to be mixed with illustration clients in dealing with house accounts.

Termination raises another difficult issue, since the agent may feel that commissions should continue to be paid for assignments obtained by the designer after termination from clients originally contacted by the agent. There are several approaches to resolve this. The agent may be given a continuing right to commissions for a limited time depending on how long the representation lasted. Or the designer may make a payout to the agent, either in a lump sum or in installments over several years. If the relationship was brief and unsuccessful, of course, the agent should have no rights at termination except to collect commissions for assignments obtained prior to termination.

The agent would usually handle billings and provide accountings, although the designer may wish to take care of this if staffing permits. The designer would want to be able to review the books and records of the agent. Since both the designer and agent provide personal services, the contract should not be assignable.

A distinction has to be made between an agent obtaining assignments and obtaining a book contract. The agent for an author receives a commission of 10–15 percent, compared to the 25 percent charged by the agent for an illustrator. If an agent arranges an assignment for a book jacket or a limited number of illustrations in a book, the 25 percent commission is reasonable. But if the designer is to be the author or co-author of a book, it might be fairer to reduce the commission to the 10–15 percent range. One consideration might be whether the designer receives a flat fee or a royalty, since a royalty makes the designer more like an author. If the designer does receive a royalty, it would be best if upon termination with the agent the designer receives direct payment from the publisher of the percentage of the royalty due.

Filling in the Form

In the Preamble fill in the date and the names and addresses of the designer and agent. In Paragraph 1 indicate the geographical area and markets in which the agent will represent the designer, the types of work covered, and whether the representation will be exclusive or nonexclusive. Be very specific when indicating the type of art or design covered by the contract, since design (and perhaps certain types of illustration) will normally be excluded from the coverage of the contract and this may require some precision of definition. In Paragraph 4 fill in the length of the term. In Paragraph 5 fill in the commission rates. In Paragraph 6 check the party responsible for billings. In Paragraph 7 indicate the time for payment after receipt of fees and the interest rate for late payments. In Paragraph 8 indicate how promotional expenses will be shared. In Paragraph 11 state when and for how long the agent shall have a right to commissions after termination. In Paragraph 13 give the names of arbitrators and the place for arbitration, as well as filling in the maximum amount which can be sued for in small claims court. In Paragraph 17 fill in which state's laws will govern the contract. Both parties should sign the contract and, if necessary, fill in the Schedule of House Accounts by listing the names and addresses of clients.

Negotiation Checklist

❏ Limit the scope of the agent's representation by geography and types of markets, including coverage of electronic rights. (Paragraph 1)

❏ Limit the scope of the agent's representation with respect to the nature of the work, including the exclusion of design from the scope of the representation except in unusual cases. (Paragraph 1)

❏ State whether the representation is exclusive or nonexclusive. (Paragraph 1) If the representation is exclusive, the agent will have a right to commissions on assignments obtained by other agents. Assignments obtained by the designer would fall under the House Account provision in Paragraph 5.

❏ If the agent uses other agents for certain markets (for example, for foreign sales or film sales), review the impact of this on the amount of commissions.

❏ State that sales through galleries or sales of original art in general are not within the scope of the agency agreement.

❏ Any rights not granted to the agent should be reserved to the designer. (Paragraph 1)

❏ Require that the agent use best efforts to sell the work of the designer. (Paragraph 2)

❏ Require that the agent shall keep the designer promptly and regularly informed with respect to negotiations and other matters, and shall submit all offers to the designer.

❏ State that any contract negotiated by the agent is not binding unless signed by the designer.

❏ If the designer is willing to give the agent a power of attorney so the agent can sign on behalf of the designer, the power of attorney should be very specific as to what rights the agent can exercise.

❏ Require that the agent keep confidential all matters handled for the designer.

❏ Give the designer the right to accept or reject any assignment which is obtained by the agent. (Paragraph 2)

❏ Specify the amount of samples to be supplied to the agent by the designer. (Paragraph 3)

❏ If samples are valuable, specify the value.

❏ Require the agent to insure the samples at the value agreed to.

❏ Raise the agent's responsibility for the samples to strict liability for any loss or damage.

❏ Provide for a short term, such as one year. (Paragraph 4) This interplays with the termination provision. Since termination is permitted on thirty days notice in Paragraph 11, the length of the term is of less importance in this contract.

❏ If the contract has a relatively long term and cannot be terminated on notice at any time, allow termination if the agent fails to generate a certain level of sales on a quarterly, semiannual, or annual basis.

❏ If the contract has a relatively long term and cannot be terminated on notice at any time, allow for termination if a certain agent dies or leaves the agency.

❏ Specify the commission percentage for assignments obtained by the agent during the term of the contract. This is usually 25 percent of the fee, and may be 2½ to 5 percent higher for out-of-town assignments. (Paragraph 5)

❏ Define house accounts, probably as accounts obtained by other agents prior to the contract or obtained by the designer at any time, and specify the commission to be paid on such accounts. A reasonable commission might be 10 percent, especially if the agent does the billing. The designer may not want to pay any commission on these accounts, while the agent may want the full commission. (Paragraph 5)

❏ List house accounts by name on the Schedule of House Accounts. This can be supplemented if house accounts are developed after the contract is signed. (Paragraph 5)

❏ State that the commission shall be computed on the billing less any expenses incurred by the designer, especially if expenses are substantial and are not reimbursed by the client. (Paragraph 5)

❏ State that commissions are not payable on billings which have not been collected. (Paragraph 5)

❏ Confirm that the agent will not collect a commission for the designer's speaking fees, grants, or prizes.

❏ Distinguish between an assignment to contribute to a book and being the author or coauthor of a book. Agents representing authors charge 10–15 percent of proceeds from the book as the commission. While the dividing line may be a fine one, designers likely to make substantial contributions to a book should consider whether treatment as an author may be appropriate in terms of the agent's commission rate. (Paragraph 5)

❏ In the case of an agent for a book, consider letting the agency do only that particular title or project.

❏ Determine who will bill and collect from the client. This would usually be a service provided by the agent, but a design firm is likely to be more capable of handling this than an individual illustrator. (Paragraph 6)

❏ If the agent is collecting billings, give the designer the right to collect his or her share directly from clients. This might provide some protection against the agent's insolvency or holding of money in the event of a dispute.

❏ Require payments to be made quickly after billings are collected. (Paragraph 7)

❏ Charge interest on late payments, but avoid a usurious interest rate. (Paragraph 7)

❏ Require the agent to treat money due the designer as trust funds and hold it in an account separate from accounts for the funds of the agency. (Paragraph 7)

❏ Share promotional expenses, such as direct mail campaigns or paid page advertising in directories. The agent may contribute 25 percent or more to these expenses. (Paragraph 8)

❏ State that both parties must agree before promotional expenses may be incurred by the agent. (Paragraph 8)

❏ Require the agent to pay for a specified minimum amount of promotional expenses, perhaps without any sharing on the part of the designer.

❏ If expenses incurred by the agent benefit several designers (or illustrators), be certain there is a fair allocation of expenses.

❏ Require the agent to bear miscellaneous marketing expenses, such as messengers, shipping, and the like. (Paragraph 8)

❏ If the agent insists that the designer bear certain expenses, require the designer's approval for expenses in excess of a minimum amount.

❏ If the agent is billing, state that the designer shall receive a copy of the invoice given to the client. (Paragraph 9)

❏ Provide for full accountings on a regular basis, such as every six months, if requested. (Paragraph 9)

❏ Give a right to inspect books and records on reasonable notice. (Paragraph 10)

❏ Allow for termination on thirty days notice to the other party. (Paragraph 11)

❏ State that the agreement will terminate in the event of the agent's bankruptcy or insolvency. (Paragraph 11)

❏ Specify for how long, if at all, the agent will receive commissions from assignments obtained by the designer from clients developed by the agent during the time the contract was in effect. (Paragraph 11) For example, if the agency contract lasted for less than a year, the agent might have such a right for three months after termination. If the agency contract lasted more than a year but less than two years, the right might continue for six months after termination. If the agent has a right to commissions after termination for too long a period, the designer may find it difficult to find another agent.

❏ Do not give the agent any rights to commissions from house accounts after termination.

❏ For book contracts, it is customary for the agent to continue to collect royalties and deduct the agent's commission even after termination of the agency contract. However, it would be better for the designer to have the right to direct payment of his or her share after such termination.

❏ Instead of allowing the agent to collect commissions for some period of time after termination, a fixed amount might be stated in the original contract. For example, 20 percent of the average annual billings for the prior three years might be payable in three installments over a year. The percentages and payment schedule are negotiable, but the designer must avoid any agreement which would make it difficult either to earn a living or find another agent. The percentage to be paid might increase if the agent has represented the designer for a longer period (or decrease for a shorter period), but should be subject to a cap or maximum amount.

❏ Do not allow assignment of the contract, since both the agent and the designer are rendering personal services. (Paragraph 12)

❏ Allow the designer to assign payments due to him or her under the contract. (Paragraph 12)

❏ If the agent represents creators who are competitive with one another, decide what precautions might be taken against favoritism. Whether it is advantageous or disadvantageous to have an agent represent competing talent will depend on the unique circumstances of each case.

❏ If the agent requires a warranty and indemnity clause under which the designer states that he or she owns the work and has the right to sell it, limit the liability of the designer to actual breaches resulting in a judgment and try to place a maximum amount on the potential liability.

❏ Provide for arbitration of disputes in excess of the amount which can be sued for in small claims court. (Paragraph 13)

❏ Compare the standard provisions in the introductory pages with Paragraphs 14–17.

Designer–Sales Agent Contract

AGREEMENT, entered into as of this _____ day of _____, 20_____, between _____ (hereinafter referred to as the "Designer"), located at _____, and _____ (hereinafter referred to as the "Agent"), located at _____;

WHEREAS, the Designer is an established designer of proven talents; and

WHEREAS, the Designer wishes to have an agent represent him or her in marketing certain rights enumerated herein; and

WHEREAS, the Agent is capable of marketing the work produced by the Designer; and

WHEREAS, the Agent wishes to represent the Designer;

NOW, THEREFORE, in consideration of the foregoing premises and the mutual covenants hereinafter set forth and other valuable consideration, the parties hereto agree as follows:

1. **Agency.** The Designer appoints the Agent to act as his or her representative:

   (A) in the following geographical area: _____

   (B) for the following markets:

   ❏ Advertising   ❏ Corporate   ❏ Book Publishing   ❏ Magazines

   ❏ Other, specified as _____

   (C) for the following types of art or design: _____

   (D) to be the Designer's ❏ exclusive ❏ nonexclusive agent for the area, markets, and types of work indicated. Electronic rights are ❏ outside the scope of this agency contract ❏ covered by this agency contract insofar as the sale of such rights is incidental to the sale of nonelectronic rights ❏ covered by this agency contract. For purposes of this agreement, electronic rights are defined as rights in the digitized form of works that can be encoded, stored, and retrieved from such media as computer disks, CD-ROM, computer databases, and network servers. Any rights not granted to the Agent are reserved to the Designer.

2. **Best Efforts.** The Agent agrees to use his or her best efforts in submitting the Designer's work for the purpose of securing assignments for the Designer. The Agent shall negotiate the terms of any assignment that is offered, but the Designer may reject any assignment if he or she finds the terms thereof unacceptable.

3. **Samples.** The Designer shall provide the Agent with such samples of work as are from time to time necessary for the purpose of securing assignments. These samples shall remain the property of the Designer and be returned on termination of this Agreement. The Agent shall take reasonable efforts to protect the work from loss or damage, but shall be liable for such loss or damage only if caused by the Agent's negligence.

4. **Term.** This Agreement shall take effect as of the date first set forth above, and remain in full force and effect for a term of _____, unless terminated as provided in Paragraph 11.

5. **Commissions.** The Agent shall be entitled to the following commissions: **(A)** On assignments obtained by the Agent during the term of this Agreement, _____ percent of the billing. **(B)** On house accounts, _____ percent of the billing. For purposes of this Agreement, house accounts are defined as accounts obtained by the Designer at any time or obtained by another agent representing the Designer prior to the commencement of this Agreement and are listed in the Schedule of House Accounts attached to this Agreement. **(C)** For books which the Designer authors or coauthors, _____ percent of the royalties or licensing proceeds paid to the Designer by the publisher or its licensees.

   It is understood by both parties that no commissions shall be paid on assignments rejected by the Designer or for which the Designer fails to receive payment, regardless of the reason payment is not made. Further, no commissions shall be payable in either **(A)** or **(B)** above for any part of the billing that is due to expenses incurred by the Designer in performing the assignment, whether or not such expenses are reimbursed by the client. In the event that a flat fee is paid by the client, it shall be reduced by the amount of expenses incurred by the Designer in performing the assignment, and the Agent's commission shall be payable only on the fee as reduced for expenses.

6. Billing. The ❏ Designer ❏ Agent shall be responsible for all billings.

7. Payments. The party responsible for billing shall make all payments due within _____ days of receipt of any fees covered by this Agreement. Such payments due shall be deemed trust funds and shall not be intermingled with funds belonging to the party responsible for billing and payment. Late payments shall be accompanied by interest calculated at the rate of _____ percent per month thereafter.

8. Promotional Expenses. Promotional expenses, including but not limited to promotional mailings and paid advertising, shall be mutually agreed to by the parties and paid _____ percent by the Agent and _____ percent by the Designer. The Agent shall bear the expenses of shipping, insurance, and similar marketing expenses.

9. Accountings. The party responsible for billing shall send copies of invoices to the other party when rendered. If requested, that party shall also provide the other party with semiannual accountings showing all assignments for the period, the clients' names and addresses, the fees paid, expenses incurred by the Designer, the dates of payment, the amounts on which the Agent's commissions are to be calculated, and the sums due less those amounts already paid.

10. Inspection of the Books and Records. The party responsible for the billing shall keep the books and records with respect to payments due each party at his or her place of business and permit the other party to inspect these books and records during normal business hours on the giving of reasonable notice.

11. Termination. This Agreement may be terminated by either party by giving thirty (30) days written notice to the other party. If the Designer receives assignments after the termination date from clients originally obtained by the Agent during the term of this Agreement, the commission specified in Paragraph 5(A) shall be payable to the Agent under the following circumstances. If the Agent has represented the Designer for _____ months or less, the Agent shall receive a commission on such assignments received by the Designer within _____ days of the date of termination. This period shall increase by thirty (30) days for each additional _____ months that the Agent has represented the Designer, but in no event shall such period exceed _____ days. In the event of the bankruptcy or insolvency of the Agent, this Agreement shall also terminate. The rights and obligations under Paragraphs 3, 6, 7, 8, 9, and 10 shall survive termination.

12. Assignment. This Agreement shall not be assigned by either of the parties hereto, except that the Designer shall have the right to assign any monies due the Designer under this Agreement.

13. Arbitration. Any disputes arising under this Agreement shall be settled by arbitration before _____ under the rules of the American Arbitration Association in the City of _____, except that the parties shall have the right to go to court for claims of $_____ or less. Any award rendered by the arbitrator may be entered in any court having jurisdiction thereof.

14. Notices. All notices shall be given to the parties at their respective addresses set forth above.

15. Independent Contractor Status. Both parties agree that the Agent is acting as an independent contractor. This Agreement is not an employment agreement, nor does it constitute a joint venture or partnership between the Designer and Agent.

16. Amendments, Mergers, Successors, and Assigns. All amendments to this Agreement must be written. This Agreement incorporates the entire understanding of the parties. It shall be binding on and inure to the benefit of the successors, administrators, executors, or heirs of the Agent and Designer.

17. Governing Law. This Agreement shall be governed by the laws of the State of _____.

IN WITNESS WHEREOF, the parties have signed this Agreement as of the date set forth above.

Designer_____   Agent_____
            Company name   Company name

By_____   By_____
     Authorized Signatory, Title   Authorized Signatory, Title

Schedule of House Accounts

Date_____

1. _____
   (name and address of client)

2. _____

3. _____

4. _____

5. _____

6. _____

7. _____

8. _____

9. _____

10. _____

11. _____

12. _____

13. _____

14. _____

15. _____

16. _____

17. _____

18. _____

19. _____

20. _____

Designer's Lecture Contract

Many designers find lecturing to be both a source of income and a rewarding opportunity to express their feelings about their work and being a designer. High schools, colleges, conferences, professional societies, and other institutions often invite designers to lecture. Slides of the designs may be used during these lectures and, in some cases, an exhibition may be mounted during the designer's visit.

A contract ensures that everything goes smoothly. For example, who should pay for slides that the designer has to make for that particular lecture? Who will pay for transportation to and from the lecture? Who will supply materials for a demonstration of technique? Will the designer have to give one lecture in a day or, as the institution might prefer, many more? Will the designer have to review portfolios of students? Resolving these kinds of questions, as well as the amount of and time to pay the fee, will make any lecture a more rewarding experience.

Filling in the Form

In the Preamble give the date and the names and addresses of the parties. In Paragraph 1 give the dates when the designer will lecture, the nature and extent of the services the designer will perform, and the form in which the designer is to bring examples of his or her work. In Paragraph 2 specify the fee to be paid to the designer and when it will be paid during the designer's visit. In Paragraph 3 give the amounts of expenses to be paid (or state that none or all of these expenses are to be paid), specify which expenses other than travel and food and lodging are covered, and show what will be provided by the sponsor (such as food or lodging). In Paragraph 10 indicate which state's law will govern the contract. Then have both parties sign the contract. On the "schedule of designs," list the works to be brought to the lecture and their insurance value.

Negotiation Checklist

❏ How long will the designer be required to stay at the sponsoring institution in order to perform the required services? (Paragraph 1)

❏ What are the nature and extent of the services the designer will be required to perform? (Paragraph 1)

❏ What slides, original designs, or other materials must the designer bring? (Paragraph 1)

❏ Specify the work facilities which the sponsor will provide the designer. (Paragraph 2)

❏ Specify the fee to be paid to the designer. (Paragraph 2)

❏ Give the time to pay the fee. (Paragraph 2)

❏ Require part of the fee be paid in advance.

❏ Specify the expenses which will be paid by the sponsor, including the time for payment of these expenses. (Paragraph 3)

❏ Indicate what the sponsor may provide in place of paying expenses, such as giving lodging, meals, or a car. (Paragraph 3)

❏ If illness prevents the designer from coming to lecture, state that an effort will be made to find another date. (Paragraph 4)

❏ If the sponsor must cancel for a reason beyond its control, indicate that the expenses incurred by the designer must be paid and there will be an attempt to reschedule. (Paragraph 4)

❏ If the sponsor cancels within 48 hours of the time designer is to arrive, consider requiring the full fee as well as expenses be paid.

❏ Provide for the payment of interest on late payments by the sponsor. (Paragraph 5)

❏ Retain for the designer all rights, including copyrights, in any recordings of any kind which may be made of designer's visit. (Paragraph 6)

❏ If the sponsor wishes to use a recording of the designer's visit, such as a video, require that the sponsor obtain the designer's written permission and that, if appropriate, a fee be negotiated for this use. (Paragraph 6)

❏ Provide that the sponsor is strictly responsible for loss or damage to any designs from the time they leave the designer's studio until they are returned there. (Paragraph 7)

❏ Require the sponsor to insure the designs and specify insurance values. (Paragraph 7)

❏ Consider which risks may be excluded from the insurance coverage.

❏ Consider whether the designer should be the named beneficiary of the insurance coverage for his or her works.

❏ Provide who will pay the cost of packing and shipping the works to and from the sponsor. (Paragraph 8)

❏ Provide who will take the responsibility to pack and ship the works to and from the sponsor.

❏ Compare the standard provisions in the introductory pages with Paragraphs 9–10.

Designer's Lecture Contract

AGREEMENT, dated the _____ day of _____, 20_____, between_____ (hereinafter referred to as the "Designer"), located at _____and _____(hereinafter referred to as the "Sponsor"), located at _____.

WHEREAS, the Sponsor is familiar with and admires the work of the Designer; and

WHEREAS, the Sponsor wishes the Designer to visit the Sponsor to enhance the opportunities for its students to have contact with working professional designer; and

WHEREAS, the Designer wishes to lecture with respect to his or her work and perform such other services as this contract may call for;

NOW, THEREFORE, in consideration of the foregoing premises and the mutual covenants hereinafter set forth and other valuable considerations, the parties hereto agree as follows:

1. **Designer to Lecture.** The Designer hereby agrees to come to the Sponsor on the following date(s):_____ _____ and perform the following services: _____.

   The Designer shall use best efforts to make his or her services as productive as possible to the Sponsor. The Designer further agrees to bring examples of his or her own work in the form of _____ _____.

2. **Payment.** The Sponsor agrees to pay as full compensation for the Designer's services rendered under Paragraph 1 the sum of $_____. This sum shall be payable to the Designer on completion of the _____ day of the Designer's residence with the Sponsor.

3. **Expenses.** In addition to the payments provided under Paragraph 2, the Sponsor agrees to reimburse the Designer for the following expenses:

   (A) Travel expenses in the amount of $_____.

   (B) Food and lodging expenses in the amount of $_____.

   (C) Other expenses listed here:_____in the amount of $_____.

   The reimbursement for travel expenses shall be made fourteen (14) days prior to the earliest date specified in Paragraph 1. The reimbursement for food, lodging, and other expenses shall be made at the date of payment specified in Paragraph 2, unless a contrary date is specified here:_____.

   In addition, the Sponsor shall provide the Designer with the following:

   (A) Tickets for travel, rental car, or other modes of transportation as follows: _____ _____

   (B) Food and lodging as follows: _____ _____

   (C) Other hospitality as follows: _____ _____

4. **Inability to Perform.** If the Designer is unable to appear on the dates scheduled in Paragraph 1 due to illness, the Sponsor shall have no obligation to make any payments under Paragraphs 2 and 3, but shall attempt to reschedule the Designer's appearance at a mutually acceptable future date. If the Sponsor is prevented from

having the Designer appear by Acts of God, hurricane, flood, governmental order, or other cause beyond its control, the Sponsor shall be responsible only for the payment of such expenses under Paragraph 3 as the Designer shall have actually incurred. The Sponsor agrees in such a case to attempt to reschedule the Designer's appearance at a mutually acceptable future date.

5. **Late Payment.** The Sponsor agrees that, in the event it is late in making payment of amounts due to the Designer under Paragraphs 2, 3, or 8, it will pay as additional liquidated damages _____ percent in interest on the amounts it is owing to the Designer, said interest to run from the date stipulated for payment in Paragraphs 2, 3, or 8 until such time as payment is made.

6. **Copyrights and Recordings.** Both parties agree that the Designer shall retain all rights, including copyrights, in relation to recordings of any kind made of the appearance or any works shown in the course thereof. The term "recording" as used herein shall include any recording made by electronic transcription, tape recording, wire recording, film, videotape, or other similar or dissimilar methods of recording, whether now known or hereinafter developed. No use of any such recording shall be made by the Sponsor without the written consent of the Designer and, if stipulated therein, additional compensation for such use.

7. **Insurance and Loss or Damage.** The Sponsor agrees that it shall provide wall-to-wall insurance for the works listed on the Schedule of Designs for the values specified therein. The Sponsor agrees that it shall be fully responsible and have strict liability for any loss or damage to the designs from the time said designs leaves the Designer's residence or studio until such time as it is returned there.

8. **Packing and Shipping.** The Sponsor agrees that it shall fully bear any costs of packing and shipping necessary to deliver the works specified in Paragraph 7 to the Sponsor and return them to the Designer's residence or studio.

9. **Modification.** This contract contains the full understanding between the parties hereto and may only be modified in a written instrument signed by both parties.

10. **Governing Law.** This contract shall be governed by the laws of the State of _____.

IN WITNESS WHEREOF, the parties hereto have signed this Agreement as of the date first set forth above.

Designer_____   Sponsor_____
                                                            Company Name

                                               By_____
                                                       Authorized Signatory, Title

Schedule of Designs

	Title	Medium	Size	Value
1.				
2.				
3.				
4.				
5.				
6.				
7.				

Licensing Contract to Merchandise Designs

Licensing is the granting of rights to use designs created by the designer on posters, calendars, greeting cards and stationery, apparel, wall paper, mugs and other household items, or any of innumerable other applications. Needless to say, this can be very lucrative for the designer. So many of the products used in everyday life depend on visual qualities to make them attractive to purchasers. These qualities may reside in the design of the product itself or in the use of designs on the product. For the designer to enter the world of manufactured, mass-produced goods offers the opportunity for new audiences and new modes of production and distribution. The best guide for designers on the subject of licensing is *Licensing Art & Design* by Caryn Leland (Allworth Press). The potentially large sums of money involved, as well as the possible complexity of licensing agreements, make *Licensing Art & Design* a valuable resource for designers who either are licensing designs or would like to enter the field of licensing.

Form 29, the Licensing Contract to Merchandise Designs, is adapted from a short-form licensing agreement contained in *Licensing Art & Design*, which also offers a long-form licensing agreement.

Filling in the Form

In the Preamble fill in the date and the names and addresses of the parties. In Paragraph 1 indicate whether the rights are exclusive or nonexclusive, give the name and description of the image, state what types of merchandise the image can be used for, specify the geographical area for distribution, and limit the term of the distribution. In Paragraph 3 specify the advance, if any, and the royalty percentage. State the date on which payments and statements of account are to begin in Paragraph 4.

Indicate the number of samples to be given to the designer in Paragraph 6. In Paragraph 13 specify which state's laws will govern the contract. Give addresses for correspondence relating to the contract in Paragraph 14. Have both parties sign the contract.

Negotiation Checklist

❑ Carefully describe the image to be licensed. (Paragraph 1)

❑ State whether the rights given to the licensee are exclusive or nonexclusive. (Paragraph 1)

❑ Indicate which kinds of merchandise the image is being licensed for. (Paragraph 1)

❑ State the area in which the licensee may sell the licensed products. (Paragraph 1)

❑ Give a term for the licensing contract. (Paragraph 1)

❑ Reserve all copyrights in the image to the designer. (Paragraph 2)

❑ Require that credit and copyright notice in the designer's name appear on all licensed products. (Paragraph 2)

❑ Require that credit and copyright notice in the designer's name appear on packaging, advertising, displays, and all publicity.

❑ Have the right to approve packaging, advertising, displays, and publicity.

❑ Give the licensee the right to use the designer's name and, in an appropriate case, picture, provided that any use must be to promote the product using the image and must be in dignified taste.

❏ Determine whether the royalty should be based on retail price or, as is more commonly the case, on net price which is what the manufacturer actually receives. (Paragraph 3)

❏ If any expenses are to reduce the amount on which royalties are calculated, these expenses must be specified.

❏ Specify the royalty percentage. (Paragraph 3)

❏ Require the licensee to pay an advance against royalties to be earned. (Paragraph 3)

❏ Indicate that any advance is nonrefundable. (Paragraph 3)

❏ Require minimum royalty payments for the term of the contract, regardless of sales.

❏ Require monthly or quarterly statements of account accompanied by any payments which are due. (Paragraph 4)

❏ Specify the information to be contained in the statement of account, such as units sold, total revenues received, special discounts, and the like. (Paragraph 4)

❏ Give the designer a right to inspect the books and records of the licensee. (Paragraph 5)

❏ Provide that if an inspection of the books and records uncovers an error to the disadvantage of the designer and that error is more than 5 percent of the amount owed designer, then the licensee shall pay for the cost of the inspection and any related costs.

❏ Provide for a certain number of samples to be given to the designer by the manufacturer. (Paragraph 6)

❏ Give the designer a right to purchase additional samples at manufacturing cost or, at least, at no more than the price paid by wholesalers. (Paragraph 6)

❏ Consider whether the designer will want the right to sell the products at retail price, rather than being restricted to using the samples and other units purchased for personal use.

❏ Give the designer a right of approval over the quality of the reproductions to protect the designer's reputation. (Paragraph 7)

❏ Require the licensee give best efforts to promoting the licensed products. (Paragraph 8)

❏ Specify an amount of money that the licensee must spend on promotion.

❏ Specify the type of promotion that the licensee will provide.

❏ Reserve all rights to the designer which are not expressly transferred. (Paragraph 9)

❏ If the licensee's usage may create trademarks or other rights in the product, it is important that these rights be owned by the designer after termination of the license.

❏ Require the licensee to indemnify the designer for any costs arising out of the use of the image on the licensed products. (Paragraph 10)

❏ Have the licensee provide liability insurance with the designer as a named beneficiary to protect against defects in the products.

❏ Forbid assignment by the licensee, but let the designer assign royalties. (Paragraph 11)

❏ Specify the grounds for terminating the contract, such as the bankruptcy or insolvency of the licensee, failure of the licensee to obey the terms of the contract, cessation of manufacture of the product, or insufficent sales of the licensed products. (This partially covered in Paragraph 4.)

❏ Compare the standard provisions in the introductory pages with Paragraphs 10–15.

Licensing Contract to Merchandise Designs

AGREEMENT made this _____ day of _____, 20_____, between _____ (hereinafter referred to as the "Designer"), located at _____ and _____ (hereinafter referred to as the "Licensee"), located at _____ with respect to the use of a certain design created by the Designer (hereinafter referred to as the "Design") for manufactured products (hereinafter referred to as the "Licensed Products").

WHEREAS, the Designer is a professional designer of good standing; and

WHEREAS, the Designer has created the Design which the Designer wishes to license for purposes of manufacture and sale; and

WHEREAS, the Licensee wishes to use the Design to create a certain product or products for manufacture and sale; and

WHEREAS, both parties want to achieve the best possible quality to generate maximum sales;

NOW, THEREFORE, in consideration of the foregoing premises and the mutual covenants hereinafter set forth and other valuable consideration, the parties hereto agree as follows:

1. **Grant of Merchandising Rights.** The Designer grants to the Licensee the ❑ exclusive ❑ nonexclusive right to use the Design, titled _____ and described as _____, which was created and is owned by the Designer, as or as part of the following type(s) of merchandise:_____ _____ for manufacture, distribution, and sale by the Licensee in the following geographical area:_____ _____ and for the following period of time: _____.

2. **Ownership of Copyright.** The Designer shall retain all copyrights in and to the Design. The Licensee shall identify the Designer as the creator of the Design on the Licensed Products and shall reproduce thereon a copyright notice for the Designer which shall include the word "Copyright" or the symbol for copyright, the Designer's name, and the year date of first publication.

3. **Advance and Royalties.** Licensee agrees to pay Designer a nonrefundable advance in the amount of $_____ upon signing this Agreement, which advance shall be recouped from first royalties due hereunder. Licensee further agrees to pay Designer a royalty of _____ (_____ %) percent of the net sales of the Licensed Products. "Net Sales" as used herein shall mean sales to customers less prepaid freight and credits for lawful and customary volume rebates, actual returns, and allowances. Royalties shall be deemed to accrue when the Licensed Products are sold, shipped, or invoiced, whichever first occurs.

4. **Payments and Statements of Account.** Royalty payments shall be paid monthly on the first day of each month commencing _____, 20_____, and Licensee shall with each payment furnish Designer with a monthly statement of account showing the kinds and quantities of all Licensed Products sold, the prices received therefor, and all deductions for freight, volume rebates, returns, and allowances. The Designer shall have the right to terminate this Agreement upon thirty (30) days notice if Licensee fails to make any payment required of it and does not cure this default within said thirty (30) days, whereupon all rights granted herein shall revert immediately to the Designer.

5. **Inspection of Books and Records.** Designer shall have the right to inspect Licensee's books and records concerning sales of the Licensed Products upon prior written notice.

6. Samples. Licensee shall give the Designer _____ samples of the Licensed Products for the Designer's personal use. The Designer shall have the right to purchase additional samples of the Licensed Products at the Licensee's manufacturing cost.

7. Quality of Reproductions. The Designer shall have the right to approve the quality of the reproduction of the Design on the Licensed Products, and the Designer agrees not to withhold approval unreasonably.

8. Promotion. Licensee shall use its best efforts to promote, distribute, and sell the Licensed Products.

9. Reservation of Rights. All rights not specifically transferred by this Agreement are reserved to the Designer.

10. Indemnification. The Licensee shall hold the Designer harmless from and against any loss, expense, or damage occasioned by any claim, demand, suit, or recovery against the Designer arising out of the use of the Image for the Licensed Products.

11. Assignment. Neither party shall assign rights or obligations under this Agreement, except that the Designer may assign the right to receive money due hereunder.

12. Nature of Contract. Nothing herein shall be construed to constitute the parties hereto joint venturers, nor shall any similar relationship be deemed to exist between them.

13. Governing Law. This Agreement shall be construed in accordance with the laws of _____; Licensee consents to the jurisdiction of the courts of _____.

14. Addresses. All notices, demands, payments, royalty payments, and statements shall be sent to the Designer at the following address _____ and to the Licensee at _____.

15. Modifications in Writing. This Agreement constitutes the entire agreement between the parties hereto and shall not be modified, amended, or changed in any way except by a written agreement signed by both parties hereto.

IN WITNESS WHEREOF, the parties have signed this Agreement as of the date first set forth above.

Designer_____   Licensee_____
              Company Name   Company Name

By_____   By_____
          Authorized Signatory, Title   Authorized Signatory, Title

Release Form for Models

Designs often portray people. Whether these images are created by the designer or by photographers or illustrators, the designer must be aware of individual's rights to privacy and publicity. While the intricacies of these laws can be reviewed in *Legal Guide for the Visual Artist*, this summary will help alert the designer to potential dangers.

The right to privacy can take a number of forms. For example, it is forbidden by state laws and court decisions to use a person's name, portrait, or picture for purposes of advertising or trade. This raises the question of the definitions for advertising and trade. It would also violate the right of privacy to bring before the public an image which showed or implied something embarrassing and untrue about someone. And physically intruding into private spaces such as a home, perhaps to take a photograph for use as a reference, can be an invasion of privacy.

The right of publicity is the right which a celebrity creates in his or her name, image, and voice. To use the celebrity's image for commercial gain violates this right of publicity. And, while the right of privacy generally protects only living people, a number of states have enacted laws to protect the publicity rights of celebrities even after death. These state laws supplement court decisions which held that celebrities who exploited the commercial value of their names and images while alive had publicity rights after death.

On the other hand, use of people's images for newsworthy and editorial purposes is protected by the First Amendment. No releases need be obtained for such uses which serve the public interest.

What should the designer do about all this? The wisest course is to obtain a model release from anyone who will be recognizable in a design, including people who can be recognized from parts of their body other than the face.

Even if the initial use of the design is editorial and does not create a privacy issue, there is always the possibility that an image will be reproduced in other ways such as for posters, postcards, and T-shirts, all of which are clearly trade uses, or for advertising. Only by having a model release can the designer guarantee the right to exploit the commercial value of the image in the future (subject, of course, to the agreement with the photographer or illustrator who may have created the image).

If the designer is creating the image, form 30 allows the designer (and others who obtain the designer's permission, such as clients) to use the model's image for advertising and trade. The designer should insist that a form like form 30 also be used by photographers or illustrators working for the designer (and extend the coverage of the release to the designer and his or her clients). While some states may not require written releases or the payment of money for a release, it is always wise to use a written release and make at least a small payment as consideration. By the way, form 30 is intended for use with friends and acquaintances who pose as well as with professional models.

If the release is drafted to cover one use, but the image is then used in a distorted and embarrassing way for a different purpose, the release may not protect the designer regardless of what it says. For example, a model signed a model release for a bookstore's advertisement in which she was to appear in bed reading a book. This advertisement was later changed and used by a bedsheet manufacturer known for its salacious advertisements. The title on the book became pornographic and a leering old man was placed next to the bed looking at the model. This invaded the model's privacy despite her having signed a release.

In general, a minor must have a parent or guardian give consent. While the designer should check the law in his or her state, the age of majority in most states is eighteen.

The designer should be certain to obtain the release when the image is received (or created), since it is easy to forget if left for later. Also, releases should kept systematically so that they can be related to the design in which the person appears who gave the release. A simple numbering system can be used to connect the releases to the designs. While a witness isn't a necessity, having one can help if a question is later raised about the validity of the release.

If the designer is given a release form to use by a client, the designer must make certain that the form protects the designer. The Negotiation Checklist will be helpful in reviewing any form provided to the designer and suggesting changes to strengthen the form.

Filling in the Form

Fill in the dollar amount being paid as consideration for the release. Then fill in the name of the model and the name of the designer. Have the model and a witness sign the form. Obtain the addresses for both the model and the witness and date the form. If the model is a minor, have the parent or guardian sign. Have the witness sign and give the addresses of the witness and the parent or guardian as well as the date.

Negotiation Checklist

❏ Be certain that some amount of money, even a token amount, is actually paid as consideration for the release.

❏ Have the release be given not only to the designer, but also to the designer's estate and anyone else the designer might want to assign rights to such as a client or a manufacturer of posters or T-shirts.

❏ If the release is obtained by a photographer or illustrator, be certain that the release extends to the designer and his or her clients.

❏ Likewise, if the release form is provided by a client, be certain its coverage offers protection for the designer.

❏ Recite that the grant is irrevocable.

❏ Cover use of the name as well as the image of the person.

❏ Include the right to use the image in all forms, media, and manners of use.

❏ Include the right to make distorted or changed versions of the image as well as composite images.

❏ Allow advertising and trade uses.

❏ Allow any other lawful use.

❏ Have the model waive any right to review the finished artwork, including written copy to accompany the artwork.

❏ Have the model recite that he or she is of full age.

❏ If the model is a minor, have a parent or guardian sign the release.

❏ Attach to the release an image that identifies the model to avoid any confusion at a later time as to who gave consent.

❏ If the model will be working in an unusually dangerous situation, such as being photographed with a potentially dangerous animal or near the rim of a canyon, consider having the model agree to indemnify and hold harmless the designer against any losses or lawsuits that might arise from this aspect of the shoot.

❏ If the images will be used in relation to sensitive issues such as diseases, sexuality, or political and religious beliefs, it would be wise to state what the use will be in the release (stating that the uses "include but are not limited to" the particular intended use).

Release Form for Models

In consideration of _____ Dollars ($_____), and other valuable consideration, receipt of which is acknowledged, I, _____ (print Model's name), do hereby give _____ (the Designer), his or her assigns, licensees, successors in interest, legal representatives, and heirs the absolute and irrevocable right to use my name (or any fictional name), picture, portrait, or photograph in all forms, including in whole or in part, in all manners, and in all media, whether now known or hereinafter discovered, without any restriction as to changes or alterations (including but not limited to composite or distorted representations or derivative works made in any medium) for advertising, trade, commercial, promotion, exhibition, editorial, or any other lawful purposes. I acknowledge that I have no rights with respect to the photograph(s) and I waive any right to inspect or approve the photograph(s) or finished version(s) incorporating the photograph(s), including written copy, if any, that may be created and appear in connection therewith. I hereby release and agree to hold harmless the Designer, his or her assigns, licensees, successors in interest, legal representatives and heirs from any liability by virtue of any blurring, distortion, alteration, optical illusion, or use in composite form whether intentional or otherwise, that may occur or be produced in the taking of the photographs, or in any processing tending toward the completion of the finished product, unless it can be shown that they and the publication thereof were maliciously caused, produced, and published solely for the purpose of subjecting me to conspicuous ridicule, scandal, reproach, scorn, and indignity. I agree that the Designer owns the copyright in these photographs and I hereby waive any claims I may have based on any usage of the photographs or works derived therefrom, including but not limited to claims for either invasion of privacy or libel. I am of full age* and competent to sign this release. I agree that this release shall be binding on me, my legal representatives, heirs, and assigns. I have read this release and am fully familiar with its contents.

Witness_____   Signed_____
                                                                     Model
Address_____   Address_____

                                             Date _____, 20 ___

———————————————— **Consent (if applicable)** ————————————————

I am the parent or guardian of the minor named above and have the legal authority to execute the above release. I approve the foregoing and waive any rights in the premises.

Witness_____   Signed_____
            Parent or Guardian
Address_____   Address_____

                                             Date _____, 20 ___

*Delete this sentence if the subject is a minor. The parent or guardian must then sign the consent.

Attach visual reference for model here,
such as a photocopy of a driver's license
or other identifying image.

Property Release Form

Property does not have rights of privacy or publicity. A public building, a horse running in a field, or a bowl of fruit are all freely available to be portrayed in a design.

Nonetheless, there may be times when the designer will want to obtain a release for the use of property belonging to others (or have a photographer or illustrator obtain such a release, in the case of work done on assignment). This might include personal property, such as jewelry or clothing, or the interiors of private buildings, especially if admission is charged. The most important reason for the release is to have a contract which details the terms of use of the property.

If the designer is lent property to use in a work, it is important to obtain a release if the designer has any intention of using that artwork in some way other than the commission. For example, if an designer were hired to create a Christmas card with the image of the client's favorite dog on the front of the card, it would be a breach of an implied provision of the contract for the designer to then sell that image to a manufacturer of dog food for use as product packaging. Such a use certainly would require the owner's permission, which could be obtained by using form 31.

As with releases for models, property releases should be obtained at the time the property is used and payment, even if only a token payment, should be made to the owner of the property. If a form is supplied by either the client or a photographer or illustrator, be certain its coverage protects the designer.

Filling in the Form

Fill in the amount being paid for use of the property, as well as the name and address of the owner and the name of the designer. Then specify the property which will be used. Finally have both parties sign the release, obtain a witness to each signature (if possible), and give the date.

Negotiation Checklist

❑ Make some payment, however small, as consideration for the release.

❑ Be certain the release runs in favor of the designer's assigns (such as clients) and estate as well as the designer.

❑ If the release is provided by the client, be certain it protects the designer.

❑ If the release is obtained by a photographer or illustrator, be certain its coverage extends to the designer and the designer's clients.

❑ State that the release is irrevocable.

❑ Include the right to copyright and publish the image made from the property.

❑ Include the right to use the image in all forms, media, and manners of use.

❑ Permit advertising and trade uses as well as any other lawful use.

❑ State that the owner has full and sole authority to give the release.

❑ Obtain the right to make distorted versions of the image as well as composite images.

❑ Allow use of the owner's name or a fictional name with the image of the property.

❑ Permit color or black and white images, as well as any type of derivative work.

❑ Have the owner waive any right to review the finished artwork, including written copy to accompany the artwork.

❑ Make certain the owner is of full age and has the capacity to give the release.

Property Release Form

In consideration of the sum of _____Dollars ($_____),
receipt of which is hereby acknowledged, I, _____, located at _____, do irrevocably
authorize _____, his or her assigns, licensees, heirs, and legal representatives, to copyright, publish, and use in all forms and media and in all manners for advertising, trade, or any other lawful purpose, images of
t   h   e
following property which I own and have full and sole authority to license for such uses: _____
_____,
regardless of whether said use is composite or distorted in character or form, whether said use is made in conjunction with my own name or with a fictitious name, or whether said use is made in color or otherwise or other derivative
works are made through any medium.

I waive any right that I may have to inspect or approve the finished version(s), including written copy that may be used
in connection therewith.

I am of full age and have every right to contract in my own name with respect to the foregoing matters. I have read
the above authorization and release prior to its execution and I am fully cognizant of its contents.

Witness_____   Owner_____

Address_____   Date_____,20_____

Permission Form

Many projects require obtaining permission from the owners of copyrighted materials such as graphics, photographs, paintings, articles, or excerpts from books. The designer ignores obtaining such permissions at great peril. Not only is it unethical to use someone else's work without permission, it can also lead to liability for copyright infringement.

Of course, some copyrighted works have entered the public domain, which means that they can be freely copied by anyone. What is included in the public domain is a complicated matter because the copyright term has changed several times, and so have the requirements for copyright notice and the consequences of omitting such notice. Works created by United States authors in 1922 and earlier are now in the public domain in the United States. Works created by United States authors between January 1, 1923, and December 31, 1977, now have a term of ninety-five years; however, works published prior to January 1, 1964, had to be renewed after twenty-eight years and could have fallen into the public domain if not renewed. The Copyright Office can review its records to determine whether a copyright was renewed.

For works published on or after January 1, 1978, the term of protection is usually the life of the author plus 70 years, so these works would only be in the public domain if copyright notice had been omitted or improper. This complicated topic is discussed fully in *Legal Guide for the Visual Artist*. The absence of a copyright notice on works published between January 1, 1978 and February 28, 1989 (when the United States joined the Berne Copyright Union) does not necessarily mean the work is in the public domain. On or after March 1, 1989, copyright notice is no longer required to preserve copyright protection, although such notice does confer some benefits under the copyright law. A basic rule is to obtain permission for using any work, unless the designer is certain the work is in the public domain or determines that the planned use would be a fair use.

Fair use offers another way in which the designer may avoid having to obtain a permission, even though the work is protected by a valid copyright. The copyright law states that copying "for purposes such as criticism, comment, news reporting, teaching (including multiple copies for classroom use), scholarship, or research, is not an infringement of copyright." To evaluate whether a use is a fair use depends on four factors set forth in the law: "(1) the purpose and character of the use, including whether such use is of a commercial nature or is for nonprofit educational purposes; (2) the nature of the copyrighted work; (3) the amount and substantiality of the portion used . . . and (4) the effect of the use upon the potential market for or value of the copyrighted work." These guidelines have to be applied on a case-by-case basis. If there is any doubt, it is best to seek permission to use the work.

One obstacle to obtaining permissions is locating the person who owns the rights. A good starting point, of course, is to contact the publisher of the material, since the publisher may have the right to grant permissions. If the creator's address is available, the creator can be contacted directly. In some cases, permissions may have to be obtained from more than one party. Creator's societies and agents may be helpful in tracking down the owners of rights.

For an hourly fee, the Copyright Office will search its records to aid in establishing the copyright status of a work. Copyright Office Circular 22, "How to Investigate the Copyright Status of a Work," explains more fully what the Copyright Office can and cannot do. Circulars and forms can be ordered from the Copyright Office by calling (202) 707-9100. The Copyright Office also gives extensive information about copyright and provides online registration on its website at www.copyrightoffice.gov.

Permissions can be time-consuming to obtain, so starting early in a project is wise. A log should be kept of each request for a permission. In the log, each request is given a number. The log describes the material to be used, lists the name and address of the owner of the rights, shows when the request was made and when any reply was received, indicates if a fee must be paid, and includes any special conditions required by the owner.

Fees may very well have to be paid for certain permissions. If the client is to pay these fees, the designer should certainly specify this in the contract with the client. If the client (such as a publisher) has an agreement making the designer liable if lawsuits arise over permissions which should have been obtained by the designer, the designer should resist such a provision or at least limit the amount of liability. For example, the designer might limit his or her liability to the amount of the design fee paid (but this will not stop the designer being named as a defendant by the owner of the work which was infringed). In any case, the designer should keep in mind that permission fees are negotiable and vary widely in amount. For a project that will require many permissions, advance research as to the amount of the fees is a necessity.

Filling in the Form

The form should be accompanied by a cover letter requesting that two copies of the form be signed and one copy returned. The name and address of the designer, the type of use, and the name of the designer's client, should be filled in. Then the nature of the material should be specified, such as text, photograph, illustration, poem, and so on. The source should be described along with an exact description of the material. If available, fill in the date of publication, the publisher, and the author. Any copyright notice or credit line to accompany the material should be shown. State after Other Provisions any special limitations on the rights granted and also indicate the amount of any fee to be paid. If all the rights are not controlled by the person giving the permission, then that person will have to indicate who else to contact. If more than one person must

approve the permission, make certain there are enough signature lines. If the rights are owned by a corporation, add the company name and the title of the authorized signatory. A stamped, self-addressed envelope and a photocopy of the material to be used might make a speedy response more likely.

Negotiation Checklist

❏ State that the permission extends not only to the designer, but also to the designer's successors and assigns. Certainly the permission must extend to the designer's client.

❏ Describe the material to be used carefully, including a photocopy if that would be helpful.

❏ Obtain the right to use the material in future editions, derivations, revisions, or electronic versions of the book or other product, as well as in the present version.

❏ State that nonexclusive world rights in all languages are being granted.

❏ In an unusual situation, seek exclusivity for certain uses of the material. This form does not seek exclusivity.

❏ Negotiate a fee, if requested. Whether a fee is appropriate, and its amount, will depend on whether the project is likely to earn a substantial return.

❏ If a fee is paid, add a provision requiring the party giving the permission to warrant that the material does not violate any copyright or other rights and to indemnify the designer against any losses caused if the warranty is incorrect.

❏ Keep a log on all correspondence relating to permission forms and be certain one copy of each signed permission has been returned for the designer's files.

Permission Form

The Undersigned hereby grant(s) permission to _____ (hereinafter

referred to as the "Designer"), located at _____, and

to the Designer's successors and assigns, to use the material specified in this Permission Form for the following book

or other product _____

for use by the following publisher or client _____

This permission is for the following material:

Nature of material _____

Source _____

Exact description of material, including page numbers_____

If published, date of publication _____

Publisher _____

Author(s) _____

This material may be used for the book or product named above and in any future revisions, derivations, or electronic versions thereof, including nonexclusive world rights in all languages.

It is understood that the grant of this permission shall in no way restrict republication of the material by the Undersigned or others authorized by the Undersigned.

If specified here, the material shall be accompanied on publication by a copyright notice as follows_____

_____

and a credit line as follows _____

Other provisions, if any _____

If specified here, the requested rights are not controlled in their entirety by the Undersigned and the following owners must be contacted _____

_____

One copy of this Permission Form shall be returned to the Designer and one copy shall be retained by the Undersigned.

_____   _____
Authorized Signatory   Date

_____   _____
Authorized Signatory   Date

Nondisclosure Agreement for Submitting Ideas

What can be more frustrating than having a great idea and not being able to share it with anyone? Especially if the idea has commercial value, sharing it is often the first step on the way to realizing the remunerative potential of the concept. The designer wants to show the idea to a client, publisher, manufacturer, or producer. But how can the idea be protected?

Ideas are not protected by copyright, because copyright only protects the expression of an idea. The idea to create a design which includes an image of the White House is not copyrightable, while the design itself certainly is protected by copyright. The idea to have a television series in which each program would have a designer teach at a well-known landmark in his or her locale is not copyrightable, but each program would be protected by copyright. Of course, copyright is not the only form of legal protection. An idea might be patentable or lead to the creation of a trademark, but these are less likely cases and certainly require expert legal assistance. How does a designer disclose an idea for an image, a format, a product, or other creations without risking that the other party will simply steal the idea?

This can be done by the creation of an express contract, an implied contract (revealed by the course of dealing between the parties), or a fiduciary relationship (in which one party owes a duty of trust to the other party). Form 33, the Nondisclosure Agreement, creates an express contract between the party disclosing the idea and the party receiving it who agrees to negotiate in good faith if the idea is used. Form 33 is adapted from a letter agreement in *Licensing Art & Design* by Caryn Leland (Allworth Press).

What should be done if a company refuses to sign a nondisclosure agreement or, even worse, has its own agreement for the designer to sign? Such an agreement might say that the company will not be liable for using a similar idea and will probably place a maximum value on the idea (such as a few hundred dollars). At this point, the designer has to evaluate the risk. Does the company have a good reputation or is it notorious for appropriating ideas? Are there other companies willing to sign a nondisclosure agreement that could be approached with the idea? If not, taking the risk may make more sense than never exploiting the idea at all. A number of steps, set out in the negotiation checklist, should then be taken to try and gain some protection. The designer will have to make these evaluations on a case-by-case basis.

Filling in the Form

In the Preamble fill in the date and the names and addresses of the parties. In Paragraph 1 describe the information to be disclosed without giving away what it is. Have both parties sign the agreement.

Negotiation Checklist

❑ Disclose what the information concerns without giving away what is new or innovative. For example, "an idea for a new format for a series to teach design" might interest a producer but would not give away the idea of using different designers teaching at landmarks in different locales. (Paragraph 1)

❑ State that the recipient is reviewing the information to decide whether to embark on commercial exploitation. (Paragraph 2)

❑ Require the recipient to agree not to use or transfer the information. (Paragraph 3)

❑ State that the recipient receives no rights in the information. (Paragraph 3)

❏ Indicate that if the agreement terminates, or if the designer requests it, the recipient shall delete all digital files and destroy all tangible copies containing the information. (Paragraph 3)

❏ Require the recipient to keep the information confidential. (Paragraph 4)

❏ State that the recipient acknowledges that disclosure of the information would cause irreparable harm to the designer. (Paragraph 4)

❏ Require good faith negotiations if the recipient wishes to use the information after disclosure. (Paragraph 5)

❏ Allow no use of the information unless agreement is reached after such negotiations. (Paragraph 5)

If the designer wishes to disclose the information despite the other party's refusal to sign the designer's nondisclosure form, the designer should take a number of steps:

❏ First, before submission, the idea should be sent to a neutral third party (such as a notary public or professional design society) to be held in confidence.

❏ Anything submitted should be marked with copyright and trademark notices, when appropriate. For example, the idea may not be copyrightable, but the written explanation of the idea certainly is. The copyright notice could be for that explanation, but might make the recipient more hesitant to steal the idea.

❏ If an appointment is made, confirm it by letter in advance and sign any log for visitors.

❏ After any meeting, send a letter which covers what happened at the meeting (including any disclosure of confidential information and any assurances that information will be kept confidential) and, if at all possible, have any proposal or followup from the recipient be in writing.

Nondisclosure Agreement for Submitting Ideas

AGREEMENT, entered into as of this _____ day of _____, 20___, between_____ (hereinafter referred to as the "Designer"), located at _____, and _____ (hereinafter referred to as the "Recipient"), located at _____.

WHEREAS, the Designer has developed certain valuable information, concepts, ideas, or designs, which the Designer deems confidential (hereinafter referred to as the "Information"); and

WHEREAS, the Recipient is in the business of using such Information for its projects and wishes to review the Information; and

WHEREAS, the Designer wishes to disclose this Information to the Recipient; and

WHEREAS, the Recipient is willing not to disclose this Information, as provided in this Agreement.

NOW, THEREFORE, in consideration of the foregoing premises and the mutual covenants hereinafter set forth and other valuable considerations, the parties hereto agree as follows:

1. **Disclosure.** Designer shall disclose to the Recipient the Information, which concerns:_____
_____

2. **Purpose.** Recipient agrees that this disclosure is only for the purpose of the Recipient's evaluation to determine its interest in the commercial exploitation of the Information.

3. **Limitation on Use.** Recipient agrees not to manufacture, sell, deal in, or otherwise use or appropriate the disclosed Information in any way whatsoever, including but not limited to adaptation, imitation, redesign, or modification. Nothing contained in this Agreement shall be deemed to give Recipient any rights whatsoever in and to the Information. Recipient shall not copy, including digitally, the Information except as necessary for the Purpose stated in Paragraph 2 hereof. Upon termination of this Agreement or upon the Designer's request, Recipient shall return all original Information and shall permanently delete all digital copies and destroy all tangible copies of the Information.

4. **Confidentiality.** Recipient understands and agrees that the unauthorized disclosure of the Information by the Recipient to others would irreparably damage the Designer. As consideration and in return for the disclosure of this Information, the Recipient shall keep secret and hold in confidence all such Information and treat the Information as if it were the Recipient's own proprietary property by not disclosing it to any person or entity.

5. **Good Faith Negotiations.** If, on the basis of the evaluation of the Information, Recipient wishes to pursue the exploitation thereof, Recipient agrees to enter into good faith negotiations to arrive at a mutually satisfactory agreement for these purposes. Until and unless such an agreement is entered into, this nondisclosure Agreement shall remain in force.

6. **Miscellany.** This Agreement shall be binding upon and shall inure to the benefit of the parties and their respective legal representatives, successors, and assigns.

IN WITNESS WHEREOF, the parties have signed this Agreement as of the date first set forth above.

Designer_____   Recipient_____
                                                                    Company Name

                                                              By_____
                                                                    Authorized Signatory, Title

Copyright Transfer Form

The copyright law defines a transfer of copyright as an assignment "of a copyright or of any of the exclusive rights comprised in a copyright, whether or not it is limited in time or place of effect, but not including a nonexclusive license." A transfer is, in some way, exclusive. The person receiving a transfer has a right to do what no one else can do. For example, the transfer might be of the right to make copies of the work in the form of posters for distribution in the United States for a period of one year. While this transfer is far less than all rights in the copyright, it is nonetheless exclusive within its time and place of effect.

Any transfer of an exclusive right must be in the form of a writing signed either by the owner of the rights being conveyed or by the owner's authorized agent. While not necessary to make the assignment valid, notarization of the signature is *prima facie* proof that the assignment was signed by the owner or agent.

Form 34 can be used in a variety of situations. If the designer wanted to receive back rights which the designer had transferred in the past, the designer could take an all rights transfer. If the designer enters into a contract involving the transfer of an exclusive right, the parties may not want to reveal all the financial data and other terms contained in the contract. Form 34 could then be used as a short form to be executed along with the contract for the purpose of recordation in the Copyright Office. For example, form 34 could be used with form 37 (licensing rights), form 38 (licensing electronic rights), or any other transfer of rights. The assignment in form 34 should conform exactly to the assignment in the contract itself.

Recordation of copyright transfers with the Copyright Office can be quite important. Any transfer should be recorded within one month if executed in the United States, or within two months if executed outside the United States. Otherwise, a later conflicting transfer, if recorded first and taken in good faith without knowledge of the earlier transfer, will prevail over the earlier transfer. Simply put, if the same exclusive rights are sold twice and the first buyer doesn't record the transfer, it is quite possible that the second buyer who does record the transfer will be found to own the rights.

Any document relating to a copyright, whether a transfer of an exclusive right or only a nonexclusive license, can be recorded with the Copyright Office. Such recordation gives constructive notice to the world about the facts in the document recorded. Constructive notice means that a person will be held to have knowledge of the document even if, in fact, he or she did not know about it. Recordation gives constructive notice only if the document (or supporting materials) identifies the work to which it pertains so that the recorded document will be revealed by a reasonable search under the title or registration number of the work and registration has been made for the work.

Another good reason to record exclusive transfers is that a nonexclusive license, whether recorded or not, can have priority over a conflicting exclusive transfer. If the nonexclusive license is written and signed and was taken before the execution of the transfer or taken in good faith before recordation of the transfer and without notice of the transfer, it will prevail over the transfer.

A fee must be paid to record documents. Once paid, the Register of Copyrights will record the document and return a certificate of recordation.

Filling in the Form

Give the name and address of the party giving the assignment (the assignor) and the name and address of the party receiving the assignment. Specify the rights transferred. Describe the work or works by title, registration number, and the nature of the work. Date the transfer and have the assignor sign it. If the assignor is a corporation, use a corporate form for the signature.

Negotiation Checklist

❏ Be certain that consideration (something of value, whether a promise or money) is actually given to the other party.

❏ Have the transfer benefit the successors in interest of the assignee.

❏ If the designer is making the transfer, limit the rights transferred as narrowly as possible.

❏ Describe the works as completely as possible, including title, registration number, and the nature of the work.

❏ Have the assignor or the authorized agent of the assignor sign the assignment.

❏ Notarize the assignment to gain the presumption the signature is valid.

❏ If the assignment is to the designer, such as an assignment back to the designer of rights previously conveyed, an all rights provision can be used. (See other provisions)

❏ If the designer is receiving the assignment, make certain that the term is not only for the copyright but also for any extensions and renewals.

Other provisions that can be added to form 34:

❏ Rights transferred. When indicating the rights transferred, the following provision could be used if the designer is to receive all

rights. Obviously, the designer should avoid giving such an assignment of rights to another party.

Rights Transferred. All right, title, and interest, including: (1) any statutory copyright together with the right to secure renewals and extensions of such copyright through the world; (2) any and all works derived from the work protected by the said copyright, whether in traditional or digital form and whether now known or hereinafter invented or discovered; and (3) any and all rights that the Assignor now has or may become entitled to in the future under federal, state, or foreign laws. In addition, the assignment includes any and all causes of action for infringement of the work, whether past, present, or future, and any and all proceeds from such causes accrued and unpaid and hereafter accruing.

Copyright Transfer Form

FOR VALUABLE CONSIDERATION, the receipt of which is hereby acknowledged, _____ (hereinafter referred to as the "Assignor"), located at _____, does hereby transfer and assign to _____, located at _____, his or her heirs, executors, administrators, and assigns, the following rights: _____ _____ in the copyrights, and any renewals or extensions thereof, in the works described as follows:

Title	Registration Number	Nature of Work
_____	_____	_____
_____	_____	_____
_____	_____	_____
_____	_____	_____
_____	_____	_____

IN WITNESS WHEREOF, the Assignor has executed this instrument on the _____ day of _____, 20____.

Assignor_____

Applications for Copyright Registration of Designs

The Copyright Office has built an excellent online presence at www.copyright.gov. Their website has extensive information about copyright, including numerous publications, forms, the federal copyright law, copyright regulations, legislative proposals, reports, and more. The designer should be able to find the answers to most questions about copyright there, including how to register copyrights.

Registration has always required a correctly filled-in application form, the specified fee, and deposit materials that show the content of what is being copyrighted. The registration process has been streamlined and the Copyright Office now prefers to have registration completed electronically on their website through what is called the eCO Online System (eCO abbreviates electronic Copyright Office). The use of paper forms is expensive for the Copyright Office, so the fee for online registration is now less than the fee for registration using paper forms, as a way of encouraging designers and other authors to file electronically. To further discourage the use of the paper application forms, the Copyright Office no longer makes them available on their website. To obtain the paper forms, a special request must be made to the Copyright Office (which can be done through the website).

Among the advantages of eCO online registration are the aforementioned lower basic registration fee (currently $35), the quickest time to complete the registration, status tracking online, secure online payment, the ability to upload certain deposit materials as electronic files, and 24/7 availability. Anyone can use eCO and most types of works are eligible for eCO (but note that groups of contributions to periodicals cannot be registered using eCO). Currently eCO will accept registrations for (1) a single work; (2) a group of unpublished works by the same author and owned by the same copyright claimant; or (3) multiple works contained in the same unit of publication and owned by the same claimant (such as a book of photographs). The eCO registration process requires filling in the online application form, paying the application fee, and submitting deposit copies.

The deposit copies for eCO can be electronic in a number of situations, including if the work being registered is unpublished, has only been published electronically, or is a published work for which identifying material would be used instead of the work itself. Identifying material for a work of visual art might be used if the work is three-dimensional or oversized (more than ninety-six inches in any dimension). The deposit requirements, including the use of identifying material, are set forth in Circular 40A, "Deposit Requirements for Registration of Claims to Copyright in Visual Arts Material." If a work is eligible for eCO registration but the deposit cannot be reproduced electronically, a hard copy may be used and sent to the Copyright Office. General guidelines to registration can be found in Circular 40, "Copyright Registration for Works of the Visual Arts."

The least preferable method for registration is to use paper forms, such as Form VA (for a work of visual art). As mentioned above, the fee for such an application is the highest—currently $65. Since eCO is an online process, copies of Form VA with instructions and Short Form VA with instructions have been included as form 35 and form 36. The goal of the Copyright Office is to phase out paper forms, but for the moment they can be used and have instructional value in terms of understanding the components of the online processes.

Of great interest to designers is the possibility of registering groups of designs. This is a way to dramatically reduce the cost of registering each design individually. Unpublished designs always benefited from being eligible for registration as an unpublished group. This remains true whether registration is done through eCO or use of the paper Form VA. To qualify for registration as an unpublished group (1) the group must have a title; (2) the designs must be assembled neatly; (3) one author must have created or contributed to all the designs; and (4) the same party must be the copyright claimant for all the designs.

For a more extensive discussion of the legal aspects of copyright, the designer can consult *Legal Guide for the Visual Artist* by Tad Crawford (Allworth Press).

Form VA

Detach and read these instructions before completing this form.
Make sure all applicable spaces have been filled in before you return this form.

When to Use This Form: Use Form VA for copyright registration of published or unpublished works of the visual arts. This category consists of "pictorial, graphic, or sculptural works," including two-dimensional and three-dimensional works of fine, graphic, and applied art, photographs, prints and art reproductions, maps, globes, charts, technical drawings, diagrams, and models.

What Does Copyright Protect? Copyright in a work of the visual arts protects those pictorial, graphic, or sculptural elements that, either alone or in combination, represent an "original work of authorship." The statute declares: "In no case does copyright protection for an original work of authorship extend to any idea, procedure, process, system, method of operation, concept, principle, or discovery, regardless of the form in which it is described, explained, illustrated, or embodied in such work."

Works of Artistic Craftsmanship and Designs: You may register "Works of artistic craftsmanship" on Form VA, but the statute makes clear that protection extends to "their form" and not to "their mechanical or utilitarian aspects." The "design of a useful article" is considered copyrightable "only if, and only to the extent that, such design incorporates pictorial, graphic, or sculptural features that can be identified separately from, and are capable of existing independently of, the utilitarian aspects of the article."

Labels and Advertisements: Works prepared for use in connection with the sale or advertisement of goods and services may be registered if they contain "original work of authorship." Use Form VA if the copyrightable material in the work you are registering is mainly pictorial or graphic; use Form TX if it consists mainly of text. **Note:** Words and short phrases such as names, titles, and slogans cannot be protected by copyright, and the same is true of standard symbols, emblems, and other commonly used graphic designs that are in the public domain. When used commercially, material of that sort can sometimes be protected under state laws of unfair competition or under the federal trademark laws. For information about trademark registration, call the U.S. Patent and Trademark Office, at 1-800-786-9199 (toll free) or go to *www.uspto.gov*.

Architectural Works: Copyright protection extends to the design of buildings created for the use of human beings. Architectural works created on or after December 1, 1990, or that on December 1, 1990, were unconstructed and embodied only in unpublished plans or drawings are eligible. Request Circular 41, *Copyright Claims in Architectural Works*, for more information. Architectural works and technical drawings cannot be registered on the same application.

Deposit to Accompany Application: An application for copyright registration must be accompanied by a deposit consisting of copies representing the entire work for which registration is to be made.

Unpublished Work: Deposit one complete copy.

Published Work: Deposit two complete copies of the best edition.

Work First Published Outside the United States: Deposit one complete copy of the first foreign edition.

Contribution to a Collective Work: Deposit one complete copy of the best edition of the collective work.

The Copyright Notice: Before March 1, 1989, the use of copyright notice was mandatory on all published works, and any work first published before that date should have carried a notice. For works first published on and after March 1, 1989, use of the copyright notice is optional. For more information about copyright notice, see Circular 3, *Copyright Notice*.

For Further Information: To speak to a Copyright Office staff member, call (202) 707-3000 or 1-877-477-0778. Recorded information is available 24 hours a day. Order forms and other publications from the address in space 9 or call the Forms and Publications Hotline at (202) 707-9100. Access and download circulars, forms, and other information from the Copyright Office website at *www.copyright.gov*.

Please type or print using black ink. The form is used to produce the certificate.

SPACE 1: Title

Title of This Work: Every work submitted for copyright registration must be given a title to identify that particular work. If the copies of the work bear a title (or an identifying phrase that could serve as a title), transcribe that wording *completely* and *exactly* on the application. Indexing of the registration and future identification of the work will depend on the information you give here. For an architectural work that has been constructed, add the date of construction after the title; if unconstructed at this time, add "not yet constructed."

Publication as a Contribution: If the work being registered is a contribution to a periodical, serial, or collection, give the title of the contribution in the "Title of This Work" space. Then, in the line headed "Publication as a Contribution," give information about the collective work in which the contribution appeared.

Nature of This Work: Briefly describe the general nature or character of the pictorial, graphic, or sculptural work being registered for copyright. Examples: "Oil Painting"; "Charcoal Drawing"; "Etching"; "Sculpture"; "Map"; "Photograph"; "Scale Model"; "Lithographic Print"; "Jewelry Design"; "Fabric Design."

Previous or Alternative Titles: Complete this space if there are any additional titles for the work under which someone searching for the registration might be likely to look, or under which a document pertaining to the work might be recorded.

SPACE 2: Author(s)

General Instruction: After reading these instructions, decide who are the "authors" of this work for copyright purposes. Then, unless the work is a "collective work," give the requested information about every "author" who contributed any appreciable amount of copyrightable matter to this version of the work. If you need further space, request Continuation Sheets (Form CON). In the case of a collective work, such as a catalog of paintings or collection of cartoons by various authors, give information about the author of the collective work as a whole.

Name of Author: The fullest form of the author's name should be given. Unless the work was "made for hire," the individual who actually created the work is its "author." In the case of a work made for hire, the statute provides that "the employer or other person for whom the work was prepared is considered the author."

What Is a "Work Made for Hire"? A "work made for hire" is defined as: (1) "a work prepared by an employee within the scope of his or her employment"; or (2) "a work specially ordered or commissioned for use as a contribution to a collective work, as a part of a motion picture or other audiovisual work, as a translation, as a supplementary work, as a compilation, as an instructional text, as a test, as answer material for a test, or as an atlas, if the parties expressly agree in a written instrument signed by them that the work shall be considered a work made for hire." If you have checked "Yes" to indicate that the work was "made for hire," you must give the full legal name of the employer (or other person for whom the work was prepared). You may also include the name of the employee along with the name of the employer (for example: "Elster Publishing Co., employer for hire of John Ferguson").

"Anonymous" or "Pseudonymous" Work: An author's contribution to a work is "anonymous" if that author is not identified on the copies or phonorecords of the work. An author's contribution to a work is "pseudonymous" if that author is identified on the copies or phonorecords under a fictitious name. If the work is "anonymous" you may: (1) leave the line blank; or (2) state "anonymous" on the line; or (3) reveal the author's identity. If the work is "pseudonymous" you may: (1) leave the line blank; or (2) give the pseudonym and identify it as such (for example: "Huntley Haverstock, pseudonym"); or (3) reveal the author's name, making clear which is the real name and which is the pseudonym (for example: "Henry Leek, whose pseudonym is Priam Farrel"). However, the citizenship or domicile of the author *must* be given in all cases.

Dates of Birth and Death: If the author is dead, the statute requires that the year of death be included in the application unless the work is anonymous or pseudonymous. The author's birth date is optional but is useful as a form of identification. Leave this space blank if the author's contribution was a "work made for hire."

Author's Nationality or Domicile: Give the country of which the author is a citizen or the country in which the author is domiciled. Nationality or domicile *must* be given in all cases.

Nature of Authorship: Categories of pictorial, graphic, and sculptural authorship are listed below. Check the box(es) that best describe(s) each author's contribution to the work.

3-Dimensional sculptures: Fine art sculptures, toys, dolls, scale models, and sculptural designs applied to useful articles.

2-Dimensional artwork: Watercolor and oil paintings; pen and ink drawings; logo illustrations; greeting cards; collages; stencils; patterns; computer graphics; graphics appearing in screen displays; artwork appearing on posters, calendars, games, commercial prints and labels, and packaging, as well as 2-dimensional artwork applied to useful articles, and designs reproduced on textiles, lace, and other fabrics; on wallpaper, carpeting, floor tile, wrapping paper, and clothing.

Reproductions of works of art: Reproductions of preexisting artwork made by, for example, lithography, photoengraving, or etching.

Maps: Cartographic representations of an area, such as state and county maps, atlases, marine charts, relief maps, and globes.

Photographs: Pictorial photographic prints and slides and holograms.

Jewelry designs: 3-dimensional designs applied to rings, pendants, earrings, necklaces, and the like.

Technical drawings: Diagrams illustrating scientific or technical information in linear form, such as architectural blueprints or mechanical drawings.

Text: Textual material that accompanies pictorial, graphic, or sculptural works, such as comic strips, greeting cards, games rules, commercial prints or labels, and maps.

Architectural works: Designs of buildings, including the overall form as well as the arrangement and composition of spaces and elements of the design.

NOTE: You must apply for registration for the underlying architectural plans on a separate Form VA. Check the box "Technical drawing."

3 SPACE 3: Creation and Publication

General Instructions: Do not confuse "creation" with "publication." Every application for copyright registration must state "the year in which creation of the work was completed." Give the date and nation of first publication only if the work has been published.

Creation: Under the statute, a work is "created" when it is fixed in a copy or phonorecord for the first time. If a work has been prepared over a period of time, the part of the work existing in fixed form on a particular date constitutes the created work on that date. The date you give here should be the year in which the author completed the particular version for which registration is now being sought, even if other versions exist or if further changes or additions are planned.

Publication: The statute defines "publication" as "the distribution of copies or phonorecords of a work to the public by sale or other transfer of ownership, or by rental, lease, or lending"; a work is also "published" if there has been an "offering to distribute copies or phonorecords to a group of persons for purposes of further distribution, public performance, or public display." Give the full date (month, day, year) when, and the country where, publication first occurred. If first publication took place simultaneously in the United States and other countries, it is sufficient to state "U.S.A."

4 SPACE 4: Claimant(s)

Name(s) and Address(es) of Copyright Claimant(s): Give the name(s) and address(es) of the copyright claimant(s) in this work even if the claimant is the same as the author. Copyright in a work belongs initially to the author of the work, including, in the case of a work make for hire, the employer or other person for whom the work was prepared. The copyright claimant is either the author of the work or a person or organization to whom the copyright initially belonging to the author has been transferred.

Transfer: The statute provides that, if the copyright claimant is not the author, the application for registration must contain "a brief statement of how the claimant obtained ownership of the copyright." If any copyright claimant named in space 4 is not an author named in space 2, give a brief statement explaining how the claimant(s) obtained ownership of the copyright. Examples: "By written contract"; "Transfer of all rights by author"; "Assignment"; "By will." Do not attach transfer documents or other attachments or riders.

5 SPACE 5: Previous Registration

General Instructions: The questions in space 5 are intended to find out whether an earlier registration has been made for this work and, if so, whether there is any basis for a new registration. As a rule, only one basic copyright registration can be made for the same version of a particular work.

Same Version: If this version is substantially the same as the work covered by a previous registration, a second registration is not generally possible unless: (1) the work has been registered in unpublished form and a second registration is now being sought to cover this first published edition; or (2) someone other than the author is identified as a copyright claimant in the earlier registration, and the author is now seeking registration in his or her own name. If either of these two exceptions applies, check the appropriate box and give the earlier registration number and date. Otherwise, do not submit Form VA. Instead, write the Copyright Office for information about supplementary registration or recordation of transfers of copyright ownership.

Changed Version: If the work has been changed and you are now seeking registration to cover the additions or revisions, check the last box in space 5, give the earlier registration number and date, and complete both parts of space 6 in accordance with the instruction below.

Previous Registration Number and Date: If more than one previous registration has been made for the work, give the number and date of the latest registration.

6 SPACE 6: Derivative Work or Compilation

General Instructions: Complete space 6 if this work is a "changed version," "compilation," or "derivative work," and if it incorporates one or more earlier works that have already been published or registered for copyright, or that have fallen into the public domain. A "compilation" is defined as "a work formed by the collection and assembling of preexisting materials or of data that are selected, coordinated, or arranged in such a way that the resulting work as a whole constitutes an original work of authorship." A "derivative work" is "a work based on one or more preexisting works." Examples of derivative works include reproductions of works of art, sculptures based on drawings, lithographs based on paintings, maps based on previously published sources, or "any other form in which a work may be recast, transformed, or adapted." Derivative works also include works "consisting of editorial revisions, annotations, or other modifications" if these changes, as a whole, represent an original work of authorship.

Preexisting Material (space 6a): Complete this space *and* space 6b for derivative works. In this space identify the preexisting work that has been recast, transformed, or adapted. Examples of preexisting material might be "Grunewald Altarpiece" or "19th century quilt design." Do not complete this space for compilations.

Material Added to This Work (space 6b): Give a brief, general statement of the *additional* new material covered by the copyright claim for which registration is sought. In the case of a derivative work, identify this new material. Examples: "Adaptation of design and additional artistic work"; "Reproduction of painting by photolithography"; "Additional cartographic material"; "Compilation of photographs." If the work is a compilation, give a brief, general statement describing both the material that has been compiled *and* the compilation itself. Example: "Compilation of 19th century political cartoons."

7, 8, 9 SPACE 7, 8, 9: Fee, Correspondence, Certification, Return Address

Deposit Account: If you maintain a Deposit Account in the Copyright Office, identify it in space 7a. Otherwise, leave the space blank and send the fee with your application and deposit.

Correspondence (space 7b): Give the name, address, area code, telephone number, email address, and fax number (if available) of the person to be consulted if correspondence about this application becomes necessary.

Certification (space 8): The application cannot be accepted unless it bears the date and the *handwritten signature* of the author or other copyright claimant, or of the owner of exclusive right(s), or of the duly authorized agent of the author, claimant, or owner of exclusive right(s).

Address for Return of Certificate (space 9): The address box must be completed legibly since the certificate will be returned in a window envelope.

Copyright Office fees are subject to change. For current fees, check the Copyright Office website at *www.copyright.gov,* write the Copyright Office, or call (202) 707-3000.

Privacy Act Notice: Sections 408-410 of title 17 of the *United States Code* authorize the Copyright Office to collect the personally identifying information requested on this form in order to process the application for copyright registration. By providing this information you are agreeing to routine uses of the information that include publication to give legal notice of your copyright claim as required by 17 U.S.C. §705. It will appear in the Office's online catalog. If you do not provide the information requested, registration may be refused or delayed, and you may not be entitled to certain relief, remedies, and benefits under the copyright law.

Ⓒ Form VA
For a Work of the Visual Arts
UNITED STATES COPYRIGHT OFFICE
REGISTRATION NUMBER

_____

VA   VAU
EFFECTIVE DATE OF REGISTRATION

_____

Month   Day   Year

DO NOT WRITE ABOVE THIS LINE. IF YOU NEED MORE SPACE, USE A SEPARATE CONTINUATION SHEET.

1

TITLE OF THIS WORK ▼

NATURE OF THIS WORK ▼ See instructions

PREVIOUS OR ALTERNATIVE TITLES ▼

PUBLICATION AS A CONTRIBUTION If this work was published as a contribution to a periodical, serial, or collection, give information about the collective work in which the contribution appeared. **Title of Collective Work ▼**

If published in a periodical or serial give: **Volume ▼**   **Number ▼**   **Issue Date ▼**   **On Pages ▼**

2

a

NAME OF AUTHOR ▼

DATES OF BIRTH AND DEATH
Year Born ▼   Year Died ▼

WAS THIS CONTRIBUTION TO THE WORK A "WORK MADE FOR HIRE"?
☐ Yes
☐ No

AUTHOR'S NATIONALITY OR DOMICILE
Name of Country
OR { Citizen of _____
Domiciled in _____

WAS THIS AUTHOR'S CONTRIBUTION TO THE WORK
Anonymous? ☐ Yes ☐ No
Pseudonymous? ☐ Yes ☐ No
If the answer to either of these questions is "Yes," see detailed instructions.

NATURE OF AUTHORSHIP Check appropriate box(es). **See instructions**
☐ 3-Dimensional sculpture   ☐ Map   ☐ Technical drawing
☐ 2-Dimensional artwork   ☐ Photograph   ☐ Text
☐ Reproduction of work of art   ☐ Jewelry design   ☐ Architectural work

NOTE
Under the law, the "author" of a "work made for hire" is generally the employer, not the employee (see instructions). For any part of this work that was "made for hire," check "Yes" in the space provided, give the employer (or other person for whom the work was prepared) as "Author" of that part, and leave the space for dates of birth and death blank.

b

NAME OF AUTHOR ▼

DATES OF BIRTH AND DEATH
Year Born ▼   Year Died ▼

WAS THIS CONTRIBUTION TO THE WORK A "WORK MADE FOR HIRE"?
☐ Yes
☐ No

AUTHOR'S NATIONALITY OR DOMICILE
Name of Country
OR { Citizen of _____
Domiciled in _____

WAS THIS AUTHOR'S CONTRIBUTION TO THE WORK
Anonymous? ☐ Yes ☐ No
Pseudonymous? ☐ Yes ☐ No
If the answer to either of these questions is "Yes," see detailed instructions.

NATURE OF AUTHORSHIP Check appropriate box(es). **See instructions**
☐ 3-Dimensional sculpture   ☐ Map   ☐ Technical drawing
☐ 2-Dimensional artwork   ☐ Photograph   ☐ Text
☐ Reproduction of work of art   ☐ Jewelry design   ☐ Architectural work

3

a **YEAR IN WHICH CREATION OF THIS WORK WAS COMPLETED**
Year ▶ _____
This information must be given in all cases.

b **DATE AND NATION OF FIRST PUBLICATION OF THIS PARTICULAR WORK**
Complete this information ONLY if this work has been published.
Month ▶ _____ Day ▶ _____ Year ▶ _____
Nation ▶ _____

4

See instructions before completing this space.

COPYRIGHT CLAIMANT(S) Name and address must be given even if the claimant is the same as the author given in space 2. ▼

TRANSFER If the claimant(s) named here in space 4 is (are) different from the author(s) named in space 2, give a brief statement of how the claimant(s) obtained ownership of the copyright. ▼

DO NOT WRITE HERE OFFICE USE ONLY

APPLICATION RECEIVED

ONE DEPOSIT RECEIVED

TWO DEPOSITS RECEIVED

FUNDS RECEIVED

MORE ON BACK ▶   • Complete all applicable spaces (numbers 5-9) on the reverse side of this page.
• See detailed instructions.   • Sign the form at line 8.

DO NOT WRITE HERE
Page 1 of _____ pages

EXAMINED BY	FORM VA
CHECKED BY	
CORRESPONDENCE ☐ Yes	FOR COPYRIGHT OFFICE USE ONLY

DO NOT WRITE ABOVE THIS LINE. IF YOU NEED MORE SPACE, USE A SEPARATE CONTINUATION SHEET.

PREVIOUS REGISTRATION Has registration for this work, or for an earlier version of this work, already been made in the Copyright Office?

☐ Yes ☐ No If your answer is "Yes," why is another registration being sought? (Check appropriate box.) ▼

a. ☐ This is the first published edition of a work previously registered in unpublished form.

b. ☐ This is the first application submitted by this author as copyright claimant.

c. ☐ This is a changed version of the work, as shown by space 6 on this application.

If your answer is "Yes," give: **Previous Registration Number** ▼   **Year of Registration** ▼

5

DERIVATIVE WORK OR COMPILATION Complete both space 6a and 6b for a derivative work; complete only 6b for a compilation.

a. Preexisting Material Identify any preexisting work or works that this work is based on or incorporates. ▼

b. Material Added to This Work Give a brief, general statement of the material that has been added to this work and in which copyright is claimed. ▼

6

a

b

See instructions before completing this space.

DEPOSIT ACCOUNT If the registration fee is to be charged to a Deposit Account established in the Copyright Office, give name and number of Account.

Name ▼   **Account Number** ▼

7

a

CORRESPONDENCE Give name and address to which correspondence about this application should be sent. Name/Address/Apt/City/State/Zip ▼

b

Area code and daytime telephone number   (   )   Fax number   (   )

Email

CERTIFICATION* I, the undersigned, hereby certify that I am the

check only one ▶ {

☐ author

☐ other copyright claimant

☐ owner of exclusive right(s)

☐ authorized agent of _____

Name of author or other copyright claimant, or owner of exclusive right(s) ▲

of the work identified in this application and that the statements made by me in this application are correct to the best of my knowledge.

8

Typed or printed name and date ▼ If this application gives a date of publication in space 3, do not sign and submit it before that date.

_____   Date _____

Handwritten signature (X) ▼

X _____

Certificate will be mailed in window envelope to this address:	Name ▼	**YOU MUST:** · Complete all necessary spaces · Sign your application in space 8
	Number/Street/Apt ▼	**SEND ALL 3 ELEMENTS IN THE SAME PACKAGE:** 1. Application form 2. Nonrefundable filing fee in check or money order payable to Register of Copyrights 3. Deposit material
	City/State/Zip ▼	**MAIL TO:** Library of Congress Copyright Office-VA 101 Independence Avenue SE Washington, DC 20559

9

*17 U.S.C. §506(e): Any person who knowingly makes a false representation of a material fact in the application for copyright registration provided for by section 409, or in any written statement filed in connection with the application, shall be fined not more than $2,500.

Form VA–Full   Rev: 05/2012   Print: 05/2012—8,000   Printed on recycled paper   U.S. Government Printing Office: 2012-372-482/80,911

Instructions for Short Form VA

For pictorial, graphic, and sculptural works

USE THIS FORM IF—

1. You are the *only* author and copyright owner of this work, *and*
2. The work was *not* made for hire, *and*
3. The work is completely new (does not contain a substantial amount of material that has been previously published or registered or is in the public domain).

If any of the above does not apply, you may register online at www.copyright.gov or use Form VA.

NOTE: *Short Form VA is not appropriate for an anonymous author who does not wish to reveal his or her identity.*

HOW TO COMPLETE SHORT FORM VA

- Type or print in black ink.
- Be clear and legible.
- Give only the information requested.

Note: You may use a continuation sheet (Form __/CON) to list individual titles in a collection. Complete space A and list the individual titles under space C on the back page. Space B is not applicable to short forms.

---

1 Title of This Work

You must give a title. If there is no title, state "UNTITLED." If you are registering an unpublished collection, give the collection title you want to appear in our records (for example: "Jewelry by Josephine, 1995 Volume"). Alternative title: If the work is known by two titles, you also may give the second title. If the work has been published as part of a larger work (including a periodical), give the title of that larger work instead of an alternative title, in addition to the title of the contribution.

2 Name and Address of Author and Owner of the Copyright

Give your name and mailing address. You may include your pseudonym followed by "pseud." Also, give the nation of which you are a citizen or where you have your domicile (i.e., permanent residence).

Give daytime phone and fax numbers and email address, if available.

3 Year of Creation

Give the latest year in which you completed the work you are registering at this time. A work is "created" when it is "fixed" in a tangible form. Examples: drawn on paper, molded in clay, stored in a computer.

4 Publication

If the work has been published (i.e., if copies have been distributed to the public), give the complete date of publication (month, day, and year) and the nation where the publication first took place.

5 Type of Authorship in This Work

Check the box or boxes that describe your authorship in the material you are sending. For example, if you are registering illustrations but have not written the story yet, check only the box for "2-dimensional artwork."

6 Signature of Author

Sign the application in black ink and check the appropriate box. The person signing the application should be the author or his/her authorized agent.

7 Person to Contact for Rights/Permissions

This space is optional. You may give the name and address of the person or organization to contact for permission to use the work. You may also provide phone, fax, or email information.

8 Certificate Will Be Mailed

This space must be completed. Your certificate of registration will be mailed in a window envelope to this address. Also, if the Copyright Office needs to contact you, we will write to this address.

9 Deposit Account

Complete this space only if you currently maintain a deposit account in the Copyright Office.

MAIL WITH THE FORM

- The filing fee in the form of a check or money order (*no cash*) payable to *Register of Copyrights*. (Copyright Office fees are subject to change. For current fees, check the Copyright Office website at *www.copyright.gov*, write the Copyright Office, or call (202) 707-3000 or 1-877-476-0778 (toll free)).

- One or two copies of the work or identifying material consisting of photographs or drawings showing the work. See table (right) for requirements for most works. **Note:** Read Circular 40a for the requirements for other works. Copies submitted become the property of the U.S. government.

Mail everything (application form, copy or copies, and fee) *in one package* to: Library of Congress
Copyright Office-VA
101 Independence Avenue SE
Washington, DC 20559

Questions? Call (202) 707-3000 or 1-877-476-0778 (toll free). Recorded information is available 24 hours a day. Order forms and other publications from *Library of Congress, Copyright Office-COPUBS, 101 Independence Avenue, SE, Washington, DC 20559*, or call (202) 707-9100. Download circulars and other information or register online at *www.copyright.gov.*

If you are registering:	And the work is *unpublished/published,* send:
• 2-dimensional artwork in a book, map, poster, or print	a. And the work is *unpublished,* send one complete copy or identifying material b. And the work is *published,* send two copies of the best published edition
• 3-dimensional sculpture • 2-dimensional artwork applied to a T-shirt	a. And the work is *unpublished,* send identifying material b. And the work is *published,* send identifying material
• a greeting card, pattern, commercial print or label, fabric, or wallpaper	a. And the work is *unpublished,* send one complete copy or identifying material b. And the work is *published,* send one copy of the best published edition

Copyright Office fees are subject to change. For current fees, check the Copyright Office website at *www.copyright.gov*, write the Copyright Office, or call (202) 707-3000 or 1-877-476-0778.

Privacy Act Notice: Sections 408-410 of title 17 of the *United States Code* authorize the Copyright Office to collect the personally identifying information requested on this form in order to process the application for copyright registration. By providing this information, you are agreeing to routine uses of the information that include publication to give legal notice of your copyright claim as required by 17 U.S.C. §705. It will appear in the Office's online catalog. If you do not provide the information requested, registration may be refused or delayed, and you may not be entitled to certain relief, remedies, and benefits under the copyright law.

ⓒ Short Form VA
For a Work of the Visual Arts
UNITED STATES COPYRIGHT OFFICE

REGISTRATION NUMBER

VA   VAU
Effective Date of Registration

Application Received

Examined By

Deposit Received
One   Two

Correspondence ☐   Fee Received

TYPE OR PRINT IN BLACK INK. DO NOT WRITE ABOVE THIS LINE.

1 Title of This Work:
Alternative title or title of larger work in which this work was published:

2 Name and Address of Author and Owner of the Copyright:
Nationality or domicile:
Phone, fax, and email:

Phone (   )   Fax (   )

Email

3 Year of Creation:

4 If work has been published, Date and Nation of Publication:

a. Date _____ _____ _____   *(Month, day, and year all required)*
Month   Day   Year

b. Nation

5 Type of Authorship in This Work:
Check all that this author created.

☐ 3-Dimensional sculpture   ☐ Photograph   ☐ Map
☐ 2-Dimensional artwork   ☐ Jewelry design   ☐ Text
☐ Technical drawing

6 Signature:
Registration cannot be completed without a signature.

*I certify that the statements made by me in this application are correct to the best of my knowledge.** Check one:
☐ Author   ☐ Authorized agent

X _____

7 Name and Address of Person to Contact for Rights and Permissions:
Phone, fax, and email:

OPTIONAL

☐ Check here if same as #2 above.

Phone (   )   Fax (   )

Email

8 Certificate will be mailed in window envelope to this address:

Name ▼

Number/Street/Apt ▼

City/State/Zip ▼

Complete this space only if you currently hold a Deposit Account in the Copyright Office.

9 Deposit account #_____

Name _____

DO NOT WRITE HERE   Page 1 of _____ pages

*17 U.S.C. §506(e): Any person who knowingly makes a false representation of a material fact in the application for copyright registration provided for by section 409, or in any written statement filed in connection with the application, shall be fined not more than $2,500.

Form VA-Short   Rev: 02/2012   Printed on recycled paper

U.S. Government Printing Office: 2012-xxx-xxx/xx,xxx

License of Rights
License of Electronic Rights

If there is one striking change in the world of design since *Business and Legal Forms for Graphic Designers* first appeared in 1990, it is the advent of electronic rights (electronic works being digitized versions that can be stored or retrieved from such media as computer disks, CD-ROM, computer data bases, and network servers). Designers, especially those whose works are likely to have the possibility of re-use, stand to profit by not giving up all rights when dealing with clients. This has been the reason that the battle over work-for-hire contracts has been fought with such ferocity in contractual negotiations, legislative proposals, and litigation. The desire of users for extensive rights must constantly clash with the desire of creators to give only limited rights. As work for hire offered the most potent path for users to gain all rights (including rights which such users had no intention or ability to exercise), so electronic rights have become the latest frontier where users seek to extend their domains at the expense of creators.

Unlike form 23, the Project Confirmation Agreement, which refers to works to be created in the future, forms 37 and 38 are for works which already exist. These forms seek to maximize the opportunities of the designer for residual income. To use these forms, of course, the designer must first limit the rights which he or she grants to the first users of work. Assuming the designer has retained all usage rights that the client did not actually need, that designer then becomes the potential beneficiary of income from further sales of the work to other users.

Forms 37 and 38 are almost identical. How - ever, for both didactic and practical reasons, the distinction between electronic and nonelectronic rights is important enough to justify two forms. Just as traditional rights have come to have generally accepted definitions and familiar divisions between creators and users as to control and sharing of income, so electronic rights may someday find similar clarification and customary allocation. A tremendous effort to clarify definitions for professionals who create images, including the definitions for licensing rights, has been made by the Plus Coalition, a nonprofit group. Their website, www.useplus.com, offers terminology to clarify the licensing of and rights in images.

An electronic work might first be a computer file, then be transmitted as email, then incorporated into a multi-media product (along with text and a sound track), then uploaded to a site on the Internet, and finally downloaded into the computer of someone cruising in cyberspace. Such digital potential for shape-shifting makes contractual restrictions both more challenging to engineer and absolutely essential to negotiate.

Forms 37 and 38 are designed for when a potential user approaches the designer directly to use work that has already been previously distributed. That previous distribution might have been in traditional media or, as is becoming ever more likely, in electronic media.

Because many of the concerns with both forms 37 and 38 are the same as for commissioned works, the negotiation checklist refers to the checklist for form 23. One key point addressed in both forms is the narrow specification of the nature of the usage as well as the retention of all other rights. When electronic rights are being granted, it is important if possible to try to limit the form of the final use (such as CD-ROM) and whether consumers can make copies (as is possible with material on the Internet).

Filling in the Forms

Fill in the date and the names and addresses for the client and the designer. In Paragraph 1 describe the work in detail and indicate the form in which it will be delivered. In Paragraph 2 give the delivery date. In Paragraph 3 specify the limitations as to which rights are granted, including the nature of the use (magazine, book, advertising, CD-ROM, etc.), the language, the name of the product or publication, the territory, and the time period of use. In an unusual case, the usage might be specified to be exclusive. Also, give an outside date for the usage to take place, after which the right will terminate. For an ongoing use, fill in a minimum amount which must be paid in order for the license not to terminate. For form 37 indicate whether consumers may copy the work, or whether the electronic rights granted are for display (viewing but not copying) use only. In Paragraph 5 give the fee or the amount of the advance against a royalty (in which case the calculation of the royalty must be included). If alteration of the work is permitted, give guidelines for this in Paragraph 7. In Paragraph 8 give a monthly interest charge for late payments. Show in Paragraph 10 whether copyright notice must appear in the author's name and in Paragraph 11 whether authorship credit will be given. In Paragraph 13 specify who will arbitrate disputes, where this will be done, and give the maximum amount which can be sued for in small claims court. In Paragraph 14 give the state whose laws will govern the contract. Both parties should then sign the contract.

Negotiation Checklist

❑ Review the negotiation checklist for form 23.

❑ To limit the grant of rights, carefully specify the type of use, language, name of the product or publication, territory, and time period for the use.

❑ Since rights are being licensed in pre-existing work, do not grant exclusive rights or limit the exclusivity to very narrow and precisely described uses. (Paragraph 3)

❑ If electronic rights are licensed, try to limit the form of final use (such as a particularly named CD-ROM or site on the Internet). (Paragraph 3)

❑ For electronic rights indicate whether consumers or end users may only see a display of the work or will actually have a right to download a copy of the work. (Paragraph 3)

❑ Limit the time period for the use and specify a date by which all usage must be completed and all rights automatically revert to the author. (Paragraph 3)

❑ Specify that all rights will revert if the income stream falls below a certain level. (Paragraph 3)

❑ For form 37, reserve all electronic rights to the designer.

❑ For form 38, reserve all traditional (nonelectronic rights) to the designer.

❑ If royalties are agreed to for Paragraph 5, review the negotiation checklist for form 29 with respect to the computation of royalties.

❑ For electronic rights especially, negotiate the right of the client to enlarge, reduce, or combine the work with other works (whether literary, artistic, or musical). (Paragraph 7)

❑ For Form 38, require the client to use the best available technology to prevent infringements. (Paragraph 10)

❑ Review the standard provisions in the introductory pages and compare to Paragraph 14.

License of Rights

Agreement as of the _____ day of _____, 20 _____, between _____, located at _____ (hereinafter referred to as the "Client") and _____, located at _____ (hereinafter referred to as the "Designer") with respect to the licensing of certain rights in the Designer's writing (hereinafter referred to as the "Work").

1. **Description of Work.** The Client wishes to license certain rights in the Work which the Designer has created and which is described as follows:

   Title_____

   Subject matter_____

   _____.

   Other materials to be provided_____

   _____.

   Form in which work shall be delivered ❏ computer file (specify format _____)

   ❏ other, specified as _____

2. **Delivery Date.** The Designer agrees to deliver the Work within _____ days after the signing of this Agreement.

3. **Grant of Rights.** Upon receipt of full payment, Designer grants to the Client the following rights in the Work:

   For use as_____in the_____language

   For the product or publication named_____

   In the following territory_____

   For the following time period_____

   With respect to the usage shown above, the Client shall have nonexclusive rights unless specified to the contrary

   here_____

   _

   Other limitations _____

   If the Work is for use as a contribution to a magazine, the grant of rights shall be for one time North American serial rights only unless specified to the contrary above.

   If the Client does not complete its usage under this Paragraph 3 by the following date_____ or if payments to be made hereunder fall to less than $____ every ____ months, all rights granted shall without further notice revert to the Designer without prejudice to the Designer's right to retain sums previously paid and collect additional sums due.

4. **Reservation of Rights.** All rights not expressly granted hereunder are reserved to the Designer, including but not limited to all rights in preliminary materials and all electronic rights. For purposes of this agreement, electronic rights are defined as rights in the digitized form of works that can be encoded, stored, and retrieved from such media as computer disks, CD-ROM, computer databases, and network servers.

5. **Fee.** Client agrees to pay the following for the usage rights granted: ❏ $_____
   ❏ an advance of $_____ to be recouped against royalties to be computed as follows_____

   _____

6. Additional Usage. If Client wishes to make any additional uses of the Work, Client agrees to seek permission from the Designer and make such payments as are agreed to between the parties at that time.

7. Alteration. Client shall not make or permit any alterations, whether by adding or removing material from the Work, without the permission of the Designer. Alterations shall be deemed to include the addition of any illustrations, photographs, sound, text, or computerized effects, unless specified to the contrary here_____

8. Payment. Client agrees to pay the Designer within thirty days of the date of Designer's billing, which shall be dated as of the date of delivery of the Work. Overdue payments shall be subject to interest charges of _____ percent monthly.

9. Statements of Account. The payments due pursuant to Paragraph 8 shall be made by Client to Designer whose receipt of same shall be a full and valid discharge of the Clients' obligations hereunder only if accompanied by the following information: **(a)** amount remitted; **(b)** check or wire transfer number and date, as well as the bank and account number to which funds were deposited by wire transfer; **(c)** Client's name as payor;**(b)** title of the work for which payment is being made; **(e)** designer's name; **(f)** the identifying number, if any, for the work, or the ISBN, if any; **(g)** the period which the payment covers; **(h)** the reason for the payment, the payment's currency, and the details of any withholdings from the payment (such as for taxes, commissions, or bank charges).

10. Copyright Notice. Copyright notice in the name of the Designer ❑ shall ❑ shall not accompany the Work when it is reproduced.

11. Authorship Credit. Authorship credit in the name of the Designer ❑ shall ❑ shall not accompany the Work when it is reproduced. If the work is used as a contribution to a magazine or for a book, authorship credit shall be given unless specified to the contrary in the preceding sentence.

12. Releases. The Client agrees to indemnify and hold harmless the Designer against any and all claims, costs, and expenses, including attorney's fees, due to uses for which no release was requested, uses which exceed the uses allowed pursuant to a release, or uses based on alterations not allowed pursuant to Paragraph 7.

13. Arbitration. All disputes arising under this Agreement shall be submitted to binding arbitration before _____ in the following location _____ and settled in accordance with the rules of the American Arbitration Association. Judgment upon the arbitration award may be entered in any court having jurisdiction thereof. Disputes in which the amount at issue is less than $_____ shall not be subject to this arbitration provision.

14. Miscellany. This Agreement shall be binding upon the parties hereto, their heirs, successors, assigns, and personal representatives. This Agreement constitutes the entire understanding between the parties. Its terms can be modified only by an instrument in writing signed by both parties, except that the Client may authorize expenses or revisions orally. A waiver of a breach of any of the provisions of this Agreement shall not be construed as a continuing waiver of other breaches of the same or other provisions hereof. This Agreement shall be governed by the laws of the State of _____.

In Witness Whereof, the parties hereto have signed this Agreement as of the date first set forth above.

Designer_____

Client_____
Company Name

By:_____
Authorized Signatory, Title

License of Electronic Rights

Agreement as of the _____ day of _____, 20 _____, between _____,
located at _____ (hereinafter referred to as the "Client")
and _____, located at _____
(hereinafter referred to as the "Designer") with respect to the licensing of certain electronic rights in the Designer's writing (hereinafter referred to as the "Work").

1. **Description of Work.** The Client wishes to license certain electronic rights in the Work which the Designer has created and which is described as follows:

   Title_____

   Subject matter_____

   _____.

   Other materials to be provided_____

   _____.

   Form in which work shall be delivered   ❏ computer file (specify format _____)

   ❏ other, specified as _____

2. **Delivery Date.** The Designer agrees to deliver the Work within _____ days after the signing of this Agreement.

3. **Grant of Rights.** Upon receipt of full payment, Designer grants to the Client the following electronic rights in the Work:

   For use as_____in the_____language

   For the product or publication named_____

   In the following territory_____

   For the following time period_____

   For display purposes only without permission for digital copying by users of the product or publication unless specified to the contrary here_____

   With respect to the usage shown above, the Client shall have nonexclusive rights unless specified to the contrary here_____

   _

   Other limitations _____

   If the Client does not complete its usage under this Paragraph 3 by the following date_____,
   all rights granted but not exercised shall without further notice revert to the Designer without prejudice to the Designer's right to retain sums previously paid and collect additional sums due.

4. **Reservation of Rights.** All rights not expressly granted hereunder are reserved to the Designer, including but not limited to all rights in preliminary materials and all nonelectronic rights. For purposes of this agreement, electronic rights are defined as rights in the digitized form of works that can be encoded, stored, and retrieved from such media as computer disks, CD-ROM, computer databases, and network servers.

5. **Fee.** Client agrees to pay the following: ❏ $_____ for the usage rights granted.
   ❏ an advance of $_____ to be recouped against royalties to be computed as follows_____

6. Additional Usage. If Client wishes to make any additional uses of the Work, Client agrees to seek permission from the Designer and make such payments as are agreed to between the parties at that time.

7. Alteration. Client shall not make or permit any alterations, whether by adding or removing material from the Work, without the permission of the Designer. Alterations shall be deemed to include the addition of any illustrations, photographs, sound, text, or computerized effects, unless specified to the contrary here_____.

8. Payment. Client agrees to pay the Designer within thirty days of the date of Designer's billing, which shall be dated as of the date of delivery of the Work. Overdue payments shall be subject to interest charges of _____ percent monthly.

9. Statements of Account. The payments due pursuant to Paragraph 8 shall be made by Client to Designer whose receipt of same shall be a full and valid discharge of the Clients' obligations hereunder only if accompanied by the following information: **(a)** amount remitted; **(b)** check or wire transfer number and date, as well as the bank and account number to which funds were deposited by wire transfer; **(c)** Client's name as payor; **(d)** title of the work for which payment is being made; **(e)** designer's name; **(f)** the identifying number, if any, for the work, or the ISBN, if any; **(g)** the period which the payment covers; **(h)** the reason for the payment, the payment's currency, and the details of any withholdings from the payment (such as for taxes, commissions, or bank charges).

10. Copyright Notice. Copyright notice in the name of the Designer ❑ shall ❑ shall not accompany the Work when it is reproduced.

11. Authorship Credit. Authorship credit in the name of the Designer ❑ shall ❑ shall not accompany the Work when it is reproduced. If the work is used as a contribution to a magazine or for a book, authorship credit shall be given unless specified to the contrary in the preceding sentence.

12. Releases. The Client agrees to indemnify and hold harmless the Designer against any and all claims, costs, and expenses, including attorney's fees, due to uses for which no release was requested, uses which exceed the uses allowed pursuant to a release, or uses based on alterations not allowed pursuant to Paragraph 7.

13. Arbitration. All disputes arising under this Agreement shall be submitted to binding arbitration before _____ in the following location _____ and settled in accordance with the rules of the American Arbitration Association. Judgment upon the arbitration award may be entered in any court having jurisdiction thereof. Disputes in which the amount at issue is less than $_____ shall not be subject to this arbitration provision.

14. Miscellany. This Agreement shall be binding upon the parties hereto, their heirs, successors, assigns, and personal representatives. This Agreement constitutes the entire understanding between the parties. Its terms can be modified only by an instrument in writing signed by both parties, except that the Client may authorize expenses or revisions orally. A waiver of a breach of any of the provisions of this Agreement shall not be construed as a continuing waiver of other breaches of the same or other provisions hereof. This Agreement shall be governed by the laws of the State of _____.

In Witness Whereof, the parties hereto have signed this Agreement as of the date first set forth above.

Designer_____   Client_____

Company Name

By:_____

Authorized Signatory, Title

Trademark Application

A trademark is a distinctive word, phrase, symbol, design, emblem, or combination of these that a manufacturer places on a product to identify and distinguish in the public mind that product from the products of rival manufacturers. A service mark is like a trademark except that it identifies services instead of products. Trademarks (including service marks) can be registered with the U.S. Patent and Trademark Office for federal protection and with the appropriate state office for state protection, although even an unregistered mark can have protection under the common law simply because the mark is used in commerce. A graphic designer who is developing a line of products—for example, furniture, fabric designs, or art—might wish to seek trademark protection for a distinctive logo or motto.

The USPTO has an excellent website (www.uspto.gov) that offers extensive information, including very helpful trademark FAQs (the paper publication "Basic Facts about Trademarks" can also be requested from the USPTO). The trademark (and service mark) application can be filled out on the website and filed electronically using TEAS. The USPTO strongly prefers that the form be filed through their website. However, form 39 is the paper trademark (and service mark) application still provided on request by the USPTO and is included here in part for educational purposes (especially since TEAS is an online process). Anyone wishing to use paper forms can call the Trademark Assistance Center at (800) 786-9199.

The application will require the following: (1) a filled-in application form; (2) a drawing of the trademark, which can be in GIF or JPEG format if the filing is done electronically; (3) the filing fee (currently $275–$375 per class, with the highest rate corresponding to applications using paper forms); and (4) if the mark is in use, one specimen of the mark for each class of goods or services indicated in the application (a specimen for a mark used on goods would show the mark on the actual goods or packaging; a specimen for a mark for services would show the mark used in the sale or advertising of the services).

The designer who believes that a certain product should be trademarked will want to be certain that any chosen trademark does not infringe an already registered trademark in commercial use. This can be accomplished by conducting a trademark search prior to filling out the trademark registration application. If other names in use are too closely similar to that selected by the designer, the decision may be made to select a different name. To conduct a search, the designer can go to the USPTO website and use TESS, the Trademark Electronic Search System. While the trademark can be filed without such a search and without the help of an attorney or search service, the search and evaluation of the search may require such expert assistance.

In fact, the design firm would place itself at substantial legal risk if it were to make a mistake in a trademark search (for example, by telling a client that a mark is available when it really is not). The safest course for the design firm is to insist that an attorney with a specialty in the trademark area be retained, preferably by the client.

An important revision of the trademark law took effect on November 16, 1989. Trademarks may now be registered before use, whereas previously they could only be registered after use. The application must include a bona fide "intent to use" statement. Every six months an "intent to use" statement must be filed again and additional fees paid, and in no event can such a preregistration period exceed three years.

Trademarks can last forever if the artist keeps using the mark to identify goods or services. The federal trademark has a term of ten years, but can then be renewed for additional ten-year terms. The designer should note that to avoid having the trademark registration canceled, an affidavit must be filed between the fifth and sixth year after the initial registration. Trademarks can be licensed (see form 29), as long as the designer giving the license ensures that the quality of goods created by the licensee will be of the same quality that the public associates with the trademark. Trademarks are entitled to protection in foreign countries under treaties executed by the United States.

It is important to understand when the symbols TM, SM, and ® can and should be used. TM (for trademark) and SM (for service mark) can be used at any time, without or prior to the issuance of registration, to inform the public of the designer's claim to trademark protection for a mark. The symbol ® (for registration) should only be used only when the mark has in fact been registered with the U.S. Patent and Trademark Office. Failure to use the ® symbol properly for a federally registered mark may diminish the right of the mark's owner to collect damages in the event the trademark is infringed.

While it is not mandatory to fill in the class of goods or services when making the trademark application, some classes that would be especially relevant to designs in commerce are:

Class 14. Precious metals and their alloys and goods in precious metals or coated therewith, not included in other classes; jewelry, precious stones; horological and chronometric instruments . . .

Class 16. Paper, cardboard and goods made from these materials, not included in other classes; printed matter; bookbinding material; photographs; stationery; adhesives for stationery or household purposes; . . .

Class 20. Furniture, mirrors, picture frames; goods (not included in other classes) of wood, cork, reed, cane, wicker, horn, bone, ivory, whalebone, shell, amber, mother-of-pearl, meerschaum and substitutes for all these materials, or of plastics.

Class 21. Household or kitchen utensils and containers (not of precious metal or coated therewith); . . . glassware, porcelain and earthenware not included in other classes.

Class 24. Textiles and textile goods, not included in other classes; bed and table covers.

Class 25. Clothing, footwear, headgear.

Class 26. Lace and embroidery, ribbons and braid; buttons, hooks and eyes, pins and needles; artificial flowers.

Class 27. Carpets, rugs, mats and matting; linoleums and other materials for covering existing floors; wall hangings (nontextile).

Class 28. Games and playthings; gymnastic and sporting articles not included in other classes; decorations for Christmas trees.

Closely related to trademarks is the area of trade dress, which has special relevance for designers and other artists who create the look of products for sale to consumers. Trade dress claims arise under section 43(a) of the Lanham Act, a federal statute. A plaintiff must prove three elements to win a trade dress claim: (1) That the features of the trade dress are primarily nonfunctional (i.e., that these features primarily identify the source of the particular goods or services); (2) that the trade dress has secondary meaning (i.e., that the public has come to identify the source of goods or services due to the associations created by the trade dress); and (3) that the competing products' respective trade dresses are confusingly similar, thus giving rise to a likelihood of confusion among consumers as to their sources.

~TRADEMARK/SERVICE MARK APPLICATION (15 U.S.C. §§ 1051, 1126(d)&(e))~

BASIC INSTRUCTIONS

The following form is written in a "scannable" format that will enable the U.S. Patent and Trademark Office (USPTO) to scan paper filings and capture application data automatically using optical character recognition (OCR) technology. Information is to be entered next to identifying data tags, such as <DATE OF FIRST USE IN COMMERCE>. OCR software can be programmed to identify these tags, capture the corresponding data, and transmit this data to the appropriate data fields in the Trademark databases, largely bypassing manual data entry processes.

Please enter the requested information in the blank space that appears to the right of each tagged (< >) element. However, do not enter any information immediately after the section headers (the bolded wording appearing in all capital letters). If you need additional space, first, in the space provided on the form, enter "See attached." Then, please use a separate piece of paper on which you first list the data tag (e.g., <LISTING OF GOODS AND/OR SERVICES>), followed by the relevant information. Some of the information requested *must* be provided. Other information is either required only in certain circumstances, or provided only at your discretion. **Please consult the "Help" section following the form for detailed explanations as to what information should be entered in each blank space.**

To increase the effectiveness of the USPTO scanners, it is recommended that you use a typewriter to complete the form.

For additional information, please see the *Basic Facts about Trademarks* booklet, available at *http://www.uspto.gov/web/offices/tac/doc/basic/*, or by calling the Trademark Assistance Center, at 1-800-786-9199. You may also wish to file electronically, from *http://www.uspto.gov/teas/index.html*.

MAILING INFORMATION

Send the completed form, appropriate fee(s) (made payable to the "Commissioner of Patents and Trademarks"), and any other required materials to:

> Commissioner for Trademarks
> P.O. Box 1451
> Alexandria, VA 22313-1451

The filing fee for this application is $375.00 *per class* of goods and/or services. You must include at least $375.00 with this application; otherwise the papers and money will be returned to you. Once your application meets the minimum filing date requirements, this processing fee becomes **non-refundable**. This is true even if the USPTO does not issue a registration certificate for this mark.

You may also wish to include a self-addressed stamped postcard with your submission, on which you identify the mark and list each item being submitted (e.g., application, fee, specimen, etc.). We will return this postcard to you, stamped with your assigned serial number, to confirm receipt of your submission.

~TRADEMARK/SERVICE MARK APPLICATION (15 U.S.C. §§ 1051, 1126(d)&(e))~

~To the Commissioner for Trademarks~

<APPLICANT INFORMATION>

<Name>

<Street>

<City>

<State>

<Country>

<Zip/Postal Code>

<Telephone Number>

<Fax Number>

<e-Mail Address>

<APPLICANT ENTITY INFORMATION>~Select only ONE~

<Individual: Country of Citizenship>
<Corporation: State/Country of Incorporation>
<Partnership: State/Country under which Organized>
   <Name(s) of General Partner(s) & Citizenship/Incorporation>

<Other Entity Type: Specific Nature of Entity>
   <State/Country under which Organized>

<TRADEMARK/SERVICE MARK INFORMATION>

<Mark>

The mark may be registered in standard character format or in special form. Applicant must specify whether registration is sought for the mark in standard character format or in a special form by entering "YES" in the appropriate space below.

<Standard Character Format> The mark is presented in standard character format without claim to any particular font style, size or color.
Enter YES, if appropriate _____

<Special Form Drawing> *Enter YES, if appropriate* _____

ATTACH a separate piece of paper that displays the mark you want to register (a "drawing" page), even if the mark is simply a word or words. Display only the exact mark you want to register on the additional piece of paper. Do not display advertising material or other matter that is not part of the mark. Please see additional HELP instructions.

PTO Form 1478 (REV 01/05)
OMB Control No. 0651-0009 (Exp. 8/31/2001)

U.S. DEPARTMENT OF COMMERCE/Patent and Trademark Office
There is no requirement to respond to this collection of information
unless a currently valid OMB number is displayed.

\<BASIS FOR FILING AND GOODS/SERVICES INFORMATION\>

\<**Use in Commerce: Section 1(a)**\>~*Applicant is using or is using through a related company the mark in commerce on or in connection with the below-identified goods and/or services (15 U.S.C. § 1051(a)).~*

\<International Class Number(s)\>

\<Listing of Goods and/or Services\>~*List in ascending numerical class order. Please see sample in HELP instructions.~*

\<Date of First Use Anywhere\>

\<Date of First Use in Commerce\>
~*Submit one (1) SPECIMEN for each international class showing the mark as used in commerce.~*

\<**Intent to Use: Section 1(b)**\>~*Applicant has a bona fide intention to use or use through a related company the mark in commerce on or in connection with the below-identified goods and/or services (15 U.S.C. § 1051(b)).~*

\<International Class Number(s)\>

\<Listing of Goods and/or Services\>~*List in ascending numerical class order. Please see sample in HELP instructions.~*

\<**Foreign Priority: Section 44(d)**\>~*Applicant has a bona fide intention to use the mark in commerce on or in connection with the below-identified goods/services, and asserts a claim of priority based upon a foreign application in accordance with 15 U.S.C. § 1126(d).~*

\<International Class Number(s)\>

\<Listing of Goods and/or Services\>~*List in ascending numerical class order. Please see sample in HELP instructions.~*

\<Country of Foreign Filing\>

\<Foreign Application Number\>

\<Date of Foreign Filing\>

\<**Foreign Registration: Section 44(e)**\>~*Applicant has a bona fide intention to use the mark in commerce on or in connection with the below-identified goods/services based on registration of the mark in applicant's country of origin.~*

\<International Class Number(s)\>

\<Listing of Goods and/or Services\>~*List in ascending numerical class order. Please see sample in HELP instructions.~*

\<Country of Foreign Registration\>

\<Foreign Registration Number\>

\<Foreign Registration Date\>

\<Foreign Registration Renewal Date\>

\<Foreign Registration Expiration Date\>
~*Submit foreign registration certificate or a certified copy of the foreign registration, in accordance with 15 U.S.C. § 1126(e).~*

\<FEE INFORMATION\>

\$375.00 x \<Number of Classes\>	= \<Total Filing Fee Paid\>

\<SIGNATURE INFORMATION\>

~ Applicant requests registration of the above-identified mark in the United States Patent and Trademark Office on the Principal Register established by Act of July 5, 1946 (15 U.S.C. § 1051 et seq.) for the above-identified goods and/or services.

The undersigned, being hereby warned that willful false statements and the like so made are punishable by fine or imprisonment, or both, under 18 U.S.C. § 1001, and that such willful false statements may jeopardize the validity of the application or any resulting registration, declares that he/she is properly authorized to execute this application on behalf of the applicant; he/she believes the applicant to be the owner of the trademark/service mark sought to be registered, or, if the application is being filed under 15 U.S.C. § 1051(b), he/she believes applicant to be entitled to use such mark in commerce; to the best of his/her knowledge and belief no other person, firm, corporation, or association has the right to use the mark in commerce, either in the identical form thereof or in such near resemblance thereto as to be likely, when used on or in connection with the goods and/or services of such other person, to cause confusion, or to cause mistake, or to deceive; and that all statements made of his/her own knowledge are true; and that all statements made on information and belief are believed to be true.~

~Signature~ _____

\<Date\>

\<Name\>

\<Title\>

\<CONTACT INFORMATION\>

\<Name\>

\<Company/Firm Name\>

\<Street\>

\<City\>

\<State\>

\<Country\>

\<Zip/Postal Code\>

\<Telephone Number\>

\<Fax Number\>

\<e-Mail Address\>

LINE-BY-LINE HELP INSTRUCTIONS

APPLICANT INFORMATION

Name: Enter the full name of the applicant, i.e., the name of the individual, corporation, partnership, or other entity that is seeking registration. If a joint venture organized under a particular business name, enter that name. If joint or multiple applicants, enter the name of each. If a trust, enter the name of the trustee(s). If an estate, enter the name of the executor(s).

Street: Enter the street address or rural delivery route where the applicant is located.

City: Enter the city and/or foreign area designation where the applicant's address is located.

State: Enter the U.S. state or foreign province in which the applicant's address is located.

Country: Enter the country of the applicant's address. If the address is outside the United States, the applicant may appoint a "Domestic Representative" on whom notices or process in proceedings affecting the mark may be served.

Zip/Postal Code: Enter the applicant's U.S. zip code or foreign country postal identification code.

Telephone Number: Enter the applicant's telephone number.

Fax Number: Enter the applicant's fax number.

e-Mail Address: Enter the applicant's e-mail address.

APPLICANT ENTITY INFORMATION

Indicate the applicant's entity type by entering the appropriate information in the space to the right of the correct entity type. Please note that only one entity type may be selected.

Individual: Enter the applicant's country of citizenship.

Corporation: Enter the applicant's state of incorporation (or the applicant's country of incorporation if the applicant is a foreign corporation).

Partnership: Enter the state under whose laws the partnership is organized (or the country under whose laws the partnership is organized if the partnership is a foreign partnership).

Name(s) of General Partner(s) & Citizenship/incorporation: Enter the names and citizenship of any general partners who are individuals, and/or the names and state or (foreign) country of incorporation of any general partners that are corporations, and/or the names and states or (foreign) countries of organization of any general partners that are themselves partnerships. If the applicant is a limited partnership, then only the names and citizenship or state or country of organization or incorporation of the general partners need be provided.

Other Entity Type: Enter a brief description of the applicant's entity type (e.g., joint or multiple applicants, joint venture, limited liability company, association, Indian Nation, state or local agency, trust, estate). The following sets forth the information required with respect to the most common types of "other" entities:

For *joint or multiple applicants,* enter the name and entity type of each joint applicant. Also, enter the citizenship of those joint applicants who are individuals, and/or the state or (foreign) country of incorporation of those joint applicants that are corporations, and/or the state or (foreign) country of organization (and the names and citizenship of the partners) of those joint applicants that are partnerships. The information regarding each applicant should be preceded by a separate heading tag (<APPLICANT INFORMATION>).

For *sole proprietorship,* enter the name and citizenship of the sole proprietor, and indicate the state where the sole proprietorship is organized.

For *joint venture,* enter the name and entity type of each entity participating in the joint venture. Also, enter the citizenship of those joint venture participants who are individuals, and/or the state or (foreign) country of incorporation of those joint venture participants that are corporations, and/or the state or (foreign) country of organization (and the names and citizenship of the partners) of those joint venture participants that are partnerships. The information regarding each entity should be preceded by a separate heading tag (<APPLICANT INFORMATION>).

For *limited liability company or association*, enter the state or (foreign) country under whose laws the entity is established.

For *state or local agency*, enter the name of the agency and the state and/or locale of the agency (e.g., Maryland State Lottery Agency, an agency of the State of Maryland).

For *trusts*, identify the trustees and the trust itself, using the following format: The Trustees of the XYZ Trust, a California trust, the trustees comprising John Doe, a U.S. citizen, and the ABC Corp., a Delaware corporation. (Please note that the trustees, and not the trust itself, must be identified as the applicant in the portion of the application designated for naming the applicant).

For *estates*, identify the executors and the estate itself using the following format: The Executors of the John Smith estate, a New York estate, the executors comprising Mary Smith and John Smith, U.S. citizens. (Please note that the executors, and not the estate itself, must be identified as the applicant in the portion of the application designated for naming the applicant).

State/Country under Which Organized: Enter the state or country under whose laws the entity is organized.

TRADEMARK/SERVICE MARK INFORMATION

Standard Character Format: Use this mark format to register word(s), letter(s), number(s), or any combination thereof, without claim to any particular font style, size, or color, and absent any design element. The application must also include the following statement:

> "The mark is presented in standard character format without claim to any particular font style, size or color.

Registration of a mark in the standard character format will provide broad rights, namely use in any manner of presentation. A mark is eligible for a claim of the standard character format if, (1) The mark does not include a design element; (2) All letters and words in the mark are depicted in Latin characters; (3) All numerals in the mark are depicted in Roman or Arabic numerals; and (4) The mark includes only common punctuation or diacritical marks.

Stylized or Design Format: Use this mark format if (1) you wish to register a mark with a design element or word(s) or letters(s) having a particular stylized appearance that you wish to protect; otherwise, choose the Standard Character Format, above.

Requirements for DISPLAY of mark on a separate piece of paper:
(a) Use non-shiny white paper that is separate from the application;

(b) Use paper that is 8 to 8.5 inches wide and 11 to 11.69 inches long. One of the shorter sides of the sheet should be regarded as its top edge. The image must be no larger than 3.15 inches high by 3.15 inches wide;

(c) Include the caption "DRAWING PAGE" at the top of the drawing beginning one inch from the top edge; and

(d) Depict the mark in black ink, or in color if color is claimed as a feature of the mark.

(e) Drawings must be typed or made with a pen or by a process that will provide high definition when copied. A photolithographic, printer's proof copy, or other high quality reproduction of the mark may be used. All lines must be clean, sharp and solid, and must not be fine or crowded.

BASIS FOR FILING AND GOODS/SERVICES INFORMATION

Use in Commerce: Section 1(a): Use this section only if you have actually used the mark in commerce on or in connection with *all* of the goods and/or services listed.

International Class Number(s): Enter the international class number(s) of the goods and/or services associated with the mark; e.g., 14; 24; 25. If unknown, leave blank and the USPTO will assign the number(s).

Listing of Goods and/or Services: Enter the *specific* goods and/or services associated with the mark. Do NOT enter the broad class number here, such as 9 or 42 (this information belongs in the field above, namely International Class Number(s)). If the goods and/or services are classified in more than one class, the goods and/or services should be listed in ascending numerical class order, with both the class number and the specific goods and/or services. For example, 14: jewelry

24: towels

25: pants, shirts, jackets, shoes

For more information about acceptable wording for the goods/services, see USPTO's on-line *Acceptable Identification of Goods and Services Manual,* at *http://www.uspto.gov/web/offices/tac/doc/gsmanual/*.

Date of First Use Anywhere: Enter the date on which the goods were first sold or transported or the services first rendered under the mark if such use was in the ordinary course of trade. For every applicant (foreign or domestic), the date of first use is the date of the first such use *anywhere,* in the United States or elsewhere. Please note this date may be earlier than, or the same as, the date of the first use of the mark in commerce.

Date of First Use in Commerce: Enter the date on which the applicant first used the mark in commerce, i.e., in interstate commerce, territorial commerce, or commerce between the United States and a foreign country.

Specimen: You must submit one (1) specimen showing the mark as used in commerce on or in connection with any item listed in the description of goods and/or services; e.g., tags or labels for goods, and/or advertisements for services. If the goods and/or services are classified in more than one international class, a specimen must be provided showing the mark used on or in connection with at least one item from each of these classes. The specimen must be flat and no larger than 8 ½ inches (21.6 cm.) wide by 11.69 inches (29.7 cm.) long.

Intent to Use: Section 1(b): Use this section if the applicant only has a bona fide intention to use the mark in commerce in the future as to all or some of the goods and/or services, rather than having actually already made use of the mark in commerce as to *all* of the goods and/or services.

International Class Number(s): Enter the international class number(s) of the goods and/or services associated with the mark; e.g., 14; 24; 25. If unknown, leave blank and the USPTO will assign the number(s).

Listing of Goods and/or Services: Enter the *specific* goods and/or services associated with the mark. Do NOT enter the broad class number here, such as 9 or 42 (this information belongs in the field above, namely International Class Number(s)). If the goods and/or services are classified in more than one class, the goods and/or services should be listed in ascending numerical class order, with both the class number and the specific goods and/or services. For example, 14: jewelry

24: towels

25: pants, shirts, jackets, shoes

For more information about acceptable wording for the goods/services, see USPTO's on-line *Acceptable Identification of Goods and Services Manual,* at *http://www.uspto.gov/web/offices/tac/doc/gsmanual/*.

Foreign Priority: Section 44(d): Use this section if you are filing the application within six (6) months of filing the first foreign application to register the mark in a defined treaty country.

International Class Number(s): Enter the international class number(s) of the goods and/or services associated with the mark; e.g., 14; 24; 25. If unknown, leave blank and the USPTO will assign the number(s).

Listing of Goods and/or Services: Enter the *specific* goods and/or services associated with the mark. Do NOT enter the broad class number here, such as 9 or 42 (this information belongs in the field above, namely International Class Number(s)). If the goods and/or services are classified in more than one class, the goods and/or services should be listed in ascending numerical class order, with both the class number and the specific goods and/or services. For example, 14: jewelry

24: towels

25: pants, shirts, jackets, shoes

For more information about acceptable wording for the goods/services, see USPTO's on-line *Acceptable Identification of Goods and Services Manual,* at *http://www.uspto.gov/web/offices/tac/doc/gsmanual/*.

Country of Foreign Filing: Enter the country where the foreign application upon which the applicant is asserting a claim of priority has been filed.

Foreign Application Number: Enter the foreign application serial number, if available.

Filing Date of Foreign Application: Enter the date (two digits each for both the month and day, and four digits for the year) on which the foreign application was filed. To receive a priority filing date, you must file the U.S. application within six (6) months of filing the first foreign application in a defined treaty country.

Foreign Registration: Section 44(e): Use this section if applicant is relying on a foreign registration certificate or a certified copy of a foreign registration currently in force. You must submit this foreign registration certificate or a certified copy of the foreign registration.

International Class Number(s): Enter the international class number(s) of the goods and/or services associated with the mark; e.g., 14; 24; 25. If unknown, leave blank and the USPTO will assign the number(s).

Listing of Goods and/or Services: Enter the *specific* goods and/or services associated with the mark. Do NOT enter the broad class number here, such as 9 or 42 (this information belongs in the field above, namely International Class Number(s)). If the goods and/or services are classified in more than one class, the goods and/or services should be listed in ascending numerical class order, with both the class number and the specific goods and/or services. For example, 14: jewelry

24: towels
25: pants, shirts, jackets, shoes

For more information about acceptable wording for the goods/services, see USPTO's on-line *Acceptable Identification of Goods and Services Manual,* at *http://www.uspto.gov/web/offices/tac/doc/gsmanual/*.

Country of Foreign Registration: Enter the country of the foreign registration.

Foreign Registration Number: Enter the number of the foreign registration.

Foreign Registration Date: Enter the date (two digits each for both the month and day, and four digits for the year) of the foreign registration.

Foreign Registration Renewal Date: Enter the date (two digits each for both the month and day, and four digits for the year) of the foreign registration renewal.

Foreign Registration Date: Enter the expiration date (two digits each for both the month and day, and four digits for the year) of the foreign registration.

FEE INFORMATION

The filing fee for this application is $375.00 *per class* of goods and/or services. You must include at least $375.00 with this application; otherwise the papers and money will be returned to you. Once your application meets the minimum filing date requirements, this processing fee becomes **non-refundable**. This is true even if the USPTO does not issue a registration certificate for this mark.

Number of Classes: Enter the total number of classes (*not* the international class number(s)) for which the applicant is seeking registration. For example, if the application covers Classes 1, 5 and 25, then enter the number "3."

Total Filing Fee Paid: Enter the fee amount that is enclosed (either in the form of a check or money order in U.S. currency, made payable to "Commissioner of Patents and Trademarks"), or to be charged to an already-existing USPTO deposit account.

SIGNATURE INFORMATION

Signature: The appropriate person must sign the form. A person who is properly authorized to sign on behalf of the applicant is: (1) a person with legal authority to bind the applicant; or (2) a person with firsthand knowledge of the facts and actual or implied authority to act on behalf of the applicant; or (3) an attorney who has an actual or implied written or verbal power of attorney from the applicant.

Date Signed: Enter the date the form is signed.

Name: Enter the name of the person signing the form.

Title: Enter the signatory's title, if applicable, e.g., Vice President, General Partner, etc.

CONTACT INFORMATION

Although this may be the same as provided elsewhere in the document, please enter the following required information for where the USPTO should mail correspondence.

Name: Enter the full name of the contact person.

Company/Firm Name: Enter the name of the contact person's company or firm.

Street: Enter the street address or rural delivery route where the contact person is located.

City: Enter the city and/or foreign area designation where the contact person's address is located.

State: Enter the U.S. state or Canadian province in which the contact person's address is located.

Country: Enter the country of the contact person's address.

Zip Code: Enter the U.S. zip code or Canadian postal code.

Telephone Number: Enter the appropriate telephone number.

Fax Number: Enter the appropriate fax number, if available.

e-Mail Address: Enter the appropriate e-mail address, if available.

Contract with an Independent Contractor

Designers often hire independent contractors, such as computer page formatters, business planners, copyeditors, and talent (see form 25). Independent contractors run their own businesses and hire out on a job by job basis. They are not employees, which saves the designer in terms of employee benefits, payroll taxes, and paperwork. By not being an employee, the independent contractor does not have to have taxes withheld and is able to deduct all business expenses directly against income.

A contract with an independent contractor serves two purposes. First, it shows the intention of the parties to have the services performed by an independent contractor. Second, it shows the terms on which the parties will do business.

As to the first purpose of the contract—showing the intention to hire an independent contractor, not an employee, the contract can be helpful if the Internal Revenue Service (IRS) decides to argue that the independent contractor was an employee. The tax law automatically classifies as independent contractors physicians, lawyers, general building contractors, and others who follow an independent trade, business, or profession, in which they offer their services to the public on a regular basis. However, many people do not fall clearly into this group. IRS guidelines as to the employee-independent contractor distinction are discussed in relation to form 44.

The second purpose of the contract is to specify the terms agreed to between the parties. What services will the contractor provide and when will the services be performed? On what basis and when will payment be made by the designer? Will there be an advance, perhaps to help defray expenses?

The designer should consult with his or her insurance agent with respect to the insurance the designer should carry when dealing with independent contractors. Certainly the designer should make sure there is adequate coverage for property damage or liability arising from lawsuits for injuries. The contractor should definitely have its own liability policy as well as workers' compensation and any state disability coverage.

Independent contractors can perform large jobs or render a day's services. Form 40 is designed to help designers deal with small independent contractors who are performing a limited amount of work. The negotiation checklist is also directed toward this situation. However, some further discussion is necessary to cover the issues arising when the designer has a larger project to complete, such as a major studio renovation.

If the designer were dealing with a substantial renovation to the studio or other construction, the contract would have to be more complex. First, it is always wise to have references for a contractor who is new to the designer. Keep deposits small, since it can be hard to get a deposit back if the contractor does not perform. There should also be clarity as to the quality and perhaps even the brands of any materials to be used.

The contractor can be asked to post a surety bond, which is a bond to guarantee full performance. However, many small contractors may have difficulty obtaining such a bond, since the insurance company may require the posting of collateral. In any event, the designer might explore with his or her own insurance agent the feasibility of demanding this from the contractor. A point to keep in mind is that the contractor's failure to pay subcontractors or suppliers of material can result in a lien against the designer's property for work done to that property. A lien is like a mortgage on a building; it must be satisfied or removed before the property can be sold. A surety bond would avoid problems with liens.

A contractor should be required to give a bid. That bid will be the basis for the terms of the contract. The contractor may want to wait until after completing the work to determine a fee. Obviously this is unacceptable. The contractor may want to charge a fee for labor, but charge cost plus a markup for materials. This is probably also unacceptable, since the designer has a budget and needs to know that budget can be met. Another variation is for the contractor to allow for a ten percent variation in the bid or the costs of materials based on what actually happens. This should be carefully evaluated by the designer, but is less desirable than a firm fee.

The fee and the job description should only be modified by a written amendment to the contract. If this isn't required, disputes are likely to result.

The designer should, if possible, require the contractor to warrant a number of facts, such as the contractor being licensed if necessary, the materials being new and of good quality, the contractor being responsible for any damages arising from its work, and any construction being guaranteed for some period of time. The contractor would agree to protect the designer (by paying losses, damages, and any attorney's fees) in the event any of these warranties were breached.

Keep in mind that form 40 is designed for day-to-day dealings with freelancers, not the hiring of builders for major renovations.

Filling in the Form

In the preamble fill in the date and the names and addresses of the parties. In Paragraph 1 show in detail what services are to be performed. Attach another sheet of description or a list of procedures, diagram, or a plan to the contract, if needed. In Paragraph 2 give a schedule. In Paragraph 3 deal with the fee and expenses. In Paragraph 4 specify a time for payment. In Paragraph 5 indicate how cancellations will be handled. In Paragraph 6[E] fill in any special criteria that the contractor should warrant as true. In Paragraph 7

fill in any insurance the contractor must carry. In Paragraph 10 specify who will arbitrate, where the arbitration will take place, and, if local small claims court would be better than arbitration, give amounts under the small claims court dollar limit as an exclusion from arbitration. In Paragraph 11 give the state whose laws will govern the contract. Have both parties sign the contract.

Negotiation Checklist

❑ Carefully detail the services to be performed. If necessary, attach an additional sheet of description, a list of procedures, or a plan or diagram. (Paragraph 1)

❑ Give a schedule for performance. (Paragraph 2)

❑ State the method for computing the fee. (Paragraph 3)

❑ If the contractor is to bill for expenses, limit which expenses may be charged. (Paragraph 3)

❑ Require full documentation of expenses in the form of receipts and invoices. (Paragraph 3)

❑ Place a maximum amount on the expenses that can be incurred. (Paragraph 3)

❑ Pay an advance against expenses, if the amount of the expenses are too much for the contractor to wait to receive back at the time of payment for the entire job. (Paragraph 3)

❑ State a time for payment. (Paragraph 4)

❑ Deal with payment for cancellations. (Paragraph 5)

❑ If expenses are billed for, consider whether any markup should be allowed.

❏ Require warranties that the contractor is legally able to perform the contract, that all services will be done in a professional manner, that any subcontractor or employee hired by the contractor will be professional, that the contractor will pay all taxes for the contractor and his or her employees, and any other criteria for the proper performance of the services. (Paragraph 6)

❏ If a photographer, illustrator, author, or other creator is to create a work protected by copyright, trademark (such as an actual trademark or perhaps a character or other identity symbol), or other form of intellectual property, make certain any needed rights of usage or ownership are obtained. (Paragraph 7)

❏ Review insurance coverage with the designer's insurance agent.

❏ Specify what insurance coverage the contractor must have. (Paragraph 8)

❏ State that the parties are independent contractors and not employer-employee. (Paragraph 9)

❏ Do not allow assignment of rights or obligations under the contract. (Paragraph 10)

❏ The designer should check with his or her attorney as to whether arbitration is better than suing in the local courts, and whether small claims court might be better than arbitration. (Paragraph 11)

❏ Allow for an oral modification of either the fee or expense agreement, if such oral change is necessary to move the project forward quickly. (Paragraph 12)

❏ Compare Paragraph 12 with the standard provisions in the introduction.

Contract with an Independent Contractor

AGREEMENT entered into as of the_____day of _____, 20____, between _____

located at _____ (hereinafter referred to as the "Designer")

and _____, located at _____

(hereinafter referred to as the "Contractor").

The parties hereto agree as follows:

1. Services to be Rendered. The Contractor agrees to perform the following services for the Designer:

_____

_____

_____

_____

_____

_____

If needed, a list of procedures, diagram, or plan for the services shall be attached to and made part of this Agreement.

2. Schedule. The Contractor shall complete the services pursuant to the following schedule: _____

_____

_____

3. Fee and Expenses. The Designer shall pay the Contractor as follows:

❏ Project rate $_____

❏ Day rate $_____/ day

❏ Hourly rate $_____/ hour

❏ Other _____ $_____

The Designer shall reimburse the Contractor only for the expenses listed here _____

_____

Expenses shall not exceed $_____. The Contractor shall provide full documentation for any expenses to be reimbursed, including receipts and invoices. An advance of $_____ against expenses shall be paid to the Contractor and recouped when Payment is made pursuant to Paragraph 4.

4. Payment. Payment shall be made: ❏ at the end of each day ❏ upon completion of the project ❏ within thirty (30) days of Designer's receipt of Contractor's invoice.

5. Cancellation. In the event of cancellation, Designer shall pay a cancellation fee under the following circumstances and in the amount specified:

----

6. Warranties. The Contractor warrants as follows:

(A) Contractor is fully able to enter into and perform its obligations pursuant to this Agreement.

(B) All services shall be performed in a professional manner.

(C) If employees or subcontractors are to be hired by Contractor they shall be competent professionals.

(D) Contractor shall pay all necessary local, state, or federal taxes, including but not limited to withholding taxes,

(E) Any other criteria for performance are as follows:

_____

_____

7. **Rights.** If the services rendered by the Contractor result in work(s) that can be protected by copyright, trademark, or other forms of intellectual property, the Client shall have the following rights of usage or ownership in these work(s):

_____

_____

8. **Insurance.** The Contractor shall maintain in force the following insurance: _____

_____

_____

9. **Relationship of Parties.** Both parties agree that the Contractor is an independent contractor. This Agreement is not an employment agreement, nor does it constitute a joint venture or partnership between the Designer and Contractor. Nothing contained herein shall be construed to be inconsistent with this independent contractor relationship.

10. **Assignment.** This Agreement may not be assigned by either party without the written consent of the other party hereto.

11. **Arbitration.** All disputes shall be submitted to binding arbitration before _____ in the following location _____ and settled in accordance with the rules of the American Arbitration Association. Judgment upon the arbitration award may be entered in any court having jurisdiction thereof. Disputes in which the amount at issue is less than $_____ shall not be subject to this arbitration provision.

12. **Miscellany.** This Agreement constitutes the entire agreement between the parties. Its terms can be modified only by an instrument in writing signed by both parties, except that oral authorizations of additional fees and expenses shall be permitted if necessary to speed the progress of work. This Agreement shall be binding on the parties, their heirs, successors, assigns, and personal representatives. A waiver of a breach of any of the provisions of this Agreement shall not be construed as a continuing waiver of other breaches of the same or other provisions hereof. This Agreement shall be governed by the laws of the State of _____.

IN WITNESS WHEREOF, the parties hereto have signed this as of the date first set forth above.

Designer_____   Contractor_____
                                                                              Company Name

                                                             By_____
                                                                           Authorized Signatory

Employment Application
Employment Agreement
Restrictive Covenant for Employment

FORM 41 FORM 42 FORM 43

Hiring new employees should invigorate and strengthen the graphic design firm. However, proper management practices have to be followed or the results can be disappointing and, potentially, open the firm to the danger of litigation. The process of advertising a position, interviewing, and selecting a candidate should be shaped in such a way that the firm maintains clarity of purpose and fortifies its legal position.

The hiring process should avoid violating any state or federal law prohibiting discrimination, including discrimination on the basis of race, religion, age, sex, or disability. Help-wanted advertising, listings of a position with an employment agency, application forms to be filled in, questions asked during an interview, statements in the employee handbook or office manual, and office forms should all comply with these anti-discrimination laws.

The firm should designate an administrator to handle human resources. That person should develop familiarity with the legal requirements and review the overall process to protect the firm and ensure the best candidates are hired. All employment matters—from résumés, applications, interview reports, documentation as to employment decisions to personnel files, and employee benefit information—should channel through this person.

The human resources administrator should train interviewers with respect both to legalities and the goals of the firm. Firms that lack job descriptions may not realize that this is detrimental to the firm as well as the potential employee. Not only will the employee have a more difficult time understanding the nature of the position, but the interviewer will have a harder task of developing a checklist of desirable characteristics to look for in the interview and use as a basis of comparison among candidates. This vagueness may encompass not only the duties required in the position, but also the salary, bonuses, benefits, duration, and grounds for discharge with respect to the position. Such ambiguity is likely to lead to dissatisfaction on both sides, which is inimical to a harmonious relationship and productive work environment.

The design firm should keep in mind that employment relationships are terminable at will by either the employee or the firm, unless the firm has promised that the employment will have a definite duration. Unless the firm intends to create a different relationship, it should take steps throughout the hiring process to make clear that the employment is terminable at will. So, for example, form 41 indicates this in the declaration signed by the applicant. The administrator should make certain that nothing in the advertisements, application, job description, interview, employee handbook, office manual, or related documents give an impression of long-term or permanent employment. Interviewers, who may be seeking to impress the applicant with the pleasant ambience and creative culture of the firm, should not make statements such as, "Working here is a lifetime career."

The application also offers the opportunity to inform the applicant that false statements are grounds for discharge. In addition, the applicant gives permission to contact the various employers, educational institutions, and references listed in the application.

Because the employment application presents the design firm with an opportunity to bolster various goals in the employment process, the application is used in addition to the résumé that the employee would also be expected to make available. The application, of course, is only the beginning of the relationship between employer and employee, but it starts the relationship in a proper way that can be bolstered by the interview, the employee handbook, and related policies that ensure clarity with respect to the employee's duties and conditions of employment.

The employment agreement evolves from the process of application and interviews. It allows the design firm to reiterate that the employment is terminable at will. It also clarifies for both parties the terms of the employment, such as the duties, salary, benefits, and reviews. By clarifying the terms, it minimizes the likelihood of misunderstandings or disputes. It can also provide for arbitration in the event that disputes do arise.

The design firm may want to protect itself against the possibility that an employee will leave and go into competition with or harm the firm. For example, the employee might start his or her own business and try to take away clients, work for a competitor, or sell confidential information. The design firm can protect against this by the use of a restrictive covenant, which can either be part of the employment agreement or a separate agreement. The restriction must be reasonable in terms of duration and geographic scope. It would be against public policy to allow a firm to ban an employee from ever again pursuing a career in graphic design. However, a restriction that for six months or a year after leaving the firm the employee will neither work for competitors nor start a competing firm in the same city would have a likelihood of being enforceable. Laws vary from state to state. It is wise to provide separate or additional consideration for the restrictive covenant to lessen the risk of its being struck down by a court (such as allocating a portion of wages to the restrictive covenant). This is best done at the time of first employment, since asking someone who is currently employed to sign a restrictive covenant may raise a red flag about relative bargaining positions and the validity of the consideration.

Certainly these agreements may be done as letter agreements, which have a less formal feeling and may appear more inviting for an employee to sign. For that reason, form 42 and form 43 take the form of letters to the employee. Regardless of whether letters countersigned by the employee or more formal agreements are used, the employment agreement and the restrictive covenant should be reviewed by an attorney with an expertise in employment law.

Two helpful books for developing successful programs with respect to employment are *From Hiring to Firing* and *The Complete Collection of Legal Forms for Employers,* both written by Steven Mitchell Sack (Legal Strategies Publications).

Filling in Form 41
This is filled in by the employee and is self-explanatory.

Filling in Form 42
Using the design firm's stationery, give the date and name and address of the prospective employee. In the opening paragraph fill in the name of the design firm. In Paragraph 1 give the position for which the person is being hired and the start date. In Paragraph 2 indicate the duties of the position. In Paragraph 3 give the annual compensation. In Paragraph 4 fill in the various benefits.

In Paragraph 8 indicate who would arbitrate, where arbitration would take place, and consider inserting the local small claims court limit so small amounts can be sued for in that forum (assuming the design firm is eligible to sue in the local small claims court). In Paragraph 9 fill in the state whose laws will govern the agreement. The design firm should sign two copies, the employee should countersign, and each party should keep one copy of the letter.

Filling in Form 43
Using the design firm's stationery, give the date and name and address of the prospective employee. In the opening paragraph fill in the

date of the Employment Agreement (which is likely to be the same date as this letter) and the name of design firm. In Paragraph 1 enter a number of months. In Paragraph 3 give the additional compensation that the design firm will pay. In Paragraph 6 fill in the state whose laws will govern the agreement. The design firm should sign two copies, the employee should countersign, and each party should keep one copy of the letter.

Checklist

❑ Appoint a human resources administrator for the firm.

❑ Avoid anything that may be discrimination in advertising the position, in the application form, in the interview, and in the employee handbook and other employment-related documents.

❑ Retain copies of all advertisements, including records on how many people responded and how many were hired.

❑ In advertisements or job descriptions refer to the position as "full-time" or "regular," rather than using words that imply the position may be long-term or permanent.

❑ Do not suggest that the position is secure (such as "career path" or "long-term growth").

❑ Never make claims about guaranteed earnings that will not, in fact, be met.

❑ Don't require qualifications beyond what are necessary for the position, since doing so may discriminate against people with lesser qualifications who could have done the job.

❑ Make certain the qualifications do not discriminate against people with disabilities who might nonetheless be able to perform the work.

❑ Carefully craft job descriptions to aid both applicants and interviewers.

❑ Train interviewers and monitor their statements and questions to be certain the firm is in compliance with anti-discrimination laws.

❑ Be precise in setting forth the salary, bonuses, benefits, duration, and grounds for discharge with respect to the position.

❑ Make certain the candidates have the immigration status to work legally in the United States.

❑ Do not ask for church references while in the hiring process.

❑ Avoid asking for photographs of candidates for a position.

❑ Never allow interviewers to ask questions of women they would not ask of men.

❑ Never say to an older candidate that he or she is "overqualified."

❑ Instruct interviewers never to speak of "lifetime employment" or use similar phrases.

❑ Have the candidate give permission for the firm to contact references, prior employers, and educational institutions listed in the application.

❑ When contacting references and others listed in the application, make certain not to slander or invade the privacy of the applicant.

❑ Have the candidate acknowledge his or her understanding that the employment is terminable at will.

❑ Stress the importance of truthful responses and have the candidate confirm his or her knowledge that false responses will be grounds for dismissal.

❑ Always get back to applicants who are not hired and give a reason for not hiring them.

The reason should be based on the job description, such as, "We interviewed many candidates and hired another individual whose background and skills should make the best match for the position."

❏ Consult with an attorney with expertise in the employment field before inquiring into arrests, asking for polygraph tests, requesting pre-employment physicals, requiring psychological or honesty tests, investigating prior medical history, or using credit reports, since this behavior may be illegal.

❏ Create an employee handbook that sets forth all matters of concern to employees, from benefits to standards for behavior in the workplace to evaluative guidelines with respect to performance.

❏ Consider whether the firm wants to have a restrictive covenant with the employee.

❏ If a restrictive covenant is to be used, decide what behavior would ideally be preventable—working for a competitor, creating a competitive business, contacting the design firm's clients, inducing other employees to leave, or using confidential information (such as customer lists or trade secrets).

❏ Give a short duration for the covenant, such as six months or one year.

❏ Make clear that additional consideration was paid to the employee for agreeing to the restrictive covenant.

❏ If there is a breach of the restrictive covenant, consult an attorney and immediately put the employee on notice of the violation.

❏ Consider whether the firm wants an arbitration clause with the employee, since such a clause allows the firm to determine where and before which arbitrators the arbitration will take place.

❏ Make certain that any contract confirming the employment specifies that the employment is terminable at will (unless the designer wishes to enter into a different arrangement). It should also clarify the duties of the employee, set forth the salary, benefits, and related information, provide for arbitration if desired, and delineate any restrictive covenant (unless that is to be in a separate document entered into at the same time).

Employment Application

Date _____

Applicant's Name _____

Address _____

_____

Daytime telephone _____ Email address _____

Social Security Number _____

Position for which you are applying _____

How did you learn about this position? _____

Are you 18 years of age or older? ❏ Yes ❏ No

If you are hired for this position, can you provide written proof that you may legally work in the United States?
❏ Yes ❏ No

On what date are you able to commence work? _____

Employment History

Are you currently employed? ❏ Yes ❏ No

Starting with your current or most recent position, give the requested information:

1. Employer _____

Address _____

Supervisor _____

Telephone number _____ Email address _____

Dates of employment _____ Salary _____

Description of your job title and duties _____

_____

Reason for leaving position _____

May we contact this employer for a reference? ❏ Yes ❏ No

2. Employer _____

Address _____

Supervisor _____

Telephone number _____ Email address _____

Dates of employment _____ Salary _____

Description of your job title and duties _____

_____

Reason for leaving position _____

May we contact this employer for a reference?   ❏ Yes   ❏ No

3. Employer _____

Address _____

Supervisor _____

Telephone number _____ Email address _____

Dates of employment _____ Salary _____

Description of your job title and duties _____

_____

Reason for leaving position _____

May we contact this employer for a reference?   ❏ Yes   ❏ No

List and explain any special skills relevant for the position for which you are applying that you have acquired from your employment or other activities (include computer software in which you are proficient).

_____
_____
_____
_____
_____
_____
_____
_____
_____

Educational History

	Name and Address of School	Study Specialty	Number of Years Completed	Degree or Diploma
High School				
College				
Graduate School				
Other Education				

Describe any internships, other specialized training (including job-related experience in the United States military), extracurricular activities, licenses, or degrees that would be particularly helpful in performing this position.

_____

_____

_____

_____

_____

_____

To make inquiries about your work record, do we need any information about your name or your use of another? ❑ Yes ❑ No If you answer yes, please explain _____

_____

References

1. Name _____ Telephone _____
   Address _____ Email address _____
   How long and in what context have you known this reference? _____

   _____

2. Name _____ Telephone _____
   Address _____ Email address _____
   How long and in what context have you known this reference? _____

   _____

3. Name _____ Telephone _____
   Address _____ Email address _____
   How long and in what context have you known this reference? _____

   _____

Applicant's Declaration

I understand that the information given in this employment application will be used in determining whether or not I will be hired for this position. I have made certain to give only true answers and understand that any falsification or willful omission will be grounds for refusal of employment or dismissal.

I understand that the employer hires on an employment-at-will basis, which employment may be terminated either by me or the employer at any time, with or without cause, for any reason consistent with applicable state and federal law. If I am offered the position for which I am applying, it will be employment-at-will, unless a written instrument signed by an authorized executive of the employer changes this.

I know that this application is not a contract of employment. I am lawfully authorized to work in the United States and, if offered the position, will give whatever documentary proof of this as the employer may request.

I further understand that the employer may investigate and verify all information I have given in this application, on related documents (including, but not limited to, my résumé), and in interviews. I authorize all individuals, educational institutions, and companies named in this application to provide any information the employer may request about me, and I release them from any liability for damages for providing such information.

Applicant's signature _____   Date _____

Employment Agreement

[Designer's Letterhead]

Date _____

Mr./Ms. New Employee

_____ [address]

_____

Dear

We are pleased that you will be joining us at _____ (hereinafter referred to as the "Company"). This letter is to set forth the terms and conditions of your employment.

1. Your employment as _____ shall commence on _____, 20___.

2. Your duties shall consist of the following: _____

_____

_____

You may also perform additional duties incidental to the job description. You shall faithfully perform all duties to the best of your ability. This is a full-time position, and you shall devote your full and undivided time and best efforts to the business of the Company.

3. You will be paid annual compensation of $_____ pursuant to the Company's regular handling of payroll.

4. You will have the following benefits:

    a) Sick days _____

    b) Personal days _____

    c) Vacation _____

    d) Bonus _____

    e) Health Insurance _____

    f) Retirement Benefits _____

    g) Other _____

5. You will familiarize yourself with the Company's rules and regulations for employees and follow them during your employment.

6. This employment is terminable at will at any time by you or the Company.

7. You acknowledge that a precondition to this employment is that you negotiate and sign a restrictive covenant prior to the commencement date set forth in Paragraph 1.

8. Arbitration. All disputes arising under this Agreement shall be submitted to binding arbitration before _____ in the following location _____ and settled in accordance with the rules of the American Arbitration Association. Judgment upon the arbitration award may be entered in any court

having jurisdiction thereof. Disputes in which the amount at issue is less than $_____ shall not be subject to this arbitration provision.

9. Miscellany. This agreement shall be binding on both us and you, as well as heirs, successors, assigns, and personal representatives. This agreement constitutes the entire understanding. Its terms can be modified only by an instrument in writing signed by both parties. Notices shall be sent by certified mail or traceable overnight delivery to you or the Company at our present addresses, and notification of any change of address shall be given prior to that change of address taking effect. A waiver of a breach of any of the provisions of this agreement shall not be construed as a continuing waiver of other breaches of the same or other provisions hereof. This agreement shall be governed by the laws of the State of _____.

If this letter accurately sets forth our understanding, please sign beneath the words "Agreed to," and return one copy to us for our files.

Agreed to:

Sincerely yours,
[Company name]

_____
Employee

By _____
Name, Title

Restrictive Covenant for Employment

[Designer's Letterhead]

Date _____

Mr./Ms. New Employee

_____ [address]

_____

Dear

By a separate letter dated _____, 20__, we have set forth the terms for your employment with _____ (hereinafter referred to as the "Company").

This letter is to deal with your role regarding certain sensitive aspects of the Company's business. Our policy has always been to encourage our employees, when qualified, to deal with our clients and, when appropriate, contact our clients directly. In addition, during your employment with the Company, you may be given knowledge of proprietary information that the Company wishes to keep confidential.

To protect the Company and compensate you, we agree as follows:

1. You will not directly or indirectly compete with the business of the Company during the term of your employment and for a period of ____ months following the termination of your employment, regardless of who initiated the termination, unless you obtain the Company's prior written consent. This means that you will not be employed by, own, manage, or consult with a business that is either similar to or competes with the business of the Company. This restriction shall be limited to the geographic areas in which the Company usually conducts its business, except that it shall apply to the Company's clients regardless of their location.

2. In addition, you will not during the term of your employment or thereafter directly or indirectly disclose or use any confidential information of the Company, except in the pursuit of your employment and in the best interest of the Company. Confidential information includes, but is not limited to, client lists, client files, trade secrets, financial data, sales or marketing data, plans, designs, and the like, relating to the current or future business of the Company. All confidential information is the sole property of the Company. This provision shall not apply to information voluntarily disclosed to the public without restrictions or which has lawfully entered the public domain.

3. As consideration for your agreement to this restrictive covenant, the Company will compensate you as follows:

_____

_____

4. You acknowledge that, in the event of your breach of this restrictive covenant, money damages would not adequately compensate the Company. You, therefore, agree that, in addition to all other legal and equitable remedies available to the Company, the Company shall have the right to receive injunctive relief in the event of any breach hereunder.

5. The terms of this restrictive covenant shall survive the termination of your employment, regardless of the reason or causes, if any, for the termination, or whether the termination might constitute a breach of the agreement of employment.

6. Miscellany. This agreement shall be binding on both us and you, as well as our heirs, successors, assigns, and personal representatives. This agreement constitutes the entire understanding. Its terms can be modified only by an instrument in writing signed by both parties. Notices shall be sent by certified mail or traceable overnight delivery to you or the Company at our present addresses, and notification of any change of address shall be given prior to that change of address taking effect. A waiver of a breach of any of the provisions of this agreement shall not be construed as a continuing waiver of other breaches of the same or other provisions hereof. This agreement shall be governed by the laws of the State of _____.

If this letter accurately sets forth our understanding, please sign beneath the words "Agreed to," and return one copy to us for our files.

Agreed to:

Sincerely yours,
[Company name]

_____
Employee

By _____
Name, Title

Project Employee Contract

A design firm may want to hire someone who falls into an intermediate position between an independent contractor (discussed with respect to form 40) and a permanent employee. If the person is to work on a project for a period of months, it is quite likely that he or she meets the legal definition of an employee. While the person may meet the IRS tests for who is an employee, the design firm may prefer not to give the person the full benefits of the typical employment contract.

The first consideration in such a situation is whether the person could be hired as an independent contractor. Since IRS reclassification from independent contractor to employee can have harsh consequences for the design firm, including payment of back employment taxes, penalties, and jeopardy to qualified pension plans, the IRS has promulgated guidelines for who is an employee.

Basically, an employee is someone who is under the control and direction of the employer to accomplish work. The employee is not only told what to do, but how to do it. On the other hand, an independent contractor is controlled or directed only as to the final result, not as to the means and method to accomplish that result. Some twenty factors enumerated by the IRS dictate the conclusion as to whether someone is an employee or an independent contractor, and no single factor is controlling. Factors suggesting someone is an independent contractor would include that the person supplies his or her own equipment and facilities; that the person works for more than one party (and perhaps employs others at the same time); that the person can choose the location to perform the work; that the person is not supervised during the assignment; that the person receives a fee or commission rather than an hourly or weekly wage; that the person can make a loss or a profit; and that the person can be forced to terminate the job for

poor performance but cannot be dismissed like an employee. The designer should consult his or her accountant to resolve any doubts about someone's status.

Assuming that these criteria suggest that a person to be hired for a project is an employee, the design firm may choose to designate him or her as a project employee. Project employees are usually hired for a minimum of four months. They may be transferred from one assignment to another. Project employees are usually eligible for most benefits offered other regular employees, such as medical/dental benefits, life insurance, long-term disability, vacation, and so on. However, project employees would not be eligible for leaves of absence and severance pay. If a project employee moves to regular status, the length of service will usually be considered to have begun on the original hire date as a project employee.

Filling in the Form

This contract would normally take the form of a letter written on the company's letterhead. Fill in the name of the project employee in the salutation. Then specify the type of work that the project employee will be doing—e.g., Designer, Illustrator, Production Artist, and so on. Indicate the start date for work and the anticipated project termination date. In the second paragraph give the salary on an annualized basis as well as on a biweekly basis. In the third paragraph state benefits for which the project employee will not be eligible, such as leaves of absence, tuition reimbursement, and severance pay. Insert the company name in the last paragraph and again after "sincerely." Both parties should sign the letter.

Project Employee Contract

Dear _____ ,

This will confirm that you have accepted a Project Job as _____

with our company. This assignment will begin on _____ , and has an expected project

termination date on or before _____ .

As we agreed, based on an annual salary of $_____ , you will be paid $_____ on a bi-weekly

basis, less applicable taxes and insurance. During the term of the assignment, this employment will be terminable at

will either by you as Project Employee or by us as Project Employer.

As a Project Employee, you are eligible for our company's benefits except for_____

_____

I cannot guarantee your employment beyond this assignment. The Project Employee status allows

you to consider finding another job within the company. An added benefit is that if your Project Employment

status changes to that of regular employee, your original Project hire date will become your start date

of continuous employment.

I am very pleased to welcome you to _____

and look forward to working with you. Please let me know if you have any questions or concerns.

Sincerely,

By:_____
Project Manager

Agreed to:

_____
Project Employee

Date:_____

Employee Performance Evaluation
Employee Warning
Employee Dismissal Notice

The purpose of the employee application process is to find and hire the best applicant for any available position. Unfortunately, despite care taken in this process, the employee may nonetheless act in such a way that it is necessary to warn and ultimately perhaps fire the employee.

Unless altered by an employment agreement, employment is terminable at will by the employer. However, such termination must not be for a reason forbidden by law. The same factors that must not influence the hiring process must not influence the process of firing either. So race, religion, age, sex, or disability cannot be the grounds for firing an employee.

The Employee Performance Evaluation, form 45, is an important part of the employer's effort to communicate with an employee as to whether the employee's performance is satisfactory. Such a written evaluation gives the employee an opportunity to improve performance by pointing to areas of weakness as well as strength. Allowing the employee to respond to the evaluation ensures that the employee is aware of the employer's concerns. The evaluation should be done on a regular basis, whether yearly or at more frequent intervals.

If the employee's performance has been found deficient in certain aspects and these deficiencies are not remedied, the employer may choose to give an Employee Warning, form 46, to the employee. Using the written warning allows the employer to build documentation as to the nature of the employee's performance and the employer's response to that performance. Ideally, the Employee Warning will point to an issue already raised in the Employee Performance Evaluation.

If the employee doesn't remedy the deficiencies pointed out in an Employee Warning, it may be necessary to dismiss the employee. In such an event, the Employee Dismissal Notice, form 46, is used to terminate the employment. This notice in the form of a letter uses the reasons given in the Employee Warning to document why the employee was dismissed. By carefully following the procedure of evaluation, warning, and then dismissal, the employer makes it far more difficult for the employee to assert that the dismissal was for an illegal reason.

Filling in Form 45
Give the name of the employee, the employee's job title or titles, the name of the evaluator, and the date of the evaluation. Then give a grade for each criterion. The evaluator should add any additional comments. The employee should then add any responses to the evaluation. Both employee and evaluator should then sign the form.

Filling in Form 46
Give the name of the employee, the employee's job title or titles, the name of the supervisor, and the date of the warning. Indicate the reason for the warning to the employee and what steps the employee can take to avoid further warnings or disciplinary action. State what the next disciplinary action is likely to be if the employee does not take action. Allow the employee to comment on the warning. The person giving the warning on behalf of the employer should sign and give his or her job title. The employee should also sign the form.

Filling in Form 47
Give the employee's name and address and fill in the salutation. Give a date for termination and the reasons for the termination. Provide a contact for the employee to review any outstanding matters in need of resolution. Sign the letter on behalf of the employer.

Checklist

❑ Review the checklist on pages 167–168, since the same legal tests that apply to hiring also apply to warnings and termination of employment.

❑ Follow the guidelines in the employee handbook with respect to what may lead to dismissal (such as obtaining employment by giving false or misleading information, maliciously destroying company property, or insubordination) and what may lead to disciplinary actions (such as unsatisfactory work, excessive absences, and using company equipment without permission).

❑ Make certain that the forms are consistent, so that the Employee Performance Evaluation includes grading that would support an Employee Warning (unless the warning is based on actions by the employee after the date of the evaluation).

❑ Likewise, make certain that the Employee Dismissal Notice is consistent with any prior Employee Warning.

❑ Keep in mind that it may be illegal to terminate an employee in order to avoid paying the employee commissions, a year-end bonus, vested financial rights, or other anticipated financial benefits.

❑ It may be illegal to fire whistle-blowers.

❑ Firing an employee after pregnancy, illness, or jury duty may violate the employee's rights.

❑ There is a risk in firing a worker in a manner other than that which is set forth in the employee handbook.

❑ Firing a worker who has a written contract for a specific term may be unlawful, and so may firing an employee who has been given verbal assurances of job security or other benefits if the employer has failed to live up to those assurances.

❑ It may be a risk to fire an employee when the punishment seems unusually severe and other workers were not held to the same standard.

❑ Never inflate employee evaluations, because firing an employee after giving an excellent performance review may be grounds for the employee to sue.

❑ In general, try to have the employee resign rather than firing the employee.

❑ It is ideal to confirm all severance arrangements in writing and have the dismissed employee sign the document in order to avoid any confusion as to the terms of the severance.

Employee Performance Evaluation

Employee _____   Job Title _____

Evaluator _____   Date of Evaluation _____

The evaluation of the various criteria is on a scale of A to F as follows:

A is for excellent performance that exceeds expectations; B is for above average performance; C is for average performance; D is for below average performance; and F is for performance that is unsatisfactory.

CRITERIA	A	B	C	D	F
1. Performance					
Speed with which work is performed					
Quality of work completed					
Productivity					
Ability to work independently					
2. Communication					
Ability to follow instructions					
Reporting to supervisor					
Communicating well with clients					
Efficiency of communications					
3. Interpersonal Skills					
Ability to work with supervisors					
Ability to supervise					
Overall relationship with clients					
4. Attendance					
Punctuality					
Overall attendance record					
5. Skills					
Has skills needed for position					
Uses skills effectively					
Works to increase skills					

Additional Comments by Evaluator: _____

_____

_____

Comments by Employee: _____

_____

_____

Signed as of the Evaluation Date by:

_____   _____
(Evaluator)   (Employee)

Employee Warning

Employee _____   Job Title _____

Supervisor _____   Date of Warning _____

This Employee Warning is being given for the following reason(s): _____
_____
_____

To avoid further warnings or disciplinary action, the employee should _____
_____
_____

In the event of the employee's failure to take appropriate remedial action, the next disciplinary measure proposed is
_____
_____
_____

The employee should enter any response to the foregoing here. _____
_____
_____

Signed for the employer as of the date set forth above by:

_____
       (Name)   Job Title _____

Signed by the employee as of the date set forth above with the understanding that signing is not an admission of any dereliction of duty but simply acknowledgement of the receipt of this Employee Warning:

_____
      (Employee)

Employee Dismissal Notice

[Employer's Letterhead]

Date _____

To _____
            (Employee)

_____
            (Address)

_____

Dear _____:

We regret to inform you that your employment shall be terminated on the following date _____

for the reasons set forth here: _____

_____.

Any accrued benefits shall be itemized in a statement which we shall provide you with within thirty days of the date of this letter. Severance pay shall be in accordance with our company personnel policy. Any insurance benefits shall be handled in accordance with state law and our company personnel policy.

Your contact for any matters relating to this termination is _____, who will explain these items and related topics and arrange for the return of any company property in your possession.

We sincerely regret that this action is necessary and wish you the best in your future endeavors.

Yours truly,

_____
(Signatory for Employer)

Commercial Lease
Sublease
Lease Assignment

Every business, whether small or large, must find suitable space for its activities. For the sole proprietor, the studio may be in the home. For a larger enterprise, the studio or office is likely to be in an office building. While some businesses may own their offices, most will rent space from a landlord. The terms of the rental lease may benefit or harm the business. Large sums of money are likely to be paid not only for rent, but also for security, escalators, and other charges. In addition, the tenant is likely to spend additional money to customize the space by building in offices, darkrooms, reception areas, and the like. Form 45 and the accompanying analysis of how to negotiate a lease are designed to protect the tenant from a variety of troublesome issues that may arise.

The old saw about real estate is, "Location, location, location." Location builds value, but the intended use of the rented premises must be legal if value is to accrue. For example, sole proprietors often work from home. In many places, zoning laws govern the uses that can be made of property. It may be that an office at home violates zoning restrictions against commercial activity. What is fine in one town—a studio in an extra room, for example—may violate the zoning in the next town. Before renting or buying a residential property with the intention of also doing business there, it's important to check with an attorney and find out whether the business activity will be legal.

In fact, it's a good idea to retain a knowledgeable real estate attorney to negotiate a lease, especially if the rent is substantial and the term is long. That attorney can also give advice as to questions of legality. For example, what if the premises are in a commercial zone, but the entrepreneur wants to live and work there? This can be illegal and raise the specter of eviction by either the landlord or the local authorities.

In addition, the lease contains what is called the "use" clause. This specifies the purpose for which the premises are being rented. Often the lease will state that the premises can be used for the specified purpose and no other use is permitted. This limitation has to be observed or the tenant will run the risk of losing the premises. The tenant therefore has to seek the widest possible scope of use, certainly a scope sufficient to permit all of the intended business activities.

Another risk in terms of legality involves waste products or emissions that may not be legal in certain areas. Again, an attorney should be able to give advice about whether a planned activity might violate environmental protection as well as zoning laws.

The premises must lend themselves to the intended use. Loading ramps and elevators must be large enough to accommodate whatever must be moved in to set up the office (unless the tenant is willing and able to use a crane to move large pieces of equipment in through windows) and any products that need to be shipped once business is underway. Electric service must be adequate for air conditioning, computers, and other machinery. It must be possible to obtain telephone service and high-speed Internet connections. If the building is commercial and the tenant intends to work on weekends and evenings, then it will necessary to ascertain whether the building is open and heated on weekends and evenings. If clients may come during off hours, it is even more important to make sure the building is open and elevator service is available.

Who will pay for bringing in electric lines, installing air conditioners, building any needed offices, installing fixtures, painting, or making other improvements? This will depend on the rental market, which dictates the relative bargaining strengths of the landlord and tenant. The lease (or an attached rider) must specify who will pay for each such improvement. It must also specify that the landlord gives the tenant permission to build what the tenant needs.

A related issue is who will own structures and equipment affixed to the premises when the lease term ends. Since the standard lease gives ownership to the landlord of anything affixed to the premises, the tenant must have this provision amended if anything of this nature is to be removed from the premises or sold to a new incoming tenant at the end of the lease term.

If the tenant has to make a significant investment in the costs of moving into and improving the premises, the tenant will want to be able to stay long enough to amortize this investment. One way to do this is to seek a long lease term, such as ten years. However, the landlord will inevitably want the rent to increase during the lease term. This leads to a dilemma for the tenant who can't be certain about the needs of the business or the rental market so far into the future.

One approach is to seek the longest possible lease, but negotiate for a right to terminate the lease. Another strategy would be to seek a shorter initial term, but have options to extend the lease for additional terms at agreed upon rents. So, instead of asking for a ten-year lease, the tenant might ask for a four-year lease with two options for additional extensions of three years each.

Yet another tactic, and probably a wise provision to insist on in any event, is to have a right to sublet all or part of the premises or to assign the lease. The lease typically forbids this, so the tenant will have to demand such rights. Having the ability to sublet or assign offers another way to take a long lease while keeping the option to exit the premises if more space is needed, the rent becomes too high, or other circumstances necessitate a move. However, the right to sublet or assign will be of little use if the real estate market turns down, so it should probably be a supplement to a right to terminate or an option to renew.

Part of the problem with making a long-term commitment is that the stated rent is likely not going to be all of the rent. In other words, the lease may say that the rent is $2,400 per month for the first two years and then escalates to $3,000 per month for the next two years. But the tenant may have to pay for other increases or services. It is common for leases to provide for escalators based on increases in real estate taxes, increases in inflation, or increases in indexes designed to measure labor or operating costs. In fact, the standard lease will make the tenant responsible for all nonstructural repairs that are needed. The tenant has to evaluate all of these charges not only for reasonableness but for the impact on what will truly be paid each month. There may also be charges for refuse removal, cleaning (if the landlord provides this), window washing, water, and other services or supplies. If the landlord has installed submeters for electricity, this may result in paying far more to the landlord than would have been paid to the utility company. It may be possible to lessen the markup, obtain direct metering, or, at the least, factor this cost into considerations for the budget.

Faced with costs that may increase, the tenant should try to determine what is realistically likely to occur. Then, as a safeguard, the tenant might ask for ceilings on the amounts that can be charged in the various potential cost categories.

Leases are usually written documents. Whenever a written agreement exists between two parties, all amendments and modifications should also be in writing and signed by both parties. For example, the lease will probably require one or two months' rent as security. The tenant will want this rent to be kept in an interest bearing account in the tenant's name. But if the parties agree to use part of the security to pay the rent at some point, this should be documented in a signed, written agreement.

The tenant should also seek to avoid having personal liability for the lease. Of course, if the tenant is doing business as a sole proprietor, the tenant by signing the lease will assume personal liability for payments. But if the tenant is a corporation, it would certainly be best not to have any officers or owners give personal guarantees that would place their personal assets at risk.

Leases can grow to become thick sheaves of paper filled with innumerable clauses of legalese. Since the lease agreement can be such an important one for a business, it is ideal to have a knowledgeable attorney as a companion when entering its maze of provisions. If an attorney is too expensive and the lease is short-term and at an affordable rent, then this discussion may give a clue that will help the tenant emerge from lease negotiations with success.

Form 48 is an educational tool. It has been drafted more favorably to the tenant than would usually be the case. Because it would be unlikely for the tenant to present a lease to the landlord, form 48 shows what the tenant might hope to obtain from the negotiations that begin with a lease form presented to the tenant by the landlord.

Forms 49 and 50 relate to a transformation of the role of the tenant. Whether to move to supe-rior space, lessen cash outflow, or make a profit, the tenant may want to assign the lease or sub-let all or a portion of the premises. Form 49 is for a sublease in which the tenant essentially becomes a landlord to a subtenant. Here the ten-ant must negotiate the same issues that were negotiated with the landlord, but from the other point of view. So, for example, while a corporate tenant would resist having its officers or owners give personal guarantees for a lease, when sub-letting the same corporate tenant might demand such personal guarantees from a corporate sub-tenant. Form 50 for the assignment of a lease is less complicated than the sublease form. It essentially replaces the tenant with an assignee who becomes the new tenant and is fully responsible to comply with the lease. A key issue in such an assignment is whether the orig-inal tenant will remain liable to the landlord if the assignee fails to perform. A related issue

with a corporate assignee would be whether the assignee would give a personal guarantee of its performance. In any event, both the sublease and the assignment will usually require the written consent of the landlord. This consent can take the form of a letter signed by both the tenant and the landlord. In the case of an assign-ment, the letter of consent could also clarify whether the original tenant would have contin-uing liability pursuant to the lease.

Filling in Form 48 (Lease)

In the Preamble fill in the date and the names and addresses of the parties. In Paragraph 1 give the suite number, the approximate square footage, and floor for the premises as well as the address for the building. In Paragraph 2 give the number of years as well as the commencement and termination dates for the lease. In Para-graph 3 give a renewal term, if any, and indicate what modifications of the lease would take effect for the renewal term. In Paragraph 5 indi-cate the annual rent. In Paragraph 6 specify the number of month's rent that will be given as a security deposit. In Paragraph 7 indicate any work to be performed by the landlord and the completion date for that work. In Paragraph 8 specify the use that the tenant will make of the premises. In Paragraph 9 give the details as to alterations and installations to be done by the tenant and also indicate ownership and right to remove or sell these alterations and installations at the termination of the term. In Paragraph 10 indicate any repairs for which the tenant shall be responsible. In Paragraph 13 check the appropriate box with respect to air condition-ing, fill in the blanks if the tenant is not paying for electricity or the landlord is not paying for water, and indicate who will be responsible for the cost of refuse removal. In Paragraph 14 state whether or not the landlord will have a key to provide it access to the premises. In Paragraph

15 indicate the amount of liability insurance the tenant will be expected to carry as well as any limitation in terms of the landlord's liability for tenant's losses due to fire or other casualty affecting the building. In Paragraph 18 indicate which state's laws shall govern the agreement. Have both parties sign and append a rider, if necessary. Leases frequently have riders, which are attachments to the lease. This gives the space to add additional provisions or amplify details that require more space such as how construction or installations will be done. If there is such a rider, it should be signed by both parties.

Negotiation Checklist for Form 48

❏ If the tenant is a corporation, do not agree that any owner or officer of the corporation will have personal liability with respect to the lease.

❏ Consider whether, in view of the rental market, it may be possible to negotiate for a number of months rent-free at the start of the lease (in part, perhaps, to allow time for construction to be done by the tenant).

❏ In addition to rent-free months, determine what construction must be done and whether the landlord will do the construction or pay for all or part of the construction. (Paragraph 7)

❏ Since landlords generally rent based on gross square footage (which may be 15–20 percent more than net or usable square footage), carefully measure the net square footage to make certain it is adequate. (Paragraph 1)

❏ Specify the location and approximate square footage of the rented premises as well as the location of the building. (Paragraph 1)

❏ Indicate the duration of the term, including starting and ending dates. (Paragraph 2)

❏ Determine what will happen, including whether damages will be payable to the

Tenant, if the landlord is unable to deliver possession of the premises at the starting date of the lease.

❏ Especially if the lease gives the tenant the right to terminate, seek the longest possible lease term. (Paragraphs 2 and 4)

❏ Specify that the lease shall become month-to-month after the term expires. (Paragraph 2)

❏ If the landlord has the right to terminate the lease because the building is to be demolished or taken by eminent domain (i.e., acquired by a governmental body), consider whether damages should be payable by the landlord based on the remaining term of the lease.

❏ If the tenant is going to move out, consider whether it would be acceptable for the landlord to show the space prior to the tenant's departure and, if so, for how long prior to the departure and under what circumstances.

❏ Seek an option to renew for a specified term, such as three or five years, or perhaps several options to renew, such as for three years and then for another three years. (Paragraph 3)

❏ Seek the right to terminate the lease on written notice to the landlord. (Paragraph 4)

❏ Although the bankruptcy laws will affect what happens to the lease in the event of the tenant's bankruptcy, do not agree in the lease that the tenant's bankruptcy or insolvency will be grounds for termination of the lease.

❏ Specify the rent and indicate when it should be paid. (Paragraph 5)

❏ Carefully review any proposed increases in rent during the term of the lease. Try to resist adjustments for inflation. In any case, if an inflation index or a porter's wage index is to be used to increase the rent, study the particular index to see if the result is likely to be acceptable in terms of budgeting.

❏ Resist being responsible for additional rent based on a prorated share of increases in real estate taxes and, if such a provision is included, make certain how it is calculated and that it applies only to increases and not the entire tax.

❏ Resist having any of landlord's cost treated as additional rent.

❏ Indicate the amount of the security deposit and require that it be kept in a separate, interest-bearing account. (Paragraph 6)

❏ Specify when the security deposit will be returned to the tenant. (Paragraph 6)

❏ If the tenant is not going to accept the premises "as is," indicate what work must be performed by the landlord and give a completion date for that work. (Paragraph 7)

❏ If the landlord is to do work, consider what the consequences should be in the event that the landlord is unable to complete the work on time.

❏ Agree to return the premises in broom clean condition and good order except for normal wear and tear. (Paragraph 7)

❏ Seek the widest possible latitude with respect to what type of businesses the tenant may operate in the premises. (Paragraph 8)

❏ Consider asking that "for no other purpose" be stricken from the use clause.

❏ If the use may involve residential as well as business use, determine whether this is legal. If it is, the use clause might be widened to include the residential use.

❏ Obtain whatever permissions are needed for tenant's alterations or installment of equipment in the lease, rather than asking for permission after the lease has been signed. (Paragraph 9)

❏ If the tenant wants to own any installations or equipment affixed to the premises (such as an air conditioning system), this should be specified in the lease. (Paragraph 9)

❏ If the tenant owns certain improvements pursuant to the lease and might sell these to an incoming tenant, the mechanics of such a sale would have to be detailed because the new tenant might not take possession of the premises immediately and the value of what is to be sold will depend to some extent on the nature of the lease negotiated by the new tenant. (Paragraph 9)

❏ Nothing should prevent the tenant from removing its furniture and equipment that is not affixed to the premises. (Paragraph 9)

❏ Make landlord responsible for repairs in general and limit the responsibility of the tenant to specified types of repairs only. (Paragraph 10)

❏ Obtain the right to sublet all or part of the premises. (Paragraph 11)

❏ Obtain the right to assign the lease. (Paragraph 11)

❏ If the landlord has the right to approve a sublease or assignment, specify the basis on which approval will be determined (such as "good character and sound finances") and indicate that approval may not be withheld unreasonably. (Paragraph 11)

❏ If the tenant has paid for extensive improvements to the premises, a sublessee or assignee might be charged for a "fixture" fee.

❏ If a fixture fee is to be charged, or if the lease is being assigned pursuant to the sale of a business, do not give the landlord the right to share in the proceeds of the fixture fee or sale of the business.

❏ Guarantee the tenant's right to quiet enjoyment of the premises. (Paragraph 12)

❏ Make certain that tenant will be able to use the office seven days a week, twenty-four hours a day. (Paragraph 12)

❏ Review the certificate of occupancy as well as the lease before agreeing to occupy the premises in accordance with the lease, the building's certificate of occupancy, and all relevant laws. (Paragraph 12)

❏ Determine who will provide and pay for utilities and services, such as air conditioning, heat, water, electricity, cleaning, window cleaning, and refuse removal. (Paragraph 13)

❏ The landlord will want the right to gain access to the premises, especially for repairs or in the event of an emergency. (Paragraph 14)

❏ Decide whether the landlord and its employees are trustworthy enough to be given keys to the premises, which has the advantage of avoiding a forced entry in the event of an emergency. (Paragraph 14)

❏ Make the landlord an additional named insured for the tenant's liability insurance policy. (Paragraph 15)

❏ Fix the amount of liability insurance that the tenant must maintain at a reasonable level. (Paragraph 15)

❏ Specify that the landlord will carry casualty and fire insurance for the building. (Paragraph 15)

❏ Indicate what limit of liability, if any, the landlord is willing to accept for interruption or harm to tenant's business. (Paragraph 15)

❏ Agree that the lease is subordinate to any mortgage or underlying lease on the building. (Paragraph 16)

❏ If the lease requires waiver of the right to trial by jury, consider whether this is acceptable.

❏ If the lease provides for payment of the legal fees of the landlord in the event of litigation, seek to have this either stricken or changed so that the legal fees of the winning party are paid.

❏ Indicate that any rider, which is an attachment to the lease to add clauses or explain the details of certain aspects of the lease such as those relating to construction, is made part of the lease.

❏ Review the standard provisions in the introductory pages and compare them with Paragraph 18.

Filling in Form 49 (Sublease)

In the Preamble fill in the date and the names and addresses of the parties. In Paragraph 1 give the information about the lease between the landlord and tenant and attach a copy of that lease as Exhibit A of the sublease. In Paragraph 2 give the suite number, the approximate square footage, and floor for the premises as well as the address for the building. If only part of the space is to be subleased, indicate which part. In Paragraph 3 give the number of years as well as the commencement and termination dates for the lease. In Paragraph 4 indicate the annual rent. In Paragraph 5 specify the number of months' rent that will be given as a security deposit. In Paragraph 7 specify the use that the subtenant will make of the premises. In Paragraph 8 indicate whether the subtenant will be excused from compliance with any of the provisions of the lease or whether some provisions will be modified with respect to the subtenant. For Paragraph 10, attach the landlord's consent as Exhibit B if that is needed. For Paragraph 11, if the tenant is leaving property for the use of the subtenant, attach Exhibit C detailing that property. If the lease has been recorded, perhaps with the county clerk, indicate where the recordation can be found in Paragraph 14. Add any additional provisions in Paragraph 15. In Paragraph 16 indicate which state's laws shall govern the agreement. Both parties should then sign the sublease.

Negotiation Checklist for Form 49

❑ If the subtenant is a corporation, consider whether to insist that owners or officers of the corporation will have personal liability with respect to the sublease. (See Other Provisions.)

❑ If possible, do not agree to rent-free months at the start of the sublease or to paying for construction for the subtenant.

❑ Specify the location and approximate square footage of the rented premises as well as the location of the building. (Paragraphs 1 and 2)

❑ Indicate the duration of the term, including starting and ending dates. (Paragraph 3)

❑ Specify that the lease shall become month-to-month after the term expires. (Paragraph 3)

❑ Disclaim any liability if, for some reason, the tenant is unable to deliver possession of the premises at the starting date of the sublease.

❑ Do not give the subtenant a right to terminate,

❑ Do not give the subtenant an option to renew.

❑ Have a right to show the space for three or six months prior to the end of the sublease.

❑ State in the sublease that the subtenant's bankruptcy or insolvency will be grounds for termination of the lease.

❑ Specify the rent and indicate when it should be paid. (Paragraph 4)

❑ Require that rent be paid to the tenant (which allows the tenant to monitor payments), unless the tenant believes that it would be safe to allow the subtenant to pay the landlord directly. (Paragraph 4)

❑ Carefully review any proposed increases in rent during the term of the lease and make certain that the sublease will at least match such increases.

❑ Indicate the amount of the security deposit (Paragraph 5)

❑ Specify that reductions may be made to the security deposit for sums owed the tenant before the balance is returned to the subtenant. (Paragraph 5)

❑ Require the subtenant to return the premises in broom clean condition and good order except for normal wear and tear. (Paragraph 6)

❑ Specify very specifically what type of businesses the tenant may operate in the premises. (Paragraph 7)

❑ Do not allow "for no other purpose" to be stricken from the use clause.

❑ Nothing should prevent the subtenant from removing its furniture and equipment that is not affixed to the premises.

❑ Require the subtenant to occupy the premises in accordance with the sublease, the lease, the building's certificate of occupancy, and all relevant laws. (Paragraph 8)

❑ Indicate if any of the lease's provisions will not be binding on the subtenant or have been modified. (Paragraph 8)

❑ State clearly that tenant is not obligated to perform the landlord's duties and that the subtenant must look to the landlord for such performance. (Paragraph 9)

❑ Agree to cooperate with the subtenant in requiring the landlord to meet its obligations, subject to a right of reimbursement from subtenant for any costs or attorney's fees the tenant must pay in the course of cooperating. (Paragraph 9)

❏ If the landlord's consent must be obtained for the sublet, attach a copy of the consent to the sublease as Exhibit B. (Paragraph 10)

❏ If tenant is going to let its property be used by the subtenant, attach an inventory of this property as Exhibit C and require that the property be returned in good condition. (Paragraph 11)

❏ Have the subtenant indemnify the tenant against any claims with respect to the premises that arise after the effective date of the sublease.

❏ Do not give the subtenant the right to subsublet all or part of the premises.

❏ Do not give the subtenant the right to assign the sublease.

❏ If the lease has been recorded with a government office, indicate how it can be located. (Paragraph 14)

❏ Add any additional provisions that may be necessary. (Paragraph 15)

❏ Review the standard provisions in the introductory pages and compare them with Paragraph 16.

Filling in Form 50 (Lease Assignment)

In the Preamble fill in the date and the names and addresses of the parties. In Paragraph 1 give the information about the lease between the landlord and tenant and attach a copy of that lease as Exhibit A of the lease assignment. In Paragraph 3 enter an amount, even a small amount such as $10, as cash consideration. For Paragraph 8, attach the landlord's consent as Exhibit B if that is needed. If the lease has been recorded, perhaps with the county clerk, indicate where the recordation can be found in Paragraph 9. Add any additional provisions in Paragraph 10. In Paragraph 11 indicate which state's laws shall govern the agreement. Both parties should then sign the assignment.

Checklist for Form 50

❏ In obtaining the landlord's consent in a simple letter, demand that the tenant not be liable for the lease and that the landlord look only to the assignee for performance. (See Other Provisions.)

❏ It would be wise to specify the amount of security deposits or any other money held in escrow by the landlord for the tenant/assignor.

❏ Consideration should exchange hands and, if the lease has extra value because of tenant's improvements or an upturn in the rental market, the consideration may be substantial. (Paragraph 3)

❏ Require the assignee to perform as if it were the original tenant in the lease. (Paragraph 4)

❏ Have the assignee indemnify the tenant/assignor with respect to any claims and costs that may arise from the lease after the date of the assignment. (Paragraph 5)

❏ Make the assignee's obligations run to the benefit of the landlord as well as the tenant. (Paragraph 6)

❏ Indicate that the assignor has the right to assign and the premises are not encumbered in any way.

❏ If the landlord's consent must be obtained for the assignment, attach a copy of the consent to the sublease as Exhibit B. (Paragraph 8)

❏ If the lease has been recorded with a government office, indicate how it can be located. (Paragraph 9)

❏ Add any additional provisions that may be necessary. (Paragraph 10)

❏ Review the standard provisions in the introductory pages and compare them with Paragraph 11.

Other Provisions That Can Be Used with Forms 49 and 50

❑ Personal Guaranty. The tenant who sublets or assigns is bringing in another party to help carry the weight of tenant's responsibilities pursuant to the lease. If the sublessee or assignee is a corporation, the tenant will only be able to go after the corporate assets if the other party fails to meet its obligations. The tenant may, therefore, want to have officers or owners agree to personal liability if the corporation breaches the lease. One or more principals could sign a guaranty, which would be attached to and made a part of the sublease or assignment. The guaranty that follows is for a sublease but could easily be altered to be for an assignment:

Personal Guaranty. This guaranty by the Undersigned is given to induce _____ _____ (hereinafter referred to as the "Tenant") to enter into the sublease dated as of the _____ day of _____, 20_____, between the Tenant and _____ (hereinafter referred to as the "Sublessee"). That sublease would not be entered into by the Tenant without this guaranty, which is made part of the sublease agreement. The relationship of the Undersigned to the Sublessee is as follows_____ _____. Undersigned fully and unconditionally guarantees to Tenant the full payment of all rent due and other amounts payable pursuant to the Sublease. The Undersigned shall remain fully bound on this guaranty regardless of any extension, modification, waiver, release, discharge or substitution any party with respect to the Sublease. The Under-signed waives any requirement of notice and, in the event of default, may be sued directly without any requirement that the

Tenant first sue the Sublessee. In addition, the Undersigned guarantees the payment of all attorneys' fees and costs incurred in the enforcement of this guaranty. This guaranty is unlimited as to amount or duration and may only be modified or terminated by a written instrument signed by all parties to the Sublease and Guaranty. This guaranty shall be binding and inure to the benefit of the parties hereto, their heirs, successors, assigns, and personal representatives.

❑ Assignor's Obligations. In the case of an assignment, the tenant/assignor may ask the landlord for a release from its obligations pursuant to the lease. If the landlord gives such a release, perhaps in return for some consideration or because the new tenant has excellent credentials, the tenant would want this to be included in a written instrument. This would probably be the letter of consent that the landlord would have to give to permit the assignment to take place. Shown here are options to release the tenant and also to do the opposite and affirm the tenant's continuing obligations.

Assignor's Obligations. Check the applicable provision: ❑ This Agreement relieves and discharges the Assignor from any continuing liability or obligation with respect to the Lease after the effective date of the lease assignment. ❑ This Agreement does not relieve, modify, discharge, or otherwise affect the obligations of the Assignor under the Lease and the direct and primary nature thereof.

COMMERCIAL LEASE, SUBLEASE, LEASE ASSIGNMENT

Commercial Lease

AGREEMENT, dated the _____ day of _____, 20 _____, between _____
_____ (hereinafter referred to as the "Tenant"),
whose address is _____
_____ and
_____(hereinafter referred to as the
"Landlord"), whose address is _____
_____

WHEREAS, the Tenant wishes to rent premises for office use;

WHEREAS, the Landlord has premises for rental for such office use;

NOW, THEREFORE, in consideration of the foregoing premises and the mutual covenants hereinafter set forth and other valuable considerations, the parties hereto agree as follows:

1. **Demised premises.** The premises rented hereunder are Suite # _____, comprising approximately _____ square feet, on the _____ floor of the building located at the following address _____ in the city or town of _____ in the state of _____.

2. **Term.** The term shall be for a period of _____ years (unless the term shall sooner cease and expire pursuant to the terms of this Lease), commencing on the ____ day of _____, 20__, and ending on the ____ day of _____, 20__. At the expiration of the term and any renewals thereof pursuant to Paragraph 3, the Lease shall become a month to month tenancy with all other provisions of the Lease in full force and effect.

3. **Option to Renew.** The Tenant shall have an option to renew the lease for a period of ____ years. Such option must be exercised in writing prior to the expiration of the term specified in Paragraph 2. During such renewal term, all other provisions of the Lease shall remain in full force and effect except for the following modifications
_____

4. **Termination.** The Tenant shall retain the right to terminate this Lease at the end of any month by giving the Landlord thirty (30) days written notice.

5. **Rent.** The annual rent shall be $_____, payable in equal monthly installments on the first day of each month to the Landlord at Landlord's address or such other address as Landlord may specify. The first month's rent shall be paid on signing this Lease.

6. **Security Deposit.** The security deposit shall be in the amount of ___ month(s) rent and shall be paid by check at the time of signing this Lease. The security deposit shall be increased at such times as the monthly rent increases, so as to maintain the security deposit at the level of ___ month(s) rent. The security deposit shall be kept in a separate interest bearing account with interest payable to the Tenant. The security deposit, after reduction for any sums owed to Landlord, shall be returned to the Tenant within ten days of the Tenant's vacating the premises.

7. **Condition of Premises.** Tenant has inspected the premises and accepts them in "as is" condition except for the following work to be performed by Landlord _____
_____ and completed by _____, 20___. At the termination of the Lease, Tenant shall remove all its property and return possession of the premises broom clean and in good order and condition, normal wear and tear excepted, to the Landlord.

8. **Use**. The Tenant shall use and occupy the premises for _____ and for no other purpose.

9. Alterations. Tenant shall obtain Landlord's written approval to make any alterations that are structural or affect utility services, plumbing, or electric lines, except that Landlord consents to the following alterations _____. In addition, Landlord consents to the installation by the Tenant of the following equipment and fixtures _____ _____. Landlord shall own all improvements affixed to the premises, except that the Tenant shall own the following improvements _____ and have the right to either remove them or sell them to a new incoming tenant. If Landlord consents to the ownership and sale of improvements by the Tenant, such sale shall be conducted in the following way _____. If Landlord consents to Tenant's ownership and right to remove certain improvements, Tenant shall repair any damages caused by such removal. Nothing contained herein shall prevent Tenant from removing its trade fixtures, moveable office furniture and equipment, and other items not affixed to the premises.

10. Repairs. Repairs to the building and common areas shall be the responsibility of the Landlord. In addition, repairs to the premises shall be the responsibility of the Landlord except for the following_____ _____.

11. Assignment and Subletting. Tenant shall have the right to assign this Lease to an assignee of good character and sound finances subject to obtaining the written approval of the Landlord, which approval shall not be unreasonably withheld. In addition, Tenant shall have the right to sublet all or a portion of the premises on giving written notice to the Landlord.

12. Quiet Enjoyment. Tenant may quietly and peaceably enjoy occupancy of the premises. Tenant shall have access to the premises at all times and, if necessary, shall be given a key to enter the building. Tenant shall use and occupy the premises in accordance with this Lease, the building's certificate of occupancy, and all relevant laws.

13. Utilities and Services. During the heating season the Landlord at its own expense shall supply heat to the premises at all times on business days and on Saturdays and Sundays. The Landlord ❑ shall ❑ shall not supply air conditioning for the premises at its own expense. The Tenant shall pay the electric bills for the meter for the premises, unless another arrangement exists as follows _____. The Landlord shall provide and pay for water for the premises, unless another arrangement exists as follows _____. Tenant shall be responsible for and pay for having its own premises cleaned, including the securing of licensed window cleaners. ❑ Tenant ❑ Landlord shall be responsible to pay for the removal of refuse from the premises. If Landlord is responsible to pay for such removal, the Tenant shall comply with Landlord's reasonable regulations regarding the manner, time, and location of refuse pickups.

14. Access to Premises. Landlord and its agents shall have the right, upon reasonable notice to the Tenant, to enter the premises to make repairs, improvements, or replacements. In the event of emergency, the Landlord and its agents may enter the premises without notice to the Tenant. Tenant ❑ shall ❑ shall not provide the Landlord with keys for the premises.

Sublease

15. Insurance. Tenant agrees to carry liability insurance and name Landlord as an additional named insured under its policy and furnish to Landlord certificates showing liability coverage of not less than $_____ for the premises. Such company shall give the Landlord ten (10) days notice prior to cancellation of any such policy. Failure to obtain or keep in force such liability insurance shall allow Landlord to obtain such coverage and charge the amount of premiums as additional rent payable by the Tenant. Landlord agrees to carry casualty and fire insurance on the building, but shall not have any liability in excess of $_____ with respect to the operation of the Tenant's business.

16. Subordination. This Lease is subordinate and subject to all ground or underlying leases and any mortgages that may now or hereafter affect such leases or the building of which the premises are a part. The operation of this provision shall be automatic and not require any further consent from Tenant. To confirm this subordination, Tenant shall promptly execute any documentation that Landlord may request.

17. Rider. Additional terms may be contained in a Rider attached to and made part of this Lease.

18. Miscellany. This Lease shall be binding upon the parties hereto, their heirs, successors, assigns, and personal representatives. This Agreement constitutes the entire understanding between the parties. Its terms can be modified only by an instrument in writing signed by both parties unless specified to the contrary herein. A waiver of a breach of any of the provisions of this Agreement shall not be construed as a continuing waiver of other breaches of the same or other provisions hereof. This Agreement shall be governed by the laws of the State of _____.

IN WITNESS WHEREOF, the parties hereto have signed this Agreement as of the date first set forth above.

Tenant _____   Landlord _____
              Company Name   Company Name

By_____   By_____
          Authorized Signatory, Title   Authorized Signatory, Title

AGREEMENT, dated the _____ day of _____, 20 _____, between _____ (hereinafter referred to as the "Tenant"), whose address is _____ _____ and _____(hereinafter referred to as the "Subtenant"), whose address is _____.

WHEREAS, the Tenant wishes to sublet certain rental premises for office use;

WHEREAS, the Subtenant wishes to occupy such rental premises for such office use;

NOW, THEREFORE, in consideration of the foregoing premises and the mutual covenants hereinafter set forth and other valuable considerations, the parties hereto agree as follows:

1. The Lease. The premises are subject to a Lease dated as of the ____ day of _____, 20___, between _____ (referred to therein as the "Tenant") and _____ (referred to therein as the "Landlord") for the premises described as _____ and located at _____ _____. A copy of the Lease is attached hereto as Exhibit A and made part hereof. Subtenant shall have no right to negotiate with the Landlord with respect to the Lease.

2. Demised premises. The premises rented hereunder are Suite # _____, comprising approximately _____ square feet, on the _____ floor of the building located at the following address _____ in the city or town of _____ in the state of _____. If only a portion of the premises subject to the Lease are to be sublet, the sublet portion is specified as follows _____.

3. Term. The term shall be for a period of ____ years (unless the term shall sooner cease and expire pursuant to the terms of this Sublease), commencing on the ____ day of _____, 20__, and ending on the ____ day of _____, 20__. At the expiration of the term and any renewals thereof pursuant to Paragraph 3, the Sublease shall become a month to month tenancy with all other provisions of the Sublease in full force and effect.

4. Rent. The annual rent shall be $_____, payable in equal monthly installments on the first day of each month to the Tenant at Tenant's address or such other address as Tenant may specify. The Subtenant shall also pay as additional rent any other charges that the Tenant must pay to the Landlord pursuant to the lease. Subtenant shall make payments of rent and other charges to the Tenant only and not to Landlord. The first month's rent shall be paid to the Tenant on signing this Sublease.

5. Security Deposit. The security deposit shall be in the amount of ___ month(s) rent and shall be paid by check at the time of signing this Sublease. The security deposit shall be increased at such times as the monthly rent increases, so as to maintain the security deposit at the level of ___ month(s) rent. The security deposit, after reduction for any sums owed to Tenant, shall be returned to the Subtenant within ten days of the Subtenant's vacating the premises.

6. Condition of Premises. Subtenant has inspected the premises and accepts them in "as is" condition. At the termination of the Sublease, Subtenant shall remove all its property and return possession of the premises broom clean and in good order and condition, normal wear and tear excepted, to the Tenant.

7. Use. The Subtenant shall use and occupy the premises for _____ and for no other purpose.

8. Compliance. Subtenant shall use and occupy the premises in accordance with this Sublease. In addition, the Subtenant shall obey the terms of the Lease (and any agreements to which the Lease, by its terms, is subject), the building's certificate of occupancy, and all relevant laws. If the Subtenant is not to be subject to certain terms of the Lease or if any terms of the Lease are to be modified for purposes of this Sublease, the specifics are as follows _____

Lease Assignment

---

9. **Landlord's Duties.** The Tenant is not obligated to perform the duties of the Landlord pursuant to the Lease. Any failure of the Landlord to perform its duties shall be subject to the Subtenant dealing directly with the Landlord until Landlord fulfills its obligations. Copies of any notices sent to the Landlord by the Subtenant shall also be provided to the Tenant. Tenant shall cooperate with Subtenant in the enforcement of Subtenant's rights against the Landlord, but any costs or fees incurred by the Tenant in the course of such cooperation shall be reimbursed by the Subtenant pursuant to Paragraph 12.

10. **Landlord's Consent.** If the Landlord's consent must be obtained for this Sublease, that consent has been obtained by the Tenant and is attached hereto as Exhibit B and made part hereof.

11. **Inventory.** An inventory of Tenant's fixtures, furnishings, equipment, and other property to be left in the premises is attached hereto as Exhibit C and made part hereof. Subtenant agrees to maintain these items in good condition and repair and to replace or reimburse the Tenant for any of these items that are missing or damaged at the termination of the subtenancy.

12. **Indemnification.** The Subtenant shall indemnify and hold harmless the Tenant from any and all claims, suits, costs, damages, judgments, settlements, attorney's fees, court costs, or any other expenses arising with respect to the Lease subsequent to the date of this Agreement. The Tenant shall indemnify and hold harmless the Subtenant from any and all claims, suits, costs, damages, judgments, settlements, attorney's fees, court costs, or any other expenses arising with respect to the Lease prior to the date of this Agreement.

13. **Assignment and Subletting.** Subtenant shall not have the right to assign this Lease or to sublet all or a portion of the premises without the written approval of the Landlord.

14. **Recordation.** The Lease has been recorded in the office of _____ on the ____ day of _____, 20___, and is located at _____.

15. **Additional provisions:** _____
_____
_____.

16. **Miscellany.** This Lease shall be binding upon the parties hereto, their heirs, successors, assigns, and personal representatives. This Agreement constitutes the entire understanding between the parties. Its terms can be modified only by an instrument in writing signed by both parties unless specified to the contrary herein. A waiver of a breach of any of the provisions of this Agreement shall not be construed as a continuing waiver of other breaches of the same or other provisions hereof. This Agreement shall be governed by the laws of the State of _____.

IN WITNESS WHEREOF, the parties hereto have signed this Agreement as of the date first set forth above.

Subtenant _____   Tenant _____
             Company Name   Company Name

By_____   By_____

Authorized Signatory, Title   Authorized Signatory, Title

Promissory Note

A promissory note is documentation of a loan that has been made either to an individual or to a company. The note includes the amount of the loan, the rate of interest, the schedule for payments of principal and interest, and the term during which the loan will be outstanding. At the end of the term, the loan must be repaid in full.

One of the key issues is how often interest will be calculated. If the loan is for a year, interest is calculated daily, and payments of interest will be made on a monthly basis. The borrower will end up having the loan amount increase with each daily addition of interest and then paying the monthly interest payment on the principal plus the added interest. This "compound interest" has been called the Eighth Wonder of the World because of the way it makes money increase. Any borrower has to take care in reviewing how often interest is charged in relation to how often interest is paid to the lender.

The way in which the principal is repaid is also important. Will there be monthly installments? If so, will the loan be repaid in full by the expiration of its term? Or will there be a partial or total balloon (i.e., a part of the loan that must be paid on the end date of the term)?

In the event of the borrower's default on the payment of either interest or principal payments when due, will the lender have the right to accelerate all of the borrower's obligations and demand immediate repayment? The note may have a specific provision dealing with this or say something like, "Time is of the essence with respect to payments due hereunder." The borrower will ideally have the right to prepay the loan so that the interest payments can be avoided if, in fact, it becomes possible to prepay the principal amount.

States have laws forbidding interest rates that are too high. Such rates are considered usury.

While usury rates vary widely from state to state, it would be wise to determine the usury limit of the state whose laws will govern the promissory note. As a precaution, form 51 includes a saving provision that would change payment of usurious interest into payments of principal in order to save the validity of the promissory note.

The promissory note may also place an obligation on the borrower to pay the lender's legal fees and other expenses in the event that litigation is necessary to enforce the note and collect monies due.

Also, the lender may insist that the promissory note be guaranteed. If an individual is signing the note, the guarantor could be someone with more substantial assets who would agree to honor the terms of the note if the borrower failed to do so. If a corporation is signing the note, the guarantor might be a shareholder of the corporation who in the absence of such a guaranty would not be liable because of the limited liability accorded to corporate shareholders.

Filling in the Form

Fill in the date and the names and addresses for the borrower and the lender. In Paragraph 1, state the amount of the loan. In Paragraph 2, indicate the duration of the loan. In Paragraph 3, give the interest rate and check the applicable box for the frequency with which the interest will be computed and charged to the loan. In Paragraph 4, indicate when payments of interest must be made, and do the same for payments of principal in Paragraph 5. In Paragraph 8, indicate which state's laws will govern whether the interest rate is usurious. This state should be where at least one or possibly both of the parties are located. The borrower should then sign the promissory note.

Negotiation Checklist

❑ Specify the loan amount. (Paragraph 1)

❑ Give the term of the loan. (Paragraph 2)

❑ Determine the frequency with which interest will be computed. The borrower prefers that the interest be computed less often, such as once a year on the anniversary of the loan. (Paragraph 3)

❑ Indicate when payments of interest shall be made. (Paragraph 4)

❑ Indicate when payments of principal shall be made and in what amounts. (Paragraph 5)

❑ State the consequences for default. The lender may wish to add, "Time is of the essence for purposes of this Promissory Note." (Paragraph 6)

❑ The borrower will want a provision allowing prepayment. (Paragraph 7)

❑ Avoid violating state usury laws. (Paragraph 8)

❑ The lender may want the borrower to pay attorney's fees and other expenses incurred by the lender in the event of the borrower's default. (Paragraph 9)

❑ Review the standard provisions in the introductory pages to see if any should be incorporated.

❑ The lender may want a guarantor for the promissory note. The borrower will have to weigh the advantages and disadvantages of agreeing to this. (See other provisions.)

Other provisions that can be added to form 51:

❑ Guaranty. A lender might require an individual other than the borrower to guarantee that the obligations of the promissory note will be honored if the borrower doesn't have solid finances, or if the borrower is a corporation (especially a small corporation with a limited number of shareholders). The guaranty would go after the signature of the borrower and would then be signed by the guarantor.

Guaranty. For value received, _____ (hereinafter referred to as the "Guarantor"), located at _____, gives an unconditional guarantee that all payments required by the above Promissory Note shall be made when and as due. The Guarantor waives any demand, notice of nonpayment, protest, notice of protest, or presentment for payment, and agrees that the Lender does not have to exhaust the Lender's rights against the Borrower before pursuing the Guarantor under this Guaranty.

IN WITNESS WHEREOF, the Guarantor has signed this Guaranty as of the _____ day of _____, 20___.

_____
Guarantor's Name

_____
Guarantor's Signature

Promissory Note

AGREEMENT entered into as of the _____ day of _____, 20____, between _____, located at _____ (hereinafter referred to as the "Borrower") and _____, located at _____ _____ (hereinafter referred to as the "Lender").

The Parties hereto agree as follows:

1. Loan Amount. The Lender shall lend to the Borrower the sum of $_____ (hereinafter referred to as the "Loan"), which Loan shall be governed by the provisions of this Promissory Note.

2. Term. The term of the Promissory Note shall be _____.

3. Interest Rate. The interest rate shall be ___%, which shall be compounded [ ] daily [ ] monthly [ ] annually [ ] other, described as _____.

4. Payments of Interest. Payments of interest due shall be made at the following intervals _____ _____, as well as at the end of the term.

5. Payments of Principal. Payments of principal shall be made in the following amount _____ at the following time _____. At the end of the term, the balance owed on the Loan shall be paid in full.

6. Default. If default is made in the payment when due of either principal or interest, then ten days after a written demand for same the entire amount of principal and interest shall become immediately due and payable at the option of the holder of this note if payment has not been made in full.

7. Prepayment. This Promissory Note may be prepaid at any time without penalty.

8. Usury. The parties hereto do not intend for the interest rate to exceed the legal interest rate permitted by the state of _____. In the event that the Borrower does pay interest in excess of the legal interest rate, any interest paid in excess of the legal interest rate shall be deemed to be a payment of principal and shall be applied to reduce the principal balance of the Promissory Note.

9. Fees and Expenses. If the Lender incurs any expenses to enforce any provision of this Note, including reasonable attorney's fees incurred either before, during, or after a lawsuit is commenced to enforce this Promissory Note, the Borrower agrees to pay the Lender's expenses and reasonable attorney's fees, including fees and expenses for any trial and also any appeal in any such lawsuit.

IN WITNESS WHEREOF, the parties hereto have signed this Agreement as of the date first set forth above.

Borrower_____
                  Borrower's Name

By_____
        Authorized Signatory, Title

General Release

Releases are helpful instruments for resolving disputes between parties and creating certainty for the future. In a general release, one party surrenders any claims against the other party. Consideration must be given for the release to be valid. For example, someone might give a release of all claims against someone else who pays them $1,000 for the release. Consideration can also take the form of specific performance, so one party could, for example, agree to deliver certain property to the other party in exchange for a general release.

Releases do not always have to be general releases. A specific release would be a release in which one party gives consideration to the other party in exchange for that party giving a release as to a specific claim. For example, the release might say that for $1,000 consideration, the party receiving the consideration releases the other party from any cause of action based on the alleged breach of a particular contract. All liabilities other than those arising from that particular contract would continue to exist and could be the basis of future lawsuits.

It is not uncommon for parties to give each other a mutual release. In this situation, both parties waive all rights that they may have against each other through the date of the release. Such a mutual release can be general (covering all rights) or specific (covering rights that would arise out of a particular incident or situation).

Filling in the Form

Fill in the date and the name and location of the releasor and the releasee. Identify the consideration (usually money) that was given to the releasor in order to have the releasor sign the release. Then have the releasor sign the release.

Checklist

❏ Make certain that consideration (something of value, usually money) is given in exchange for the releasor's signing the release.

❏ Acknowledge receipt of the consideration.

❏ Discharge the releasee.

❏ Discharge others who might stand in the shoes of the releasee, such as heirs, executors, or assignees.

❏ Require the releasor to warrant that none of the rights being released have been assigned to others.

❏ Indicate that the oral modifications of the release are invalid.

❏ If the release is a mutual release, make certain that both parties sign.

❏ If the release is a specific release, be careful in describing the exact rights or obligations being surrendered by the releasor.

❏ While not strictly required, it can be a good precaution to have the release signed in the presence of a notary public.

Other provisions that can be added to form 52:

Mutual release. If both parties are releasing each other, this should be clearly indicated.

Mutual release. The Releasor and the Releasee hereby release and discharge each other, their respective heirs, executors, administrators, successors, and assigns from all claims and obligations of either against the other, known or unknown, arising through the date of this Release. Further, the parties warrant that no claims and obligations subject to this Release have been assigned to any other party. This Release cannot be amended orally.

Specific release. A specific release is limited in terms of what rights or obligations are being released.

Specific release. The Releasor does hereby release and discharge the Releasee, the Releasee's heirs, executors, administrators, successors, and assigns from the following claims and obligations of the Releasor against the Releasee _____

_____
_____ arising through the date of this Release. Further, the Releasor warrants that no claims and obligations subject to this Release have been assigned to any other party. This Release cannot be amended orally.

General Release

On the ____ day of _____, 20___, _____ (hereinafter referred to as the "Releasor"), located at _____, for good and valid consideration described as _____, received from _____ (hereinafter referred to as the "Releasee"), located at _____, receipt of which is hereby acknowledged, does hereby release and discharge the Releasee, the Releasee's heirs, executors, administrators, successors, and assigns from all claims and obligations of the Releasor against the Releasee, known or unknown, arising through the date of this Release. Further, the Releasor warrants that no claims and obligations subject to this Release have been assigned to any other party. This Release cannot be amended orally.

IN WITNESS WHEREOF, the Releasor has signed this Release as of the date first put forth above.

_____

Releasor

Agreement to Arbitrate

Many agreements contain an arbitration provision. However, if a dispute arises and the agreement does not provide for arbitration, the parties may agree to arbitration anyway. Arbitration should be less expensive than a lawsuit for both sides. The parties have the opportunity to choose the organization or person to act as arbitrator (such as the American Arbitration Association), which can help control costs. The arbitrating group may be chosen because of a special expertise in the subject matter of the dispute (so for example, a graphic designer having a dispute with a client in California might turn to the California Lawyers for the Arts). Another reason that arbitration can save legal expenses is that the arbitration decision is final and cannot be appealed through the courts.

Of course, the absence of an arbitration provision in the original contract may make it difficult for the parties to reach an agreement to arbitrate. The party with deeper pockets may prefer to slug it out in court and wear down the opponent. But if both sides want a quick and probably less expensive way to resolve their dispute, an agreement to arbitrate can make a great deal of sense.

Mediation should also be mentioned here. In arbitration, two parties take their dispute before a neutral party for a final resolution one way or the other. In mediation, two parties take their dispute before a neutral party in an effort to work out a mutually agreeable resolution. However, the mediator merely suggests what might be a good solution. The parties are under no obligation to go along with the mediator's suggestions. Mediation is certainly worth trying before arbitration, but only arbitration makes certain that the dispute will be brought to a conclusion.

Filling in the Form

Fill in the date and the names and addresses of the parties. In Paragraph 1, describe the disagreement with specificity. In Paragraph 3, indicate what organization or person will act as arbitrator. In Paragraph 4, state where the arbitration will take place. Only fill in Paragraph 5 if the rules of the American Arbitration Association will not be used. In Paragraph 7, indicate which state's laws will govern the agreement. Then the parties should each sign.

Checklist

❏ Consider mediation as a step before arbitration.

❏ Carefully set forth the specifics of the dispute, since this is what the arbitration award will cover. (Paragraph 1)

❏ Determine the best arbitrator for the dispute. (Paragraph 3)

❏ Decide on the best location for the arbitration to take place. (Paragraph 4)

❏ Determine which rules will govern the arbitration proceeding. (Paragraph 5)

❏ State that the award of the arbitrator is final and cannot be appealed. (Paragraph 6)

❏ Compare the standard provisions in the introductory pages with Paragraph 7.

Agreement to Arbitrate

AGREEMENT entered into as of the _____ day of _____, 20____, between _____, located at _____, and _____, located at _____.

WHEREAS, the parties hereto have a disagreement; and

WHEREAS, the parties desire to avoid litigation; and

WHEREAS, the parties are willing to submit their disagreement to arbitration;

NOW, THEREFORE, in consideration of the foregoing premises and the mutual covenants hereinafter set forth and other valuable consideration, the parties hereto agree as follows:

1. Dispute. The parties are in disagreement with respect to the following matter, specifically described as _____ _____ _____.

2. Arbitration. The parties agree to submit the disagreement set forth in Paragraph 1 to binding arbitration.

3. Arbitrator. The arbitrator shall be _____.

4. Location. The arbitration shall be in the following location _____.

5. Procedure. The arbitration shall be settled in accordance with the rules of the American Arbitration Association unless specified otherwise here. _____ _____.

6. Award. Judgment upon the arbitration award shall be final, conclusive, and binding on the parties, and enforceable in any court having jurisdiction thereof.

7. Miscellany. This Agreement contains the entire understanding between the parties and may only be modified or amended by a written instrument signed by both parties. A waiver or default under any provision of this Agreement shall not permit future waivers or defaults under that or other provisions of this Agreement. Written notice can be given to the parties at the addresses shown for them. This Agreement shall be binding on the parties, their heirs, legal representatives, successors-in-interest, and assigns. This Agreement shall be governed by the laws of the state of _____.

IN WITNESS WHEREOF, the parties hereto have signed this as of the date first set forth above.

_____
Name and Title

_____
Name and Title

Selected Bibliography

Crawford, Tad (editor). *AIGA Professional Practices in Graphic Design.* New York: Allworth Press, 2008.

Crawford, Tad. *Legal Guide for the Visual Artist.* New York: Allworth Press, 2010.

Fishel, Catharine. *Inside the Business of Graphic Design.* New York: Allworth Press, 2002.

Fleishman, Michael. *Starting Your Career as a Freelance Illustrator or Graphic Designer.* New York: Allworth Press, 2001.

Foote, Cameron. *The Business Side of Creativity.* New York: W. W. Norton & Company, 2006.

Foote, Cameron. *The Creative Business Guide to Running a Graphic Design Business.* New York: W. W. Norton & Company, 2009.

Graphic Artists Guild Handbook: Pricing and Ethical Guidelines. New York: Graphic Artists Guild, 2010.

Heller, Steven (editor). *Design Disasters.* New York: Allworth Press, 2008.

Heller, Steven and Lita Talarico. *Design Firms Open for Business.* New York: Allworth Press, 2013.

Heller, Steven (editor). *The Education of a Design Entrepreneur.* New York: Allworth Press, 2002.

Leland, Caryn. *Licensing Art and Design.* New York: Allworth Press, 1995.

Lockwood, Tom (editor). *Design Thinking.* New York: Allworth Press, 2009.

Millman, Debbie. *How to Think Like a Great Graphic Designer.* New York: Allworth Press, 2007.

Perkins, Shel. *Talent Is Not Enough: Business Secrets for Designers, Second Edition.* San Francisco: New Riders, 2010.

Pocket Pal. Stamford, Connecticut: International Paper Company, 2007.

Sack, Steven Mitchell. *From Hiring to Firing.* Merrick, New York: Legal Strategies Publications, 1995.

Sack, Steven Mitchell. *The Complete Collection of Legal Forms for Employers.* Merrick, New York: Legal Strategies Publications, 1996.

Sparkman, Don. *Selling Graphic and Web Design.* New York: Allworth Press, 2006.

Shapiro, Ellen. *The Graphic Designer's Guide to Clients.* New York: Allworth Press, 2003.

Williams, Theo Stephan. *The Graphic Designer's Guide to Pricing, Estimating & Budgeting.* New York: Allworth Press, 2010.

Wilson, Lee. *The Pocket Legal Companion to Copyright.* New York: Allworth Press, 2012.

Wilson, Lee. *The Pocket Legal Companion to Trademark.* New York: Allworth Press, 2012.

Index